Eva

Literature and Translation

Literature and Translation is a series for books that address literary translation and for books of literary translation. Its emphasis is on diversity of genre, culture, period and approach. The series uses an open access publishing model to disseminate widely developments in the theory and practice of translation, as well as translations into English of literature from around the world.

Series editor: Timothy Mathews is Emeritus Professor of French and Comparative Criticism, UCL.

Eva

A Novel

Carry van Bruggen

Translated and with a Commentary by
Jane Fenoulhet

First published in 2019 by
UCL Press
University College London
Gower Street
London WC1E 6BT

Available to download free: www.uclpress.co.uk

A CIP catalogue record for this book is available from The British Library.

ISBN: 978-1-78735-331-2 (Hbk.)
ISBN: 978-1-78735-330-5 (Pbk.)
ISBN: 978-1-78735-329-9 (PDF)
ISBN: 978-1-78735-332-9 (epub)
ISBN: 978-1-78735-333-6 (mobi)
DOI: https://doi.org/10.14324/111.9781787353299

Contents

List of Figures

Acknowledgements

I first translated *Eva* around 10 years ago. I would like to express my gratitude to the many students who worked on the novel at various stages of the English translation, whether in translation or literature classes. They brought the English *Eva* to life and helped me make some crucial decisions about the translation.

Indeed I am grateful to so many colleagues and students of Dutch, Comparative Literature and Translation Studies at UCL who have shared my enthusiasm for the literatures of Europe over the many years during which I have taught and researched there.

Jane Fenoulhet
Professor Emerita of Dutch Studies

Commentary
Becoming Eva: on translating as a woman

Jane Fenoulhet

Introduction

The novel *Eva* by the Dutch writer Carry van Bruggen deserves to be recognized as a significant modernist text in the European canon. There are two main reasons why this has not so far been the case. First, Carry van Bruggen writes in Dutch, a minor European literary language that has not been much translated until recently. Secondly, as a woman and a Jew writing at the end of the nineteenth century and in the early twentieth century, van Bruggen's work received mixed reviews from her contemporaries, and she has had to wait until the late twentieth century for recognition at home; this has meant a lack of scholars championing her work. Today, the fact that she writes from her experience as a Jewish woman, taken together with her experimentation with narrative in this novel, can only serve to recommend her to a contemporary audience.

The aim of this translation project is to provide the first English translation of van Bruggen's ground-breaking novel so that it will be accessible to anyone interested in the history of modernist women's writing in Europe. As a literary experiment, *Eva*, which first appeared in 1927, is not an immediately accessible text, as I explain below. Nevertheless, the literary qualities for which I value the novel so highly need to be transferred for an English reader in such a way as to bring the work and its main character to life in a manner that is in keeping with the novel's vibrant vitalism. This was the translation brief I gave myself.

Van Bruggen's *Eva* has generally been considered a modernist novel since Fokkema and Ibsch included it in their 1987 book *Modernist*

Conjectures: A Mainstream in European Literature alongside such writers as Proust, Joyce and Woolf. However, it has until now remained inaccessible to audiences that are unable to read Dutch, though thanks to Fokkema and Ibsch, Van Bruggen's place in literary histories written in Dutch is now secure. For example, Erica van Boven and Mary Kemperink accord her a prominent place in their account of the literary avant-garde and modernism in the textbook *Literatuur van de moderne tijd* (Modern literature. 2006). Their short description of *Eva* comes closest to the view of the novel I present here: that is, as a 'so-called novel of consciousness' in which the narrative constructs a stream of consciousness to register the subjective experience of the main character, Eva.[1] This experiment with the Dutch language relays moments of epiphany, along with Eva's powerful perceptions of her surroundings and of her interactions with others. In this respect, there are parallels with the writing of Virginia Woolf in, for example, *Mrs Dalloway* (1925), which uses 'the language of what life *feels* like', according to Carol Ann Duffy.[2] Jeanette Winterson describes Woolf as 'an experimenter who managed to combine the pleasure of narrative with those forceful interruptions that the mind needs to wake itself'.[3] Both of these descriptions of Woolf's writing apply equally well to Carry van Bruggen's in *Eva*.

Carry van Bruggen's own life is transformed into this text, which tracks the growing self-awareness of Eva through the use of innovative techniques that bring readers close to the protagonist's liberation and with it her expanding subjectivity. For this reason, I start with a portrait of the writer and her writing, which culminates in *Eva*, her last published work. In my description of her life, I highlight those aspects that in some way or another play a part in the novel.

The introduction to the writer and her place in Dutch life and letters will be followed by the reading of *Eva* that informs my translation. Because perspective in the novel is restricted to what can be seen through Eva's eyes and mind, this stream of consciousness gives rise to a highly elliptical form of expression, resulting in the need to translate many silences. Even when these are translated in turn by silences, the pregnant pauses generate many meanings in readers' minds. One of the important characteristics of *Eva* is that it is a novel that can bear multiple readings, and I needed to map these so as to enable them in the translation.

Finally, I will discuss all the important translation decisions and negotiations. The shifts that took place as I revised the translation may be of particular interest to literary translators.

Carry van Bruggen

Carry van Bruggen was born Carolina Lea de Haan in 1881 in the small town of Smilde in the Netherlands. She grew up in an orthodox Jewish community in Zaandam to the north of Amsterdam. Her father was a rabbi, so the young Carry was brought up in a world of tradition and strict observance of Jewish law at a time when anti-Semitism was prevalent in the Netherlands. The Jewish community was poor and lived largely apart from Dutch society, though her schooling brought Carry into contact with the wider world. She was particularly close to her brother, Jacob Israël de Haan, who was just a year younger and also became a writer. Both of them had access to secondary education. Carry van Bruggen trained to be a primary school teacher, and she eventually took a teaching job in a poor district of Amsterdam, commuting back and forth to her parents' home in Zaandam before finally moving to Amsterdam. Jacob studied law there, and soon made a name as a poet and novelist. Despite their father's role

Figure 0.1   Portrait of Carry van Bruggen in oils by J. D. Hendriks. Reproduction from the collection of Literatuurmuseum.nl

in the Jewish community, and like many others of their generation, Carry and Jacob turned away from the faith and culture of their childhood as they became assimilated into city society. However, the break with orthodox Judaism did not mean that Van Bruggen abandoned her roots. Far from it. Her fiction grapples with the tensions between mainstream society and traditional Jewish culture, and between the generations within Jewish families.

In 1904 Carry van Bruggen married the journalist and socialist Kees van Bruggen and took his name. They moved to the Dutch East Indies, present-day Indonesia, so that Kees could take up a position as editor of the *Deli Courant*, based in Medan. It was here that Carry began writing, initially to provide the paper with a ladies' section. She also became a mother for the first time in 1905. According to J.M.J. Sicking, the couple did not settle well in the Dutch East Indies, returning to the Netherlands in 1907.[4] This was an important year for Carry: she and her husband settled in Amsterdam, their son was born and she published her first book, the social realist story *In de schaduw (van kinderleven)* (In the shadow (of children's lives)).

Before turning to Van Bruggen's published oeuvre, however, there is one precious resource that provides an impression of Carry van Bruggen as a woman writing in the early twentieth century. It is the only published interview with her, which appeared in the magazine *Den Gulden Winckel* on 15 July 1915.[5] The interviewer was the Flemish critic and essayist André de Ridder, who introduced her with the following sentence: 'Seldom have I met a female author who was so communicative, so exuberantly expressive, so full of fierce life force.'[6] The writer herself speaks very openly about her childhood, in particular the lasting effects of her sense of inferiority that derives from her keenly felt inferior social position and difference as a Jew. She explains that this lack of self-assurance had an impact on her writing, 'which is why it took some time before I began writing in the way I should have always written'.[7] What Van Bruggen is referring to here is the fact that her early novels and stories were written in a realist fictional mode, simply because it was the dominant one. 'What a damaging effect the superior, pompous critics who were holding forth at the time of my debut, had on me and on others!'[8]

The 1907 novella *In de schaduw* is a collection of scenes from the lives of ordinary working people, especially their children, whose non-standard Dutch speech is represented directly on the page, while the narrative is in an informal variant of the standard language. In the interview, Van Bruggen describes this first work as naturalist. Naturalism had been the most influential movement in Dutch literature in the latter part of the nineteenth century, often paired with an impressionist style of writing. Despite its adherence to the dominant mode, Van Bruggen's novella represents a rare, if not unique, attempt in Dutch literature to represent life in a small town that contained a Jewish community living apart from mainstream society. Furthermore, the language in which she does so – especially the dialogue in which she gives her characters distinctive voices – is rather more down to earth than that of her male colleagues. At the heart of each scene is a story of anti-Semitism – for example, non-Jewish children mock the 'nasty' food the Jews eat; teachers mock the Jewish holidays, so that Jewish children dread telling the teacher they have to be absent – revealing systematic discrimination. Given the outspokenly Jewish perspective and implicit criticism of the cruelty of others, it is perhaps not surprising that certain critics reacted unfavourably to this debut. *De verlatene* (The abandoned one. 1911) and *Het joodje* (The little Jew. 1914) continue the theme of society's unfavourable treatment of Jews.

Carry van Bruggen's second publication was another collection of scenes, this time from life in the Dutch East Indies: *Een badreisje in de tropen* (A holiday in the tropics. 1909). In the same year she also published *Goenong Djatti (Een Indische roman)* (Gunung Jati (A novel of the Indies). 1909), her first novel, a realist narrative of the stresses and strains in Dutch colonial society; it creates the strong impression that a woman as open and thoughtful as Carry van Bruggen would not have found that milieu at all conducive to a lively intellectual life. Her third Indonesian novel, *Een Indisch huwelijk* (An Indies marriage. 1916) deals with an important social problem in the colonial society of the time: the shortage of suitable women. This led to hypocritical attitudes whereby Dutch men's liaisons with Indonesian women were tolerated, while the women themselves and any mixed-race children born out of these relationships were not. The publication date of 1916 for this critique of patriarchal Dutch society suggests that Van Bruggen wisely waited until she was no longer forced to make the best of colonial society before giving expression to criticism that would have made her and her husband's position even more difficult. It is no surprise that after three years Kees van Bruggen gave up his role on the *Deli Courant* and returned to work in Amsterdam.

Another interesting group of novels are those written under the pseudonym of Justine Abbing. I have noted elsewhere that these narratives present 'independent women's pioneering lives in a readable, realist way', suggesting that a novel like *Uit het leven van een denkende vrouw* (Scenes from the life of a thinking woman. 1920) demonstrates Van Bruggen's versatility as a writer and her mission to provide serious reading matter for working women in which they might recognize their own lives.[9] The Abbing novels also show that, despite her own fierce intellectualism and literary experimentation, Van Bruggen had respect for independent women of all classes, perhaps remembering her own lower-middle-class existence as a primary school teacher before she achieved success as a writer.

I have spent time on these three groups of novels precisely because I see in them Carry van Bruggen's connectedness to many aspects of Dutch life, and the richness and multiplicity that characterizes her fiction. Furthermore, with the exception of the specifically colonial setting, all these elements can be found in Van Bruggen's last novel *Eva* and therefore inform my translation.

The remaining part of Van Bruggen's oeuvre has a special part to play in the writer's literary life and in her dynamic approach to herself. Through various becomings, she leads an intensive life of growing self-awareness; what I would describe as a becoming-woman both in the everyday sense of growing out of girlhood and becoming a wife and a mother, and in the Deleuzean sense as a vital step toward becoming minor, in other words embracing a position on the margins of society.[10] The novels that bear witness to this process begin with *Heleen: Een vroege winter* (Heleen: an early winter. 1913). As Van Bruggen herself put it, 'With Heleen I became myself; that book has been my rebirth; in it, the depiction of mental life is the main thing while the visual is secondary [...]'[11] The novel, which is narrated in the third person, has very little plot; it simply follows Heleen through her childhood days of fear and anxiety, panic even, with a mother who is not able to comfort her. The depiction of Heleen's emotional life is sometimes heart-rending precisely because it is described through the body – it is unashamedly 'enfleshed', to use a term of Rosi Braidotti's:[12]

Heleen looked up, sighed and saw that she was alone. Darkness was spreading, how wonderfully sweet were these last remnants of light. She saw the girls in twos and threes walking back and forth in front of her, the gravel crunched slightly, something caught in her throat, tears welled up, was she really sad right now? In an uncertain anguish she rubbed the back of her head against the wall, gave a little moan, closed her eyes and let her tears run into her open mouth.[13]

A few years later, when she is studying away from home, Heleen's doubts and fears almost get the better of her at times, so that she briefly thinks of suicide and worries about madness or some kind of breakdown, though she realizes that others are unaware of her extreme inner life: 'no-one saw the wounds that she intended to cut in her own heart in her pursuit of truthfulness'.[14] The novel ends when she writes to the older man she loves to end their relationship, not because she has stopped loving him, but because she loves him too much. Although the book focuses on Heleen's emotional and mental life, readers are just as aware of her physical life, since it is her physical desire for this man that makes her realize the gulf between them. This novel of female-embodied subjectivity narrated from a female perspective marks an important new departure in Dutch literature.

Een coquette vrouw (A flirtatious woman. 1915) picks up this thread in the character of Ina, who is married to the rather phlegmatic Egbert. As I explain elsewhere, 'She needs attention and extremes of emotion: not only can Egbert not give her these, he feels that this is inappropriate behaviour for a wife and mother. Ina is a faithful wife in the sexual sense, but there is always someone else in her life who makes her feel alive.'[15] Ultimately Ina forfeits her position in society and her friendships because of her insistence on the freedom to follow her own inclinations and not behave according to the patriarchal norm. The novel opens with a striking illustration of Ina's sensuality:

> The window was open -, the cool May breeze lifted the curtains gently, without force, made them swell like sails and floated them into the room - they subsided softly again - like the exhalation of a sleeping child. Ina looked at them over the bunch of damp bluebells held in both hands, nose and mouth buried in them - her heart thumped with a soft, intense delight, she felt it in her throat - and just as she did when a child, she allowed the words of her thoughts to measure her heartbeat: the winter is past ... the winter is past ... the winter is past ...[16]

Ina is in the process of becoming a writer, though Egbert finds it hard to take her first published story seriously. In fact, when she asks what he thinks about it, he insults her and criticizes her as a woman, complaining that she always wants to discuss matters when he prefers her to be quiet and leave him to his own work.

The narrative is still realist, the narrator stands outside the fictional world and readers are told how Ina thinks and feels. At the same time, the focus on Ina provides a strong female perspective and implicit criticism of the patriarchal institution of marriage. Ina's position and the unhappiness it causes her engages readers through powerful feelings of frustration at the restrictions imposed on this lively and creative woman. If becoming-woman in the Deleuzean sense means a move away from the mainstream, then this novel certainly provides an impetus for this process, even though Ina herself is still only beginning to test society's social and cultural boundaries. The novel ends when Egbert leaves her for someone else. Shock and despair make way for new feelings:

> Life threw off its everyday appearance and revealed itself in a trembling, sombre, mysterious coppery glow. The landscape of her own future, - as she had seen it just a moment ago, clear and cool, hours and years in serried ranks, all things plain and distinct as in sober afternoon light - seemed suddenly wider, full of shadows and secrets.[17]

The novel *Eva* and translation

Approaching *Eva*

What is it about Carry van Bruggen's last novel, *Eva* (1927), that means it is both a continuation of the two earlier novels of becoming-woman and yet makes a more significant contribution to Dutch and European modernist literature?

The novel displays an astonishing intellectual and affectual honesty not seen in Dutch literature before. Despite the fact that I compared Van Bruggen's narrative experiment with Virginia Woolf's fiction, the auto-biographical dimension and frank representation of female experience sets it apart. For me, the novel is a fitting high point of an intense creative life. It marks Van Bruggen's own becoming-woman in two senses: she has left behind not one, but two molar societies – the orthodox Jewish milieu in which she grew up and the mainstream Dutch society where women's subjectivity was restricted by codes of behaviour, morals and artistic practices. Gradually, as she wrote and thought, thought and wrote, Carry van Bruggen disregarded those norms and followed her own path. This entailed daring to write philosophical works about language and about the individual in literature; realist novels exposing the conditions of poor children in Amsterdam; novels examining the position of the younger generation of educated Jews and their alienation from their roots;

autobiographical sketches of childhood from the child's perspective; and most importantly of all, novels in which the narrative itself was pushed to its limits in order to give expression to female subjectivity. The experimental process that was begun with *Heleen* and *Een coquette vrouw* is completed in *Eva*.

In the afterword to an edition of selected fictional works by Van Bruggen, the editor, J.M.J. Sicking, notes that she herself regarded *Eva* as the culmination of all her literary work, noting that she had been able in the novel to express herself 'definitively and completely'.[18] This personal liberation of the writer is what gives the novel its vitality. It is the way in which Van Bruggen uses the Dutch language to express herself that makes her the 'mother' of Dutch literary modernism, which finally emerged in the Netherlands in the 1930s. Not that Van Bruggen would have identified herself as a modernist. Furthermore, like her contemporary Virginia Woolf, she did not count herself a feminist either. At the same time, Van Bruggen's insistence on transforming the narrative to render Eva's inner life and consciousness can certainly be compared with a novel such as *Mrs Dalloway* (1925). Her approach results in a discontinuous narrative that proceeds in eight separate scenes from the life of Eva, within which time flows according to Eva's thoughts in a Deleuzean 'aion' or timeless time.

In what follows I will map the novel's narrative features, linking these to the expression of Eva's subjectivity; that is, to the main character's growing awareness of herself as a socially constructed individual and as a living being experiencing the world and its richness.

The translation process

My translation strategy evolved as I became more and more familiar with the novel. I would go so far as to say that translating became a question of (re)enacting my own becoming-woman through Van Bruggen's and Eva's refusal to accept the masculine norms that aim to control a woman's creativity and her sexuality. This meant that it was impossible for me to separate the translational from the personal. From the initial position of seeing translation as impersonating Van Bruggen in order to recreate her work, I moved to one where I at least in part came to re-embody the writer I was translating, questioning my own use of English writing conventions while at the same time reflecting on the possibilities for freedom within marriage. For example, Van Bruggen repeatedly uses the evocative image of the cage into which wild ducks are lured on the island where she spends her summers in order to express the confines of marriage. I retranslated some of those passages a few times while reviewing forty years of marriage. In some ways my experience when translating *Eva* was similar to Lara Feigel's encounter with Doris Lessing in her book *Free Woman: Life, Liberation and Doris Lessing*. Feigel's own life becomes entangled with Lessing's in a way that both produces her own autobiographical writing and a surprisingly vivid sense of Doris Lessing both as a woman and a writer. As a translator, my role was to allow my own voice to infuse the translation and to revivify the text without inserting my own autobiography.

The narrator

The novel is narrated in the first, second and third person. The narrative opens with an evocation of a snowy New Year's Day in a small Dutch harbour town, narrated from a distance in the third person, but interrupted by an indeterminate second person narrator:

> Today is in the New Century - the Old Century came to an end yesterday. A hundred years have gone by. A balloon, gradually deflating, deflating - empty at last. An old chain unwound from the capstan, new a hundred years ago. These chains sink into the water when the boats anchor, you are standing in the reeds, you watch them unreel, they touch the water, they break its surface, and it closes over them ...[19]

We meet the central character soon after this: 'And she walks alone.' However, we never learn her name in the first episode, 'The New Century', whose narrator switches between the more distant third person and the appellative 'you'. Its function is to allow the narrator to speak directly to this unknown character. Is the narrator talking to herself, perhaps? The effect is certainly to zoom in, revealing the main character's reactions, thoughts and feelings:

> Why do you understand everything ... why is it that the knowledge of so many things stays with you? You can't ever rid yourself of it, you can't forget it. You can't even go back years without it being there, the whispering at school, it made you blush, it made

you blink, you got all hot and flustered … your forehead grew clammy.[20]

When the narrator discloses a childhood fantasy about becoming delirious and uttering 'bad' words, we encounter the first-person narrator for the first time: 'And it's not my fault that I know them …'. Van Bruggen also uses direct speech where the characters, including the main character, use 'I' as a matter of course.

The second episode, 'Homewards', again refers to the protagonist as 'she' and addresses her as 'you'. She is at the station with a young woman called Andy, waiting to travel back home in the evening from her new life as a teacher in the city, when the narrator uses 'I' again. Andy introduces the naïve protagonist to 'What men want'. This is her reaction:

> There is something in me that strains towards the acid light … but there is also something in me that wants to turn away from it … I want to know and not know, I want to hear and not hear … Let's, let's … close the gates … let's stand with our backs against them … let's make haste to where it is safe, where it is good …[21]

In the third episode, 'Voices', we finally learn the protagonist's name when her boyfriend calls her down into the dark garden:

> If he doesn't come, if it doesn't come, then life no longer has any meaning.
>
> 'Eva … Evie … are you there … have you come?'
>
> 'Yes, I am here … I came …'[22]

She is torn between desire for the kind of physical contact that allows the two of them to merge and her sense of self. When she senses he is not really interested in her as a person, she pulls away:

> […] oh, do you think that I desire this … is that what girls come for … And you dare, my boy … You dare to say that to me, to Me …! A burning pillar shot up and as if before her own eyes, she saw written:
>
> Me with a capital letter! Like in the Ten Commandments: 'Thou shalt not take My name in vain.'[23]

Figure 0.2 Photograph of Carry van Bruggen c. 1915 from the collection of Literatuurmuseum.nl

These examples show the crucial role the use of pronouns plays in the portrayal of Eva's growing self-awareness and self-assertion. Although normalizing the use of pronouns in English was never a possibility since their shifts are part of the fabric of the novel that I was trying to preserve, I was concerned about the narrative being perceived as messy or poorly written, which would undermine the aim of the translation. This fact influenced other translation decisions, most particularly on the occasions where I was guided by readability and acceptability. For instance, in episode five, 'May Day', Eva remembers an old dream: 'Once years and years ago, I had a bad dream [...].' The Dutch text has the equivalent of 'Once years and years ago there was a bad dream [...]', and although I wanted to keep the impersonal construction because it normally follows the 'once upon a time' formula, I opted for the more natural-sounding version.

Verb tenses

These can be just as unsettled and unsettling as the shifting narrator and are important indicators of what is going on in Eva's mind. The stream of consciousness narrates what Eva is experiencing in the moment, moving between the time and place of the main narrative and memories and impressions. Take this passage from episode five, where Eva has been reading a letter from her twin brother David:

> But he sees David's letter and goes to read the newspaper. Now it's quiet ... distant, closed voices ... more distant, open sounds ... dreamy ... dozy ... Distant lands ... distant seas ... strange names you learned ... years ago ... but they attached themselves, they chained themselves to the moments ... and return again with those moments, year in, year out ... the inflexible regularity of a calendar ...[24]

A significant moment of rupture in Eva's life is when she learns of David's death. The episode entitled 'David' opens with Eva meeting the children from school, a repeated occurrence narrated in the present tense: 'She walks with the children along the hard paths.' At the same time, sudden switches to and from the past tense of the main narrative interrupt the smooth flow of time, alerting the reader to some as yet unknown disruptive force while also delaying the moment of revelation:

> She arrived home with the children -, every afternoon she first goes to collect Claartje and together with Claartje she goes to meet Eddy from school, and with both of them, with each one holding one of her hands, a warm hand shut tight, she then walks back under the tall, bare trees [...][25]

The following paragraph again opens with the same switch to the past tense – 'And they arrived home and Ben said: "I have to speak to you alone for a moment"' – and continues in the past tense to the second occurrence of 'Ben said "Prepare for the worst. David is dead."' These examples give an idea of the complexities of Van Bruggen's use of tense. While it could have been tempting to iron out some of the shifts to render the English narrative more reader-friendly by producing a smoother read, my strategy has been to reproduce the uncomfortable effects of Van Bruggen's use of tenses. This is because the stream of consciousness brings us readers so close to Eva that we can, at least in part, experience some of what Eva feels, such as her sense of dread on hearing Ben's words.

Figure 0.3 Photographic portrait of Carry van Bruggen with her two children from the collection of Literatuurmuseum.nl

Intensities

A powerful feature of the narrative of Eva's life is the way it expresses intensities of feeling. David's death sparks the following harrowing passage, in which Eva reflects with astonishing honesty on her vulnerability:

> Sympathy destroyed me, - with the living and the dead, with the bones in the charnel house behind the old church. Gratitude ground me down, bliss crushed me … Spring burst upon me … I was the starry firmament … I was the sunset … I was it all, I bore it all. The cows lowed their complaints to me in the summer night, out of the meadow-dew, but I did not understand. Not a single thing left me in peace. Everything flowed towards me, and flowed out of me -, I was the flowing heart of all things. I suffered injustice, I avenged injustice -, I was burned with the martyrs -, I joined in

with the plotters ... I have forgiven all things and committed all things ... created all and destroyed all.[26]

This passage is also an expression of Eva's sense of connectedness with everything. It is timeless and extends to all people and represents the philosophical heart of the novel, which I link to Spinoza's philosophy of immanence, that is of the divine presence in the material world. This also explains my choice of Gilles Deleuze and Rosi Braidotti as philosophical guides for my translation of *Eva*, since they also work in this tradition. In other words, I would not want to pin down Carry van Bruggen and her last novel to a feminist agenda alone, although the concept of becoming-woman has been an important source of my translation strategy. It is intrinsically connected to vitalism, and motherhood is perhaps its most important expression in the novel. The pioneering passage in which Eva feeds her new baby is one of the most intense in the entire novel. Since it combines maternal love with various powerful bodily sensations, and is the first place in the novel where Eva overcomes her deeply ingrained sense of shame and awkwardness in intimate matters, I will quote it here at length:

And now I lift you up and cradle you in my arm ... you weigh seven pounds and you can't talk ... and you rule my life and all my happiness rests with you. My lap is your home, the crook of my arm is for your little head ... never before have I been in so confined a shaft, alone with you. You have learnt since this morning, you didn't cry, you know me already, you trust me, you know I'm always here, and that I will always be here from now on. And now I put down the candle, there! So I can see you, without it bothering you, and we are together in one chair ... oh, you are forcing me into a corner and I like it there ... and now I give myself to you, you may take me ... with your round little head and your hair fine as the March grass ...

The doors are rattling, a soft, dull sound ... the wind moves round like a weary sigh ... space calls to me, but I don't go ... you forced me into the corner and I like it there. Oh, so greedy ... so greedy ... you're almost hurting me. You were too greedy, now you can't take any more ... milk spills from your little mouth. Are your eyes really going to be like mine? Yes, the eloquent, vivacious brown has almost filled the murky greyblue emptiness. Do you yourself know this? Is that why you're looking at me like that? You never looked at me like that before tonight. Are you grateful - because you could take me when you wanted? I'm grateful too, because I can give myself when I want. And we look at one another. And I have never looked at your father like that. He took me and I gave myself ... is that how it was? It must have been like that, or you wouldn't be here now with me, in my lap. We didn't look at one another ... and we didn't recall it ... we pushed it away from us ... because we were ashamed. Worlds ... worlds turning ... each in its atmosphere of shame ...

Never more estranged, never further away than in union.

People are further apart than the stars ... we didn't get close to one another ... You little mouth is pursed ... you haven't had enough yet. How greedy ... how greedy ... your little throat undulates, *so* greedy ... greedily and steadily you drink me empty. And I've only got one hand for you, for I cover my eyes with the other, because of what I suddenly know: this must be it, to be taken while giving like this ... my heart is beating like never ever before ... and the fire spreads through me, so that my own hand can feel it and it is there ... where the secret feelings live ... there where I received you ... and that is how I know for sure.[27]

In the translation of this passage I aimed to convey the power of new life to overcome jaded social constructs such as shame, so it was vital not to shy away from the unmistakeable erotic dimension. First, Eva contrasts her feelings for the baby with those for her husband when she says 'and now I give myself to you, you may take me ...' on giving him her breast. Compare this with what she says of his conception: 'He took me and I gave myself ... is that how it was? It must have been like that, or you wouldn't be here now with me, in my lap. We didn't look at one another ... and we didn't recall it ... we pushed it away from us ... because we were ashamed.' Van Bruggen is open about the feelings of desire aroused by the baby's sucking – she speaks of the fire spreading through her 'there ... where the secret feelings live ... there where I received you ...'.

Yet again, my chosen strategy required me to resist the impulse to tone down the intensity of the passage, particularly where it reveals uncomfortable truths about the way women's bodies work.

Punctuation

As well as being a pathbreaking fictional evocation of the sensation of breastfeeding, the above passage is exceedingly daring in its intimate revelations. Knowing the straight-laced nature of mainstream Dutch society, I am intrigued that the novel was published as early as 1927, and I wonder whether its modernist mode of writing somehow made publication less risky, at least in part. Given that the elliptical style of writing was so new in Dutch literature, and the punctuation the opposite of what was considered good, fluent style, it is quite possible that readers did not follow the entire narrative, which enabled them to overlook the most shocking events, especially the anonymous sexual encounter in the dunes, which I will return to later. For now, I wish to discuss the role of the superficially boring, yet crucially important matter of punctuation in the translation of the novel.

'[T]ranslation relocates a text from the there and then in the here and now', according to Clive Scott in *Literary Translation and the Rediscovery of Reading* and an important aspect of this 'is about registering the text in my body'.[28] The importance of punctuation, certainly in relation to *Eva*, is that it points to places in the text where readers are invited to involve themselves bodily in the reading process. This becomes immediately clear when reading it aloud: the punctuation indicates where to pause, take a breath, speak louder or more emphatically, whisper, speak fast as in an aside or use a questioning intonation, for instance.

For an English readership – and perhaps also for readers of the Dutch version – the punctuation in *Eva* could be considered stylistically challenging. In particular, the regular and frequent use of '…' is difficult to tolerate, and might even be seen as poor writing by those who value full sentences. The insistence with which it is used in the novel makes it perfectly clear that it is a deliberate device with the function of pulling the reader into the narrated present. A translator could normalize the punctuation fully, preserve it fully or negotiate between those two positions. Compare the impact of the normalizing translation (i) with the extreme punctuation of (ii):

i. The doors are rattling. They make a low, dull sound. The wind moves round like a weary sigh. Quiet … quiet. He is stirring in his little white crib. Here I am. I'm here, but I've never seen your eyes like *that* before. How quietly you lie there waiting. Stay like that a moment. I'm coming. I fetch the candle and the low chair and I'm back. Did I talk too much? Wasn't I quick as a flash? And now I lift you up and cradle you in my arm. You weigh seven pounds and you can't talk. And you rule my life, and all my happiness rests with you.

ii. The doors are rattling, a deep, dull sound, the wind moves round like a weary sigh … shh … shh … he is stirring in his little white crib. Here I am … I'm here … but I've never seen your eyes like *that* before. How quietly you lie there waiting … stay like that a moment … I'm coming … I fetch the candle and the low chair and I'm back … did I talk too much, wasn't I quick as a flash? And now I lift you up and cradle you in my arm … you weigh seven pounds and you can't talk … and you rule my life and all my happiness rests with you.

It is not possible to say which of the two variants is the 'best' translation since that all depends on the aim of the translation. Given that mine was a literary aim to see Van Bruggen recognized as the significant modernist woman writer that I consider her to be, I needed to bring out the modernist qualities of the work and abandon the desire to please my readers. However, I did try out a normalizing strategy in (i) above to help me confirm my decision. This method enables a translator to register the different impacts of choices made. Reading (i) it is still clear that we are reading an internal monologue spoken by the main character: a first-person narrative in which Eva addresses her child as 'you'. The disadvantage of such a clear approach is its lack of fluidity, which in the second passage creates the sense of thinking along with the narrator and central character. We have come to know Eva as a complex character, but here we see her in a moment of simplicity and maternal solicitude. Moreover, as we saw above, the fluidity is inherently bound in with the portrayal of Eva. As her self-awareness grows, so does the use of the I-narrator: Eva is given her own voice. This is the function of the use of ellipsis: to map the incompleteness and dynamic nature of Eva's thought. This has the effect of creating the illusion of being in the midst of things, and thus leads us to read performatively.

Version (i) creates the opposite of a fluid text and gives the narrative a certain banality. The following sentence adds the explicitness of conjunctions: 'You have learnt since this morning, *for* you didn't cry *because* you know me already. You trust me. You know I'm always here, and that I will always be here from now on.' Version (ii) – 'You have learnt since this morning, you didn't cry, you know me already, you trust me, you know I'm always here, and that I will always be here from now on' – creates a string of phrases linked by commas that serves to evoke a feeling of breathlessness: 'I register the text in my body', to use Scott's phrase.[29]

Translating sex scenes

The lack of explicit narration of the sex scenes in *Eva* poses an interesting translation problem. One reason is practical and historical, namely that a readily comprehensible representation of sex would not have been acceptable in the Netherlands in the 1920s and would have precluded publication. Another more complex reason is connected with the main character's powerful sense of shame. The translator's problem is also that of the reader of the Dutch text, since he or she must actively construct narrative meaning from a web of linked images. In this case a reader-centred strategy must at least be considered, the question being how much help to give the reader. I did experiment with an interpretive approach. However, this was in conflict with my overall strategy, which chose to concentrate on a small, primarily academic readership and not to shy away from producing a challenging read in English. Initially, an interpretive approach worked well as a form of close reading to ensure that I had myself understood all the nuances of van Bruggen's text.

The first scene is between Eva and her husband Ben:

And Ben says: 'Are you lying comfortably?'

Yes, Ben, I'm lying comfortably.

The walls of the room contract, it becomes a narrow shaft, a cage, a tall, narrow cage. You ought to be able to get up … go out. Where to? Oh: into the water, for example. Or: into a cafe, for example. Right in the middle of a fight. Knives. Screams. Someone being stabbed to death. But don't you come too close to me … o bloody hell … Like a thousand iron rings tugged along a brass rod … how can you be so coarse, so mean, as to think of a fight … and for such a curse to well up inside you!

And Ben says: 'Shall I tuck you in?'[30]

This extract from the scene is painful to read. What is clear from the start is that Ben is embarrassed by his own sexual desire, which combined with Eva's deeply ingrained sense of shame produces extreme mental and physical discomfort. Despite the lack of direct narration, the scene still manages to be frank. The one remaining element that I have left in a more explicit form than in the Dutch text is the curse 'bloody hell'. The Dutch uses a shortened version 'godverd …', which is generally used by those who try not to swear and may have been required here so as not to offend the readership. I tried 'hell and [damnation]', 'bloody ...', 'Christ ...', but in the end felt that the full curse better justified Eva's subsequent comments.

The second sex scene is much longer and represents not only Eva's sexual awakening, but also the climax of the novel. Eva and her lover only know each other's first names, and they will part after their assignation in the dunes on one of the Wadden Islands off the coast of Friesland. Marius is married and he and his wife will leave the island the following day. The difficulty with this passage is that it narrates what would have been a completely forbidden love, and so it is couched in even more elusive language: in my case it needed to be read multiple times before I was completely sure what had taken place in the dunes. The following passages give an idea:

> And I lie beside you in the warm, soft sand ... and you build your path, the path to me, through kiss upon kiss, in a determined solemnity ... but this path cannot lead anywhere. With these kisses you drive me into bliss, beyond bliss and you drive me to despair. You drive yourself to despair too, because this is not yet fulfilment ...

> [...]

> I know that this is the only way to confide wholly in one another and that this is the formula for a total surrender. All is one, one-and-the-same.

> Totality ... eternally blossoming understanding, rocket against night sky, bursting into endless myriad colours. Tree of life, deathspring. Eternally disturbed, eternally restored equilibrium. Storms and Trade Winds. The unbending urge towards duty -, the hot thirst for penance, the longing for mortification ... the one-and-the-same, expressed through emotion in endless forms. And that which presents itself as Despair ... the Storm-of-Storms ...

> The cosmic Spirit, who was very much an artist ... one person must take the upward path from lowliness, the other person must take the downward path from on high, but all must arrive at the spot where life is complete in the storm of storms.

> And because this one thing, uncomprehended till now, untasted until today, is suddenly absorbed like a flame into Totality, because my emotion chimes in with my understanding, and my understanding confirms my emotion, so that now for the first time

it truly enters my life where emotion and understanding may not remain separate or Totality will shrivel to a word, I am now sailing into the safe haven before your eyes, so that my calm amazes you …[31]

The translation challenge was to preserve the indirectness of the passage while ensuring that the text would be capable of interpretation. The steps involved careful literal translation, interpretative translation, a return to indirectness and several adjustments to ensure comprehensibility. Part of van Bruggen's narrative technique is an intertextual one, for example in this passage that makes it clear Eva's damaging sense of shame has been exorcized: 'It is not love that makes bodily desire acceptable. Bodily desire makes love acceptable. I could tell it abroad. But if they should ask me what it means, I would refer them to St. Paul: He who has ears to hear, let him hear.'[32] The reference to St. Paul in this quotation is preceded by one to the Dutch author Frederik van Eeden. Eva's bodily surrender to Marius is narrated through her intellectual and cultural responses, and her childhood memories. The 'Storms and Trade Winds' in the long quotation captured Eva's imagination during a lesson at school, while 'Totality' is her philosophical grasp of life and this material world. Together with the 'cosmic Spirit', it is part of a recurring literary reference to the Dutch psychiatrist and writer Frederik van Eeden's concept of pure mind or pure understanding.[33] At the same time, interpretation depends on some details of what is happening between the two lovers. We know that they kiss, but do they go further? Does 'total surrender' mean that Eva for the first time willingly gives her body to a man? Totality is expressed in the image of the rocket against the night sky 'bursting into endless myriad colours', a suggestive cliché, perhaps, but one that can certainly be recognized as representing sexual climax. This passage is followed by a reference to Eva and Marius's first eye contact at a concert in Amsterdam twenty years earlier, and the phrases 'The violins trembled at what had been consummated' and 'we experienced the moment, endless, unbearable, until the invisible choirs were reborn in a sigh and the chorale's crescendo filled the spaces beneath the twilit vaulting'.[34] Given their place in the narrative, they must be read in at least two ways.

How to read this translation

By far the greatest challenges that came with my chosen approach to *Eva* were whether to preserve the text's multilingual nature and, closely bound up with this, whether to annotate. In addition, names posed a particular challenge. At one stage in the translation process, I anglicized the spelling of certain names, so that Ernestien became Ernestine, for example, and juffrouw Cool became Miss Cole. But this left me with the problem of names such as Claartje, which could be transposed into Clara or even Clare, and mevrouw Baarslag, which could not be easily transposed. In my final revision of the text, I reverted to the Dutch names for two very different reasons: first, the novel is so definitely set in Amsterdam society of the first two decades of the twentieth century; and second, the names of the main character, Eva, and the important men in her life – David, Ben and Marius – need no translation, which lessens the impact of my decision to foreignize in respect of names.

The overall aim of the translation is to insert this novel by Carry van Bruggen into European literary history. For this reason, I decided on a documentary approach to names and multilingualism, by which I mean one that gives access to the text as it appeared at the time. In addition to leaving names in their Dutch forms, I have left words, phrases and quotations in French, German and Hebrew, which is the closest I can get to multilingualism in the English version. On some occasions, van Bruggen includes an explanation as with '*Kol Nidrei*. All the vows' in the first and last chapters. And when Eva recalls a verse of a well-known song by Schubert, '*Es war, als hätt' der Himmel [...]*' I have left it in the German, which is how it is normally sung in the English-speaking world. However, where Eva quotes from Dutch literature, I have translated these quotations directly for the English reader. This rather pragmatic mixed approach was influenced by the fact that internet searches are available to all, and very effective. My decision not to annotate was guided by a reluctance to interfere with the English text on the page by inserting visible notes or references.

This commentary should go some way to assist readers without explaining each individual cultural reference or point of difficulty. This is in keeping with how Carry van Bruggen asks her readers to read in fresh ways, to find new reading strategies that embrace tensions and ellipses, and not to mind if the text is not always immediately accessible. In this way we are all invited to become-woman and cross over the boundary separating tradition from the dynamic life of becoming.

Notes

1. My translation of 'een zogeheten bewustzijnsroman', Erica van Boven and Mary Kemperink, *Literatuur van de moderne tijd. Nederlandse en Vlaamse letterkunde in de 19ᵉ en 20ᵉ eeuw* (Bussum: Coutinho, 2006), 210.
2. 'Carol Ann Duffy on *Mrs Dalloway*', in Virginia Woolf, *Mrs Dalloway* (London: Vintage, 2004), xii.
3. Jeanette Winterson, 'Foreword', *Mrs Dalloway*, vii.
4. Carry van Bruggen, ed. J.M.J. Sicking, *Verhalend proza* (Amsterdam: Van Oorschot, 2007), 591. Online edition at https://dbnl.org/tekst/brug004verh01_01/colofon.php.
5. Reproduced in Jan Fontijn and Diny Schouten (eds), *Carry van Bruggen. Een documentatie* ('s-Gravenhage: Nijgh & Van Ditmar, 1985), 7–17.
6. My translation of 'Ik ontmoette zelden een vrouwelijke auteur zoo spraakzaam, zoo exuberant van woord, zoo vol heftige levensdrift.' Fontijn & Schouten, 8.
7. My translation of 'vandáár ook dat ik pas later aan 't schrijven ben gegaan zooals ik altijd had móeten schrijven ...' Fontijn & Schouten, 11.
8. My translation of 'Wat 'n kwaad heeft de hooghartige, pompeuze critiek, die aan 't woord was ten tijden van mijn debut, mij en anderen berokkend! ...' Fontijn and Schouten, 12.
9. Jane Fenoulhet, *Making the Personal Political: Dutch Women Writers 1919–1970* (Oxford: Legenda, 2007), 56–7.
10. See, for example, Rosi Braidotti, *Nomadic Subjects: Embodiment and Sexual Difference in Contemporary Feminist Theory* (New York: Columbia University Press, 1994), 114.
11. My translation of 'Met Heleen ben ik mezelf geworden; dat boek is mijne wedergeboorte geweest; daar is de gemoedsbeschrijving hoofdzaak en het geziene beeld 't secundaire geworden [...]' Fontijn & Schouten, 12.
12. See, for example, Rosi Braidotti, *Nomadic Theory: The Portable Rosi Braidotti* (New York: Columbia University Press, 2011), 61.
13. My translation of 'Heleen sloeg de oogen op, zuchtte en zag, dat zij alleen was. De donkere dreef aan, hoe wonderbaarlijk zoet was nog dit laatste licht. Ze zag de meisjes in paartjes en bij drieën heen en weder langs zich gaan, het grint kraakte licht, er beet iets in haar keel, er rezen tranen, was ze nu echt bedroefd? Ze wreef in een onvaste smartelijkheid haar achterhoofd tegen den muur, kreunde even, sloot de oogen en ving haar tranen in haar open mond.' Carry van Bruggen, *Heleen: een vroege winter* (Amsterdam: Maatschappij voor Goede en Goedkope Lectuur, 1913), 58. The edition used is online at https://dbnl.org/tekst/brug004hele01_01/colofon.php.
14. My translation of 'niemand zag de wonden, die ze om waarheidswille meende te moeten slaan in haar eigen hart', Van Bruggen, *Heleen*, 187.
15. Fenoulhet, *Making the Personal Political*, 55.
16. My translation of 'Het venster stond open -, de koele Meiwind lichtte zachtzinnig, zonder geweld, de gordijnen op, bolde ze als zeilen en dreef ze tot midden in de kamer - dan zonken ze weer stil terug - het was als het uitademen van een slapend kind. Boven den bos vochtige hyacinthen, die ze in twee handen hield omklemd, mond en neus erin begraven, keek Ina ernaar - haar hart bonsde van een zacht, heftig verheugen, ze voelde het in haar keel - en als toen ze een kind was, liet ze de woorden van haar gedachten deinen op den maatslag van haar hart: de winter is voorbij ... de winter is voorbij ... de winter is voorbij ...' Carry van Bruggen, *Een coquette vrouw* (Amsterdam: P.N. van Kampen, 1916), 1. The edition used is online at https://dbnl.org/tekst/brug004coqu01_01/colofon.php.
17. My translation of 'het leven wierp zijn dagelijksche gedaante af en toonde zich in een trillenden, somberen, geheimvollen gloed als van koper -, het landschap van haar eigen toekomst, zooals ze het even te voren had gezien, klaar en koel, met de uren en de jaren als in rij en gelid, alle dingen nuchter en duidelijk als onder kleurloos middaglicht - leek plotseling verwijd, vol duisternissen en geheimen.' Van Bruggen, *Een coquette vrouw*, 255.
18. Carry van Bruggen, ed. J.M.J. Sicking, *Verhalend proza* (Amsterdam: Van Oorschot, 2007), 592. Online edition at https://dbnl.org/tekst/brug004verh01_01/colofon.php.
19. Carry van Bruggen, tr. Jane Fenoulhet, *Eva* (London: UCL Press, 2019), 27.
20. *Eva*, 29.

21 *Eva*, 47.
22 *Eva*, 70.
23 Eva, 70–1.
24 *Eva*, 94–5.
25 *Eva*, 131.
26 *Eva*, 135.
27 *Eva*, 125–6.
28 Clive Scott, *Literary Translation and the Rediscovery of Reading* (Cambridge: Cambridge University Press, 2012), 12.
29 For this section I have drawn on an earlier article: Jane Fenoulhet, 'Signs of Life. Vitalising Literary Studies', *Journal of Dutch Literature* 18/2 (2017): 11–12.
30 *Eva*, 123.
31 *Eva*, 176, 180–1.
32 *Eva*, 182.
33 See, for example, Lynn Gamwell, *Mathematics and Art: A Cultural History* (Princeton: Princeton University Press, 2015), Chapter 6.
34 *Eva*, 182.

Bibliography

Boven, Erica van and Mary Kemperink, *Literatuur van de moderne tijd. Nederlandse en Vlaamse letterkunde in de 19ᵉ en 20ᵉ eeuw* (Bussum: Coutinho, 2006).

Braidotti, Rosi, *Nomadic Subjects: Embodiment and Sexual Difference in Contemporary Feminist Theory* (New York: Columbia University Press, 1994).

Braidotti, Rosi, *Nomadic Theory: The Portable Rose Braidotti* (New York: Columbia University Press, 2011).

Bruggen, Carry van, *Heleen: Een vroege winter* (Amsterdam: Maatschappij voor Goede en Goedkope Lectuur, 1913). https://dbnl.org/tekst/brug004hele01_01.

Bruggen, Carry van, *Een coquette vrouw* (Amsterdam: P.N. van Kampen, 1916). https://dbnl.org/tekst/brug004coqu01_01.

Bruggen, Carry van, ed. J.M.J. Sicking, *Verhalend proza* (Amsterdam: Van Oorschot, 2007). https://dbnl.org/tekst/brug004verh01_01/.

Fenoulhet, Jane, *Making the Personal Political: Dutch Women Writers 1919–1970* (Oxford: Legenda, 2007).

Fenoulhet, Jane, 'Signs of Life. Vitalising Literary Studies', *Journal of Dutch Literature* 18/2 (2017): 1–13.

Fokkema, D.W. Fokkema and E. Ibsch, *Modernist Conjectures: A Mainstream in European Literature 1910–1940* (London: Hurst, 1987).

Fontijn, Jan and Diny Schouten (eds.), *Carry van Bruggen. Een documentatie* ('s-Gravenhage: Nijgh & Van Ditmar, 1985).

Gamwell, Lynn, *Mathematics and Art: A Cultural History* (Princeton: Princeton University Press, 2015).

Scott, Clive, *Literary Translation and the Rediscovery of Reading* (Cambridge: Cambridge University Press, 2012).

Sicking, J.M.J., *Overgave en verzet. De levens- en wereldbeschouwing van Carry van Bruggen* (Groningen: Passage, 1993).

Woolf, Virginia, *Mrs Dalloway* (London: Vintage, 2004).

Figure 1.1 Title page of Carry van Bruggen, *Eva* (Amsterdam: E. M. Querido, 1928)

1
The New Century

Late last night it hung over the rooftops, it glowed with the light from the street lamps, and tonight it decided to fall - snow. It is the first snow of the new year, the first snow of the new century - snow bringing renewal to the world. Today is in the New Century - the Old Century came to an end yesterday. A hundred years have gone by. A balloon, gradually deflating, deflating - empty at last. An old chain unwound from the capstan, new a hundred years ago. These chains sink into the water when the boats anchor, you are standing in the reeds, you watch them unreel, they touch the water, they break its surface, and it closes over them … then one day, you are sure, they will be raised again into the light, and the boats will once more sail out of the harbour in spring sunshine -, but the old century has sunk for ever.

Snow lies spread in a blanket, snow climbs the walls of houses, sticking to gables … and it is so quiet … and all life seems to have crept away: it is afternoon, it is new year. And she walks alone. The maid opened the door, it slammed shut with David inside and in half an hour she will pass by again. And now the echoes die away and now she returns to what is hers - the way you might seek out something kept hidden from everyone else in a little box, something that was all yours, … this secret something of hers is the walk past a certain house, and her thoughts.

She walks to the end of the low-lying little street, climbs onto the dike and into the strong smell of snow. It sweeps across from the fields, it blows over the water.

The windmills are silhouetted stark black against the whiteness, the bulky hulls of the wintering ships against the sky, against the water, immovable, grey on grey. This is his house, facing the water -, it's all shut up; it's empty now and it'll be cold and very silent -, snow-lit gloom. Inside the door, the narrow hall, the stand with his walking sticks, the hatstand with his coats. One stick and one coat are missing … he is away travelling. The first door on the right is the room with the bookcase, the hanging lamp, the round table, where they sat, where they will sit again, together, the book between them. In this square house, enclosed by his snowy garden, he lives alone. Long ago his wife lived there too. She went mad and had to be taken away, returned once, but was taken away again and eventually died. There was a daughter who went to Sweden with her Swedish husband, a trader, and a son who drowned in a calm Pacific Ocean, on a calm day, between Borneo and Japan, and no-one ever knew why or how. And in February he will be fifty years old.

It is wonderful, the sudden discovery of one another, it is wonderful and natural. You waited, you kept a place free inside yourself for it. You know this, looking back … because you felt you couldn't have waited much longer …

There is a stiff breeze blowing through the harbour, the whitish clouds hover on the horizon. The water gleams, silvery and chill, like a fish, the wooden landing-stages, skimpy little bridges, run across it in a wide arc, - away from the quay, and much further on, returning to the quay. Diagonally and horizontally the water is criss-crossed with brown wooden beams - each one with a snowy line on its rounded surface. This is her world, it has a heart that has beaten with hers for years. In the open curve of the dike the sturdy boatmen lean into the wind, and stare across the harbour in their shiny Sunday clothes. And here … here it is. The sickly sweet aroma penetrates the pure snow smell … buckets clank … water splashes … hooves stamp … coarse song, a short, crude laugh. And the confused beating of her own heart. Because this is the dread place, the lowest of the low … it houses a fat man with red puffy cheeks, who shouts out crude words after all the girls, there are crude words written in chalk on the inside of the doors and the doors are flung and pegged wide open, pushing aside mud and snow. On the outside of the doors there is nothing, the doors are like the fat stable hand's mouth, - after all, the words come from inside him, from his insides. The coach house is deep and dark, and a smoking lamp burns red in the back, and in the gloom horses are frightening animals, with their shuddering necks, their shifty eyes, their shrill whinnying, their angry snorts … the bridles and saddles on the grey walls look like instruments of torture, and coaches that aren't moving, coaches with no horses, suddenly turn into dream shapes.

Why do you understand everything … why is it that the knowledge of so many things stays with you? You can't ever rid yourself of it, you can't forget it. You can't even go back years without it being there, the whispering at school, it made you blush, it made you blink, you got all hot and flustered … your forehead grew clammy. Why does each word make such an impression on you .., why did you ever look at the doors, why is there something that scorches you, glows inside you, yet at the same time you are repelled …? Once was enough for it to get a hold on you.

Why do you consider yourself to be guilty, simply because you understand? You do not find peace until you confess this guilt.

To yourself you say … 'Do you still believe in the stork? Or do you know … do you know … or do you still believe in the stork?' Always this same thing. And it leads you to … unbearable revelations. You daren't connect it in your thoughts to father and mother -, you snapped that thread, but it was spun again and again, out of you and around you … Only by casting it off, only by making an exception for father-and-mother, while you knew better, could you bear living with them. You questioned people with your eyes, married people, and you gave the answer yourself. No … No … No. Surely not, but cutting across all your insistence -, deep certainty: what so many know cannot be denied. All people are cursed. They must suffer the most for the dearest thing … Later, bit by bit, the very worst thing happened. A sentence in a book. 'Their love was not without consequences -, fear took hold of her.'

You didn't understand it right at first -, but it hooked itself into you. It buzzed around you, like a fly. It made you dizzy, woozy, confused. Sometimes in the night, the buzzing grew to a shout. It shouted to itself. What does this mean … 'not without consequences'? The words became ghosts that whispered around you. Who can tell me … tell me, what this … has to do with love? Love … love … you kissed the back of your own hand. They were called Ewald and Dorothea, and they kissed in the rose arbour. 'Their love was not without consequences …' And there it is, it screams out at you: that consequence is: a child. The dearest thing for which you have to suffer the most? Suffer …? 'Their love was not without consequences' … and it is the very thing you may not talk about, may not think about, that the crude words shouted by the stable boy signify. But that can't be right … there must be a way out, a hidden other meaning. You shouldn't have to know all this. It ought not to have the power to hook itself into you, you ought not to understand crude words. Is it not terrible that you are so vulnerable, so receptive to what is dirty? Without even the certainty that it will stay enclosed within you. This was only really brought home to her last year.

Father had slipped and broken his ankle and Nurse Den Hertog came to massage it. They call Nurse Den Hertog 'nosey', they also call her a 'nasty piece of work', but you can't not know her. She stood talking to mother in the hall and they thought they were alone -, but she was standing behind the wardrobe door, and Nurse Den Hertog was talking about Miss Cool, the rich one from 'The Whaler', really strict, really proud, really pious. She nursed Miss Cool when she was seriously ill, she had pneumonia. It gives you a very high temperature, and people lose their senses, they lose themselves and become delirious. And sometimes they say dreadful things. Words you didn't know they knew -, terrible curses … where were they hidden? If you swallow a needle, it travels through your body and sometimes comes out after years, a pin gets stuck and you die … It must be dreadful what Miss Cool said. Nurse Den Hertog called it: 'a stream of vomit.' She also said: 'It was heart-stopping.' She and the doctor did not dare to look at one another. And Mrs Baarslag, her own niece, was present. No-one dared to look at anyone. As though what was written on the inside of the doors, was written inside Miss Cool as well, and the doors had stayed closed for years, years, it was kept 'under lock and key', but the fever broke it open and it came out and everyone got to see it …

'If anyone ever let any of it be known …' my mother said, 'she wouldn't be able to live for the shame.' 'Perhaps it would be good for her, if she heard this thing about herself, she is so hard on others.' That is what Nurse Den Hertog said. And then she left and mother quickly went into the kitchen leaving her still hidden in the wardrobe … And it can start at any moment … this evening, tonight … the pneumonia comes and your temperature gets higher and you wander away from yourself, you're not yourself any more, you're not in yourself … you're delirious, delirious … oh where do you go in your delirium? And the fever forces open the doors and bad words are written on the inside.

Unknowing, her lips have spoken them. Father and mother are present -, they hear … David hears … the doctor hears, and they dare not look at one another, they recoil from her.

And it's not my fault that I know them …

Oh yes it is, you should never have read them. And anyway, you only understand them because you're bad …

For ever afterwards she will look to see if she can read it in their eyes … what happened … what did I say? But you can never ask in so many words. There is a chance that you will die in your delirium … then it would be the last thing they heard you say, and their last memory this: She was not noble and she was not pure.

That afternoon, that evening and in the days that followed, she put on her coat for every errand, every little outing. And mother said: 'How come you suddenly feel the cold. When it isn't cold at all.'

'Well … it's that I'm so worried … that I'll get pneumonia. And I don't want to … I don't want to …'

'What don't you want …?'

Oh, if only you could tell someone, just once. But no. Never.

'I really don't want to die.'

'Silly girl, silly billy.'

The coach house doors are often washed clean, but they don't stay clean -, the fat stable hand with the red, puffy cheeks writes words on them again. But she has been washed clean … and there is nothing left to defile her.

It was a foggy day, in October. And she emerged from the corridor, where it was damp and chill, into the open air where it was milder and lighter - for a moment, you stay there musing in the open door, musing as you stare into the brightness, musing over what is out of reach - and then she went slowly down the steps, which had puddles on them that reflected the sky. You can splatter that image of the sky with your foot, which is what she did, and she had almost reached the bottom step, when she paused to let him past on his way up. He always walks along absorbed in thought -, doesn't say much more in class than is necessary, to the point, and greets you in the street the way he would greet a lady. This is what happened on that afternoon. He raised his hat and she saw his thin, smooth, grey hair, exposed in the light, she returned the greeting and was about to continue. Then his voice brought her to a halt and she stood still, with her feet on different steps. And she looked up at him and he looked down at her and she saw his eyes, blue, and she heard his voice: 'I can't seem to make sense of the fact that you write essays like this one and yet misbehave so frequently in class, that you cause everyone so much trouble.'

Her lips opened, but no sound came out and so they stood there and looked at one another. She felt her eyes opening wide to his.

'And how do you justify that to yourself?'

And then … and then … she said nothing, she jumped off the step, and raced off, but in one second a thousand flowers opened in her, a thousand vows rose to the heavens … a thousand white birds fluttered round her. A thousand vows. 'Kol Nidrei.' All the vows. Nothing ugly left … straight to unblemished purity. Once as a child you wanted to travel beyond the horizon to the Arctic Ocean, to the bears and the magic light and the green transparent mountains … And no more arguing over nothing and no more selfishness … and trying harder to do your best at home and not always forgetting everything you're asked to do, and not just pinning up the selvedge, but sewing properly … and scrubbing your nails better … to stay this way for the rest of your life, and be so utterly like this on the inside that he can come in to you, can look into you at any time of day or night, wherever you are, whatever you are doing; so that there is nothing in you, about you, that you would be afraid for him to see. Not a thought. But why did De Veer give him her essays to read?

Ten days later, in the corridor.

'Could you come to my house on Sunday morning round about eleven? I have something to say to you about your essay.'

She went. She walked past the coach house. The man shouted after her and the words were on the inside of the doors. The voice did not reach her, the words sped past her eyes, their power gone. Yes, man, I don't even hear you, you can give your lungs a rest … yes words, I don't even see you, I never knew you -, can't you tell? Now I am at the top of a tower, there is no dirt that can contaminate me this high up.

The blue exercise book lay on the round table, the room was filled with silver light, outside are the quays, the harbour … the floating planks lie criss-crossed, like cross-hatching on a drawing. He said: 'Sit down over there and read it out to me.'

It was the essay about pity. De Veer had already seen it. Oh … ten out of ten!

'You mustn't say that you've already seen your mark.'

'No, I won't say anything.'

And she read about what makes your life a misery. Because, after all, you can't do anything about it. Not about the tramps, and not about the sailors … not about Rémy and Vitalis … not about the man without a tongue, who's from Russia. And your pity swells … swells, your head is fire and flame. You feel it even with people who don't deserve it -, with the nasty boss. You had said to yourself: No, don't pity him. He must be punished, the boys avenged. But if he is imprisoned, and about to undergo punishment, your pity will force its way out and speed to him. There is nothing you can do about it. Sometimes you almost pity animals more than people - skinny horses you see being thrashed, hungry hunted dogs, old ill cats … once even that black rat in a grey nest as the Sabbath evening fell … Oh look, that chair once stood in a room beside a stove … and now it's floating there, floating over there … floating into the canal … floating out to sea where it will be lost for ever.

'It's very nice … very good … I would have given you nine out of ten for it. It doesn't do to want to make it too beautiful.'

'But as beautiful as you can?'

'As beautiful as you can … without overbeautification.'

She had never heard that word before. He also said this: 'You mustn't write "lifeless objects". You wouldn't say that, would you?'

'But there is such a thing as spoken language and written language, isn't there? That's what Mr De Veer says anyway.'

And then he gave a little laugh. 'Well, if Mr De Veer says so, then I would keep that. And I hear that you have already turned over a new leaf at school.'

'I want to carry on. I want to be even better.'

She did not look at him. Her voice was hoarse. They were standing in front of the bookcase, which covers the whole of the back wall of the room. She thought: each book has hundreds of pages, each page has hundreds of words, every word has a meaning. This is … a world, closed. A curiosity swelled in her, an unease, her eyes ran over the books from bottom to top, from left to right … fixed on them, let go of them. She turned away from them again.

The fat, superior housekeeper has come in with two cups of coffee and a plate of brown biscuits on a tray. They have drunk the coffee, eaten the biscuits, facing one another across the round table. And a charabanc full of noisy people went past the house, the windows rattled, the silver light seemed to tremble. The water stretched out, grey underneath but with a gleaming silver surface, the distant ships stood out like dark clogs in a light mist, solid, and the bridges so fragile as though constructed from matchsticks laid side-to-side without being joined together and all so alike in their wide arc that it seemed as though you kept seeing the same thing, like the stone when you play ducks and drakes. And he said: 'Perhaps you'd like to come again on Sunday morning?'

And again, and again.

But now comes the moment in which she rises higher, leaving even the tower below her, in which she rises so high that contact with life becomes unbearable.

He said: 'You can't come next Sunday, I've promised it to Loukie. She is so behind because of missing school so much. If I don't help her get back on track, she won't be able to catch up.'

Oh … so next Sunday, Loukie will be sitting here! Loukie is blond, fair-skinned and good, she is the darling of all the teachers. His too?

'Do you like Loukie more than me? Do you like Loukie best … of all the girls in the class?'

He was standing by the bookcase.

'You do ask silly things … stupid … childish things.'

The light trembled against the ceiling. She was silent … a little shamefaced, a little taken aback and … a little comforted.

They read Vondel. Controlled and sing-song, his voice followed his thin finger along the lines of the play.

'You have to learn to understand him really well before you can appreciate him.'

'Yes, I want to learn to understand him. I want to learn to understand everything.'

Understand everything. The words echoed inside her … her own words … an echo of thoughtful wonder … she stared across the purple velvet tablecover which caught the light to resemble little violet leaves. And suddenly his hand, reaching round her back, lay on her shoulder, pressed it lightly and then fled …. And his voice had an intimacy … a cracked intimacy … a voice which cracked with intimacy.

'You know well enough … well enough … I like you best … you are the only one …'

A thousand vows to heaven … a thousand white birds, a thousand solemn vows … - *Kol Nidrei* … All the vows … This she could bear, this made her happy, fulfilled, satisfied, but now all that is left is the despair of a wild disoriented desiring, the torture of a persistent longing that seeks to annihilate itself and does not know how.

Why did he stay below when she rose above the tower? How shall I make him understand that everything must change now, that things cannot go on as they were, now that this has happened, that it must be put into new words, borne along by new deeds? Oh I will never get over this. One of us will surely die before Sunday … really it would be best if we both died on Friday or Saturday, but Sunday came … they were sitting at the round table, and his right hand was resting on her left hand and their eyes dwelt together in the book.

And it was then that she had to flee. The housekeeper came in with the cups of coffee and the thin brown biscuits … the chair scraped, her fingertips were ice-cold and she stood by the window.

'Aren't you having your cup of coffee?'

Oh, don't say it … don't say it. Don't let it continue like this … let us … let us …. Oh, high above the highest towers … and her heart gasped in her like a separate being with separate pain, tearing at its pain.

'No, thank you.'

For a moment he looked up.

There were the ships in the silvery light, unrigged, sails put away for their winter sleep, the clouds had left the sky, brown rafts floated in great pools of blue. She heard him eating and drinking ... her heart gasps in its own pain, tears at its pain ... oh, this is not what I want, not what I want. On Monday in school ... she saw him ... coming out of a door. Oh misery, shackled in slavery to low things, to hidden humiliation. And the pain of wild desire, striking out in all directions and unable to orient itself, to find a goal, a name, refuses to attach itself to anything that has a name ... sometimes it happens blowing bubbles, the bubble tugs agonisingly at the pipe and you blow so it grows and swells shimmering ever more golden and silver, until it bursts and your hand is wet ...

'And this is what she means when she says I'll be back in half an hour!'

'Oh David ... am I so late? What time is it then?'

But he isn't cross, he is happy, he has great news to tell her. First of all -, why Mr Van Hasselt summoned him. There was a letter, a tutor was sought for a disabled boy in a large house just outside the town where David went to school, and David is going to be recommended for the post. Now he won't need to look for a position at a school after his examination, every day he will have free hours all to himself, he will learn Latin and Greek and will give the boy, who is ten now, lessons in them when he is twelve.

The boy is called Berthold. One morning, seven years ago now, his mother found him in bed paralysed, he had been chasing his ball through the garden the day before -, slowly, slowly life is beginning to return to his legs ... Mr Van Hasselt said: a changeable, wilful child, what they are looking for is someone, not too old, to be a friend to him, who can teach and lead, who loves studying -, because of all these things he will entrust David with the task, has chosen him, will recommend him. David will become what he wants to be in life, Berthold's father will help him. His life will shoot like a rocket way above hers -, for to her, there is a today, around which her being twines itself; the 'future' is nothing more than what you see through an opaque window, shadowy.

And now they are walking side by side as they have done for the many days of the many years that have passed, and without speaking, they know where they are going, along the harbour and around the bend, where the water is so wide, where the harbour, waterway, canal, have merged to make a lake. This is the path they used to walk, from when they were small till they were fourteen. Then he took the exam and got the scholarship and went to the school in the north, where Uncle Eli lives and from then on only came home in the holidays. Then they resumed the old walks, they walked along the harbour, counted the ships. Every autumn she had to write and tell him how many were going to spend the winter here - you can tell by the dismantled yard arms - she faithfully wrote to tell him when the 'Haidarabad' had put in again. Between them they created a whole collection of winter days in letters, but those years have come to an end now.

'Today … the New Century … the very first day of a hundred new years.'

'Isn't it like going into a big, empty room?'

'Like being under … a … yes, a dome. Like being under an enormous dome.'

'Yes … empty … empty … and the Old Century is brim-full, packed full.'

'Yesterday we could say: The Battle of Waterloo was in this century.'

'And Napoleon died on St Helena in this century.'

'And the Franco-German war was in this century.'

'And we ourselves were born in this century.'

'There's one thing it would be good to know … it would be good to know … They say that the apple tree is already contained in an apple pip … just as it will be when it is grown … the curve of its branches … and the smell and taste and shape of the apples … And would there be such a thing as the seed which contains everything … everything that will be the New Century, which is still empty …?'

'And even if there were, it would still all be unknown.'

'So, there is only one thing we can be sure of.'

'Sure of one thing …?'

'That we were born in the last century … and that we will die in this one.'

'And would we both … at the same time … like you sometimes read about twins?'

'We can't know, only the one thing …'

The wind blows cold over the fields, the chill, gleaming water stretches into the distance. There aren't many ships left this year, the hibernating few are waiting for spring, they lie as though they are growing out of the water.

Only the one thing … we can know … that we will die in this century … Somewhere in the hundred years that have just begun … one day … one day … Knowledge, knowledge, come visit me … Death, you are still far away, I can push you away from me when you make me feel anxious … Death, I want to know you now. Once I knew you

... once that knowledge planted itself right in my heart ... in the night after the day of the storm. At school we had read that poem 'One day, black sand, like the night, will cover us o'er' - the sky was so dark, it was like evening in the class, it was my turn, but I couldn't read ... I would have ... I would have started to cry ... then the schoolmaster quickly gave us that other story 'Silly Annie and clever Lizzie' ... but that night the knowledge was waiting for me, it came and settled on me. I knew death. There was a white pip in the black earth and in that pip was me. How thankful you should be that you don't always have to know what is always true ... and yet you sometimes want to summon it, though you have no power over it.

'Look, our pile of beams ... almost snowed over.'

Yes, it looks like a mound of snow on the high, empty dike and so lonely standing out above everything. We're coming to rest on you again today, old pile of beams, we're coming to keep you company! In the summer there is toadflax growing deep inside in the sand that has blown in.

'And do you remember that we once discovered a whole garland of purple vetch in it? You couldn't find its beginning or its end.'

It is wonderful to sit high up, your legs pulled in towards your body. You look out across the water, across the polders -, you see polder after polder, you see one distant view dissolve into another ...

'And we moved our heads, and then the avenues of trees moved apart ... they passed through one another.'

'Yes, that day with father, when the air trembled above the rapeseed.'

'In the middle of summer, when the Kaiser came ...'

'And that morning, with father too. Going to town on foot for the first time. And we rested over there ... close to where the big turf heap is now ... And it was so cool and sweet out in the air full of skylarks. And the town seemed so far away ... an endless walk ... seven kilometres!'

'It was seven years ago, we were eleven.'

'And do you remember this as well? We went to father. We said ... father, may we walk with you to town one day? It was April. And father thought about it and father said: in three months we will go. It sounded like: never ...'

'Three months are for ever when you're eleven ...'

'I remember this too, in the history book by Sluys and Hoofiën. It said "For nine months the Israelites had remained in the desert. In this relatively short time, much happened." I thought ... am I reading this right ... or is "months" a printing error that should say "weeks"? I did not understand that you could say that about "nine months". "A relatively short time".'

'Nine months still is a long time anyway ...'

'But how can it be ... that distances and times seem greater the smaller you are ...? Three months. Seven kilometres ...'

'Is it that you measure everything against yourself?'

'Compare it with yourself ...'

'Yes. Father had an orange each for us.'

'And do you remember ... how we ... suddenly ... heard a clock tower ... in the town that was still in the distance ...?'

'But don't you think, don't you think ... that even so, all those years, seven years, have gone by so quickly, in a flash?'

Silently the water flowed far below them, past their feet, silently the grey canal flowed to the sea ... a strange solemnity ... the New Century! The water is deep, not a murmur rises from it -, the cropped reeds do not move, do not go with the flow, they stand stock-still in shining circles and silvery foam. 'So calm today, so calm ...'

But there are noises, here and there, there is a short, fierce dog bark, tracking low across the snow, which seems to come from all directions at once .... It could be anywhere, that bad, barking animal ...

'A black dog ...'

'Yes, a black dog ...'

And now the tinkle of horse-bells. So distant, so small, like the tiny silver bells, the decorated spindles that are on the Torah scrolls. Any moment now the horse and cart must appear -, where? Still hidden. Behind the farmhouse perhaps with its hefty trees forming one dark clump.

And in every sound memory resides, it bursts out of the lightest tinkle, out of the silence itself ... like what you learnt about seed pods at school, seed pods on plants ... that burst open in a puff of wind and the seeds shoot everywhere. These are the old days, the old walks. And through the picture of winter, summer emerges, in a sigh, in a lapping of water ... which caught like a hook, pulled aside a shutter ... and you see ... blue sky, blue water ... yellow flowers, grasses ... and the shutter closes. This is how, one winter morning in bed, at the very first sound of the very first bird, she saw the stalk of a lady's smock glistening ... it was bending in the wind. And a spread of sugar Easter eggs, alternating pink-and-white, in a shop window ...

'And does it happen to you that places where you walked keep your thoughts for you?'

'And they come back to you the next time.'

This is what they talk about, until they are silent again, staring silently into the flowing water.

'This strange solemnity … today, around everything …'

'As though everything knows about the New Century.'

'You might well think that.'

'You would think it was rather wonderful, if everything was feeling the same as you, and that you both knew this of one another.'

And now they are silent again and now she knows: it is going to happen … the moment has come … He never brings it out straight away … but she has already seen the grey notebook in his pocket.

'Theo has given me another poem to read out to you.'

'Yes …'

Nowadays they can say it without laughing and without embarrassment, as though slowly they have come to believe in the existence of the friend who doesn't exist, Theo, the sickly boy, who entrusts his poems to David, who tells him to read them to her. They've been talking about him for so long … every holiday, often in a letter, saying that his illness is worse again, or that he has perked up a bit at last, and what he is reading, and what he is doing … they created him together, so that now he exists for both of them … for her he consists of David's words and her own daydreams … an image, clear and vague at the same time and so deeply engraved in her that she can no longer imagine life without it. Imagining him no longer there hurts, and she doesn't want to. 'Theo,' who consists solely of David's words and her daydreams, must stay … But that expression -, that something 'consists of something' … Air consists of oxygen and carbon dioxide … Theo consists of words and dreams … Is it … the same? Or not …?

'Shall I begin. Are you going to listen?'

'Yes, I'm listening …'

No, she isn't listening. She heard one line, and sank down through something, sank through the depths, sank to the bottom and there she finds the other words … sweet, sweet … dark and sweet. And the music of David's voice …

'You know well enough … you are the dearest … the only one …'

Or was it something else, was it: 'You know very well that you are the dearest …'

'Now listen … now the first lines are repeated:

Where by moonshine clouds are racing
To the grey horizon gone

At his window he stands gazing
In his white shirt all alone …

Do you think they are beautiful … these first lines … these last lines?'

'Yes, beautiful!' There are poplars … there is, in the sky, inky blue and silver interwoven … silvery cotton wool, absorbing the inky blue; faint, wide, coloured rings tremble round a veiled moon. A young man stands in his shirt.

And David imagined it, saw it, wrote it in the grey notebook. It is alright for her to know -, only he will not say it to her in so many words. And if she were in his place, she wouldn't either, she too would dream up a boy or a girl.

'And Theo would like to know, I was supposed to ask you … what you think about that repetition. First "at his window" and then straight afterwards "in his white shirt". "His" twice. He had wondered about: "At *the* window". What do you think?'

No, oh no … not at 'the' window. 'The' window is everyone's window -, his mother and father's window, his brothers' and sisters', 'the window' is the living room window. But if you say 'his window', then you see him in the dark, inside the four walls, lonely and enclosed.

And outside it is lighter than inside, and outside are the poplars … inkily blue-black interwoven with silver … silvery cotton wool absorbing the blue-black ink … this is what the sky is like, and wide coloured rings are trembling … an enormous target, a veiled white rose: the moon!

How beautiful the last two lines are … but why are they so beautiful …? Why is this beautiful …?'

At his window he stands gazing
In his white shirt all alone …

'Yes, I don't know myself … I mean … Theo won't know why either.'

And they stare across the water, flowing steadily, far below their feet. Not a murmur rises from it. The cropped reeds stand in light-reflecting circles and silvery foam. Behind the outer dike it looks as though the polders are sinking … sunken … the twilight forces them into the earth. Oh … look … the first light! Over there in the distant farmhouse a hand lit the lamp, shining out over the white expanse and now it is evening. And here a cart, with its lamps already lit, turns out of a yard, dragging a double track of gold across the snow. If there had been no snow, you would have heard the horse trotting, if there had been no snow, it would not be so quiet … so quiet … as it is now, suddenly, inside herself … where words were silenced, echo died, only the poplars left reaching to the coloured rings around the moon. And now it is as though the silence within her and the silence outside her flow into one another, her own breath is one breath with the snowy expanse, with the flowing water.

'Did you hear horse bells somewhere again?'

'It could be your imagination. Your expectations creating them.'

'Yes, listening invites the sound …'

'Sound that perhaps isn't there.'

'Sound that existed somewhere deeper, like the deeper stars which your eye summons to appear in the sky.'

'Yes, sometimes they seem to leap towards your eye.'

The horizons sucked the daylight towards them … it has dwindled in slow, gradual colour changes -, denser and denser shadow fills the space between sky and earth, fills the high, empty dome of the New Century. Distant windows breathe glowing gold over the snow. Solitude, loneliness … all surrenders to the new Future. The silent persistence of the steadily-flowing water … it is playing its part and is ready for the next hundred years.

'And when we are all, all of us gone … this water will still …'

'The same water …'

'Different and the same …'

Slowly the last warmth has left their bodies and clothes, they feel the cold reaching their skins.

'We're getting so stiff … we must go home …'

'Yes.'

But they cannot. The flowing water is keeping them captive, and the white unendingness under the darkening sky.

As though they will never again sit together like this if they interrupt this sitting together …

'And now, the first day of the New Century is already past.'

Yes … This is how it begins … this is how it unrolls … this is how the hours mount, and pile up into days, with their happenings, days which group themselves into years, with their events, until at last that great big empty Future will be filled. And then that Century will be finished.

Just one more moment. They stand in the twilight in front of the pile of beams and stare into the deep, flowing water … it stares up at them … eye-in-eye they stand with the water … breath-on-breath with the expanse, heart-on-heart with the silence … they are bound together with everything in one life, under the icy evening sky, under the dome of the New Century.

'But is this not exactly like … the beginning of the world?'

Yes, that's it! It's the Torah story of the Creation of the World … 'In the beginning God created the Heaven and the Earth. Now the earth was unformed and void … And darkness … And the Spirit of God hovered over the face of the waters …'

And the first day, which they watched pass before their very eyes! And a great sigh of emotion … - *vayehi-erev, vayehi-voker, yom echad* … And it was morning, and it was evening, the First Day …

2
Homewards

The sky is like the rising smoke of purple Bengal fire, it is studded with lights like red-and-silver Christmas tree baubles. She is walking on the open platform with Andy. Behind them is the long, dark roof, like a cupped hand … this is the trains' dungeon. In they thunder, out of the emptiness, and are caught as though in a trap, where they struggle to free themselves with powerless screeching, urgent panting; their groans hammer against the walls and roof. In there the evening gloom descended hours ago.

Light and sound inhabit the purple mists. Red-and-green lights bloom in the sky, yellow-and-purple lights bloom along the ground, flowers that have sprung up from far-flung seeds, and locomotives glide, heavy, slow, high-breasted swans in a sea of mist. They venture out of the dark dome … they venture out hesitantly, hold back again … they cross and turn in uncomprehended regularity … tooters call in the mist, as though distant, yet are close by, the toots flatter, the toots command, the locomotives respond, grumpy or happy, and hiss, as they release clouds of white steam.

Every day she walks here like this as evening falls, always beyond the dark roof -, to the left she looks out over the wide, quiet quay, which catches the last of the light, the houses are old and narrow, arranged in a slight curve, the houses are tall and silent, each window in its pale, yellow frame. And to the right is the water, in silvery grey motion, velvety in the mist, stippled with golden light, wandering stars on invisible masts, rowing boats like glow-worms so low in the water, so unpredictable and so quick. And away from her speeds the shining double track, cutting a way home through the polders. Every evening the return home is a good ending, every morning the departure for town a happy start. Each day the city makes her its own again, takes possession of her …

In the mornings there is the delight of the bright water, the watchful towers, the intimacy of old alleyways, the tarred house fronts with the luminous yellow of the window frames. A dull melancholia pushes its way towards you out of old warehouse facades across motionless water and forces you to stop in your tracks, like a hand. There are the bridges with their fine musculature, the supple, living bridges, rearing, leaping bridges, which cut and divide up the water, link and join the quays, which constantly change the view. And the large houses, elegantly grouped in curves, move your thoughts on to time, which passes, to people who die, to things that remain. In the afternoons there are the towers encircled in mist and rain … pigeons flapping their way home … seagulls weary of the swell in swirling mist … activity coming to a close … smells and sounds in gathering evening glow.

And then she allows some of this burgeoning love to come alive in her, take possession of her in willing intimacy … meanwhile the day just past, and the school, live on in her. It is a large, light school, which stands new and fresh at the water's edge, by the hurly-burly of the quay … The water is jubilant in the sun, and flashes splashes of light in through the windows which strike the white ceiling. There they remain, dancing sleepily or urgently, depending on the movement of the water. Little Leendert with his hunched shoulder and damp mouth is always watching them, you can tell from his little face that they make him happy … he laughs … but you must tell him not to because you are the schoolmistress. You must say: 'Leendert, pay attention to your sums, you got them all wrong again yesterday.' That wipes the smile from his face and you go over to him and look down on him and he somehow feels it: you only said that because you are 'Miss' and he surrenders his little head to you, against your stomach, against your striped pinafore, and his downy smile has returned; and you walk back to your high chair, he mustn't see you fighting back tears, for his crooked shoulder and his damp little mouth. And Truitje Waars can't stop talking, you can make her sit somewhere else, you can punish her … it is an urge, her round eyes drink in life and she is full to the brim, and what goes in must come out, it must come out in all directions, or she would burst. And the 'old boss' walks through the light-dappled corridors, humming to himself, and taps on the glass door and pulls a face under his old-fashioned cap and the children squirm and giggle on the benches at this dotty, kind, headmaster. But every day Arjen Brand grumbles more grimly through gritted teeth at the 'state of things' … he has brought unrest into the school, it is creeping through the entire city, from school to school: there should be no Heads any more, school should become a 'republic', the school assembly its government.

Daily she hears those around her talking vehemently about this, disputing fiercely, and she can't help thinking about it sometimes because as soon as she has been taken on permanently, she will have to take sides,- at the moment she can still let it settle gently on her, which is what she does and looks left to the quay and right to the water ... and then suddenly, that strange, hot, sharp-and-sweet smell that the locomotives give off ... and it assails her demanding to be given a name ... name of an autumn flower, that she smelt once, in passing, as evening fell, but she cannot find its name ... And the smell subsides and her thoughts rush ahead into the evening and she sees herself in the small town behind the sunken polders, in the little town across the water, going home through the dark, empty streets. Sometimes you carry in you the pleasant weight, the urgency of a story you plan to tell; like a headteacher came that morning to observe her teaching, or she has been summoned to another school to give a test lesson. As they leave the Heads say: 'You will be hearing from me' -, and mostly you don't hear anything, but there is always the chance, that one day soon a letter will arrive for you.

These are the peaceful days of her new existence. Each morning she arrives in the rattling train and the city opens its arms and she strides along her regular route and finds everything in its rightful place at the right time, and she greets the dear old man in his herring booth, that break-away bit of fairground on the humpback bridge over the sluice -, and there is the frightening quarrelsomeness of the white-jacketed women which suddenly breaks off into tremendous laughter ... and in school Little Leendert, who laughs at the little suns dancing dozily or angrily without knowing he is doing it, and Truitje who would burst if she had to keep silent ... and the doors close and it is quiet and the school is like a block of silence, a block consisting of silent little boxes, in the midst of the noise of freedom under the open sky ... and you put on your large pinafore and you are the schoolmistress ... you walk between the benches, bend to look at exercise books, and little mouths smile their expectation, little eyes lift up their fear to you ... and warm little hands, warm little creatures, find their way shyly into your own hands ... and now arithmetic is done for the day ... and now you climb on to your high chair and now you are going to tell a story and now all you see are eyes ... eyes ... eyes ... pools of eyes in raised faces, and there is one pair of poor, painful eyes and that is Mausje and she is sighing with pleasure before you've begun, before you've said a word.

And so the days flow, evaporate, move peacefully toward an even more peaceful evening -, but this day ends in oppressiveness and anxious tension ... Andy has left the school with her and Andy is walking beside her and Andy talks about her life, her experiences. Shock waves flow with the words from Andy's lips, enter her very ears, rise higher, fill her, fill her up. She cannot answer, it seems to her that Andy is mistaken, that the thoughts she associates with everything are wrong, the explanation she gives to everything is wrong. She says: 'All men are the same, and all men want the same thing.'

She insists, and her stories prove it: all men are the same and all men want the same thing. And there was even one ... you feel yourself pushing away the thought, as though with hands and feet, as though in mortal fear, the thought that Andy forces on you ... for the worst one of all was a clergyman!

'Yes, that evening at table I could already sense what was going to happen ... his eyes ... every time his wife looked away for a moment ... men's eyes, I know them so well ... and first thing in the morning on the stairs ... after that I barricaded my door. First I put the table in front of it, with a chair on top of it, and a tray with a pile of books, water carafe and glass on it ... you can imagine, if that lot had come down ... no-one would sleep through that ... And what do you think ...? Through the window! In his own house! A clergyman ... married ... three children ...'

There is an old dream ... a crowd of crazily misshapen animals was pushing its way along a narrow winding path between pancake stalls ... red curtains billowed ... a dull red, the colour of spilt blood ... the leader of the pack was a large, grey elephant ... You want to call out, want to say: - Andy ... are you certain that this is what he wanted, ... this thing you are talking about ... this thing you so often talk about, this thing you have been talking about today ever since school, so much that it makes me feel completely confused ... couldn't there have been another reason why he wanted to come into your room? But she cannot call out ... she knows only too well ... there can be no other reason. And yet she doesn't know. Always the same mixture of feelings: doubt about whether things really are as people say ... a deeper feeling of certainty ... yes, they really are ... an even deeper despair and shame at the overlaid certainty.

'And I was standing at the foot of my bed in an instant ... and I was standing there as good as naked ... because it was in the middle of summer.'

Andy ... Andy ... you are wearing your nightdress, surely, even in the summer ... She doesn't say this. Her eyes blink as though the light is too bright, too fierce. The tooters call out of the mist ... they flatter ... they command ... the locomotives recede and turn in uncomprehended regularity ... they shriek and hiss ... red-and-green flowers bloom up high, purple-and-yellow flowers bloom down low ... and across the water, in the distance, the boat appears ... to left and right a string of golden coins above the dark current. 'Yes ... and then ... but what are you looking at so intently? You are listening, aren't you?'

Andy's face is turned towards hers. She has glorious red hair which shines at her temples as though spun from fine metal threads, her forehead is high and white and shiny smooth -, under it are her deep-set eyes, glowing blue, like gemstones, blooming blue, like flowers. And her lips are deep red lips, that make you want to run your finger gently along them, soft and deep red, with their straight, incised little folds of soft, dark red rose petals ... and the corners are drawn like tiny snakes ... sometimes the snakes disappear suddenly and when they do, it is as though a shiver passes through her at something bitter that she can taste inside herself.

'And do you know what he had the impudence to say ... do you know what he tried to do ...?'

Yes ... Andy ... yes, tell me! Tell me what he had the impudence to say, what he tried to do! ... Take me into this world, the world of acid light. No ... Andy ... no ... don't tell me. In the book there was a girl, a girl called Ethel, an orphan, lost among bad people. A book lay on the piano ... a book with 'immoral stories' ... and with ... 'depraved pictures' ... she was alone in the room ... and no-one could have seen her ... and it would never have come to light ... But she didn't do it. 'Deeply offended, Ethel screwed up the disgusting pamphlet into a ball and threw it on the fire.' That is how I want to be, I don't want to be any worse than I am now ... Help me, Andy, don't tell me anything ... anything else about all those bad men ... about that man in the town where you lived with your parents, where you went to the girls' school, who grabbed hold of you in the park ... about the pharmacist who put bad notes in your bottle of pills ... about the doctor ... the doctor ... a doctor, even ... in whose hands you had to place yourself ... do not tell me what they say, what they are after. There is something in me that strains towards the acid light ... but there is also something in me that wants to turn away from it ... I want to know and not know, I want to hear and not hear ... Let's, let's ... close the gates ... let's stand with our backs against them ... let's make haste to where it is safe, where it is good ... Oh Andy, let's take refuge on the high ground for our own sakes ... let's do as I did when I was small, to combat the threatening shapes of night ... cling to light things ... let's talk about the school and how Arjen Brand had another go at Ebner … it's getting the old headmaster down … it must have been lovely and peaceful in the old school, once upon a time … I managed to give Leendert 'satisfactory' for his sums today … Mausje with his sore, inflamed eyes, they hurt so much now all the time … he cries with the pain … and that makes it worse … and Truitje Waars was allowed to talk for the whole of the last hour … because it was her birthday … and she spouted like a fountain … like a twirling little garden sprinkler, she spouted away …

'Did she show you her new pinafore? She said: "I'm going to show all the schoolmasters and mistresses my new pinafore."'

'Who …?'

'Truitje Waars!'

'How on earth did you arrive at Truitje Waars …?'

Andy … Andy … let's stand with our backs against the gates. I can feel that I want to hear … I'm not sure that I can be like Ethel … Andy, let's keep the gates to evil shut, what's behind them can only bring shame and scandal …

'And all those weeks I walked around with pain in my back, my left hip, and didn't dare allow myself to be examined.'

'Oh but I can understand that so well! I didn't want that either … perhaps I might have got a scholarship like my brother David if I had … but you had to have a medical examination and I didn't want that …'

'So you knew too that you can't trust them!'

'Not trust …? Our doctor …? Who always says that a doctor must above all be a good person to be a good doctor …? No Andy, but it's our own sense of shame. You don't get undressed … for another person. Wasn't it Mary of Burgundy …? That is how I want to be. Whether it's possible, if your life is in danger, is a different matter … It's the shame … and it's humiliating … I'm already dreading the medical for my permanent position, even if it is with a woman doctor here … it's still humiliating. To have to undress for another person. Actually, that goes for everything that you are made to do … you are ordered to do … everything where they don't recognize your own will … everything in which they try to make a thing, a slave, an object of you. Did I ever tell you how as a child I stayed away from a party, because in the newspaper it said that the children in the top classes would be 'arranged' on the steps of the town hall! I objected to being 'arranged'. In the same way, I wouldn't want to be laid on a table for an operation … or examination … I even have a problem with gym because of the commands … I always feel the urge to say: do it yourself! So I can quite understand that you didn't want to allow yourself to be examined ….'

But Andy doesn't answer, she takes hold of her arm, and when she next speaks, she is following her own thoughts. 'They will make life difficult for you too. Your turn will come. You have beautiful eyes.'

'Do I have … do I have beautiful eyes?' The glow races through her.

'Yes … and a lovely colour skin … brown … so warm … and your downy cheeks …'

'Do I …? Do I …? At school they called me: yellow gipsy.'

'And your short hair … your jolly boys' hair … how did you come to have short hair? Have you been ill recently?'

'No, I am never ill … Oh but this hair, it's a mad story … it still makes me laugh, the way it stopped them in their tracks that day. At home they wanted me to have plaits … they thought that was nicer … My hair was always so unkempt … but I didn't want to … and so, one day, I came up with this. And now I'm ready in five minutes every morning.'

'It makes you look like a boy … and I could take you for a boy … but I'm pleased that you aren't a boy. Boys are mean … I would be afraid of you.'

The locomotives hiss as though they have lips and a tongue … you read about snakes that hiss like that … the locomotives glide, dark high-breasted swans in a sea of mist … they dim the blooms of light and let them flare again … they toot threateningly, flatteringly, commandingly … call as though distant yet are close by … the smell assails her, wanting a name, it was an autumn flower, wet with rain, it was an evening … one single evening … a hot, empty smell … Smell, let go of me, don't plague me for a name -, I can't give you one.

The quiet houses by the quay below are tender in the dusk -, all that lives of them now is the tender and luminous yellow of the windows … the afternoon city sank … the evening city rises up, orange, red and Christmas-tree silver.

'If I think of you in boys' clothes … what an attractive boy you would be …'

Oh Andy, I feel warm all over when you say such sweet things to me …

And now they walk quietly, for Andy can't think of anything else, hasn't any more to say … they walk up and down the platform in the darkness and Andy's hand glows around hers, soft and tight. And gradually, more and more people have gathered, feet shuffle in the dark, voices crescendo, brush past, die down, and repeat the cycle -, a stream of lit faces, men, women, turned towards them in absent-minded wondering.

But now there is a rumbling in the fog, and a small, black cube emerges -, the train is shunted backwards along the platform. It jerks and lurches to a halt, and a man creeps into each of the dark boxes, lights a lamp in it, and lowers himself backwards this time out of a light box … Oh weariness, strange heaviness … Did it hurt Andy when she suddenly pulled her head to one side? Surely girls don't kiss each other on the lips.

Oh, to throw it all down beside you like a heavy parcel for a moment. To feel yourself emptying out, and to let yourself be jolted, the fiercer the better, so that you are shaken out in this little train compartment, that you know as well as your own little room, and where everything seems to be loose, a musical ensemble of tinkling, rattling and flapping that clashes all the tunes together, and your eyes shut tight as a mussel shell, as though they will never open again, … and this is how you go home, you swerve round the bend, fly across the dark water, race into the flatland and into the little station.

She almost slid off the seat and sits upright again and stares indignantly into the darkness. This suddenly seems like a strange, long journey, a journey lasting hours, through distant lands … the mist dispersed … shadows of trees near and far flit past a yellow-grey gleam on the horizon … a reedy pool, far to the west, catches the light and reflects it onward … and suddenly she recoils from her own face, so close, so clear behind the window. Beautiful eyes … downy cheeks … o but you mustn't look like that, casting your eyes upwards from under your eyebrows. They say: that look is common. But how come there is no more common a word than 'common'? It wasn't always like that, not when you were small. Then it was 'common' to tell tales and play marbles … later on it became a repulsive word, because it was always used to hint at … *that*. Mother never says it, Mother says: immoral. Mr De Veer at school always said: unbecoming. In the paper you read: depraved. Unbecoming is the best word, it is a respectable and calm word, which doesn't make you feel anything except that what is referred to is 'heartily disapproved of.' This is how Mr De Veer would want you to speak. Condemned, without that unbearable, hidden pleasure, that secretive reaching …

Slowly the dike rises towards the bridge … this is where the smell of coal begins, the autumn air, thick, sharp, rising from the low-lying polders on either side … far away to the west, the reedy pool glimmers in loneliness … Reedy pool, one day I will come to you …

Suddenly the black, rain-washed silence. Over there to the North, the train rumbles away in the dark and she stands all alone in the square. The all-too-sweet-cake smell of the lemonade factory hangs thick and dense, caught in the damp air. High up in the wall, one lone lit window. A boy goes past her whistling … How far away … how long ago it all seems … and every day this same change … an expansion and a contraction … she is much bigger here in the little town than over there in the city … she is much smaller here with Father and Mother than over there in the school.

Once she has turned the corner into their own street, she always involuntarily slows her pace. The house is over there, between the seventh and the eighth street lamp, golden rays in the velvet night -; between neighbour Bol and neighbour Bruin, that is where she lives, that is where she is expected. And she strides along the side with the houses, listens to the sounds as she passes by, dull noises behind wooden partitions, muffled voices … she knows who lives in each house … each family enclosed in its own walls. Living, living together … she takes her fleeting, unformed thoughts past the one house after the other, moving toward the one that waits, evening after evening … And then unexpectedly light streams out of the open door into the darkness, spreads a golden film over the wet cobblestones … and Father comes down the steps. Father and big Boasson have come out of the house together.

'Father …!'

They stand still … and Father explains to her … they have to go somewhere for a moment … they'll be back soon.

'But Father … what is the matter? Father … has something happened at home, to mother?'

No, nothing has happened at home, but there is something … something sad … a sudden, great upheaval has occurred, a disagreement in the congregation.

'But what is it, Father, what is it?'

Smiling, big Boasson looks at Father, but Father shakes his head. No.

She stands wide-eyed looking up at the two of them, and big Boasson smiles at her.

'How old are you, by the way …?'

'I'll be nineteen next month.'

'And do you still believe in the …?'

But Father grabs him by the arm, and pulls him along into the darkness, she hears big Boasson laughing, but Father doesn't laugh with him.

What can it be … what has happened … what upheaval …? she wonders by the coat stand. Mother's face peering round the living room door.

'Is it you …? Did you have a good day today …?'

'Yes, everything was fine.'

No, nothing was fine … shh … there was Andy. But that doesn't belong here. The cavalcade of crazily malformed animals out of her old dream, winding their way between the pancake stalls. Faded red curtains billowing, the colour of spilt blood. A grey elephant led the way … And here is Mother. 'Mother, what has happened in the congregation … what kind of disagreement?' But Mother puts her finger to her lips. There is a tangible fear and dejection … and at the table, opposite the corner with the white cloth where her plate, her fork and knife, wait as they do every day, sits Mrs Snoek. She sits slumped in her chair like an empty sack, a glass of water in front of her … she is purple and pale from crying, her eyes have been cried out, her mouth cried soggy -, her threadbare old bandeau has slipped down over her forehead, sits askew, and her forehead shines as though she had just washed it and forgotten to dry it. She looked up briefly, nodded absently and is staring in front of her again.

'Is it because of Mrs Snoek … because of her husband … the Rabbi … this disagreement?'

The question brings Mother to a halt on her way to the kitchen, hesitating.

'May I tell her?'

'Go on, tell her … she's a big girl now … almost a woman …'

She sits waiting behind her corner of the table with the white cloth and gleaming plate, she looks at Mrs Snoek. How terribly tired you must be … how unspeakably wretched, to sit like that, so hunched, so motionless …

She spoons beans from the dish on to her plate … toying with them, she would rather not eat at all.

'Now tell me, mother!'

'Well … they want to go and make a complaint against Mr Snoek at the Rabbinate …'

'Who wants to do that …?'

'The men of the Synagogue Council …'

'Mr Boasson as well?'

'No, not Mr Boasson. And not Mr Aarons really either. But Mr Israels and Mr Wolfsthal … they want to, especially Mr Wolfsthal. Mr Snoek did something recently … did something that is not allowed, at Mietje Weil's wedding.'

The beans fall off her fork back onto her plate.

'Well … but you were there yourself anyway. You know the routine. They are standing there under the tallith the bridegroom and bride, they are standing hand-in-hand and then the Rabbi takes the rice from the plate and sprinkles them with it ... and he says: "p'ru ur'vu". And that is simply not allowed, them standing there like that and the Rabbi sprinkling them with rice, if they ... if they ... if the bride ... because then it would be pointless, and in a sense a lie ... that "p'ru ur'vu" is said.'

Not comprehending ... not comprehending immediately ... what Mother means. Oh, hateful comprehension, that dawns on you in a flash, that makes you complicit in it all. But can you help it that you know what 'p'ru ur'vu' means? 'Be fruitful and multiply ...' And if she really ... if she really ... if the bride ... yes, Mother is right, then in a sense it is a lie ... a falsehood ...

Suddenly ... like a beetle you thought was dead, you left lying on the ground, that suddenly flies up and away ... as sudden as that, Mrs Snoek begins to cry again. Bitterly ... bitterly ... bitterly is how people describe it. She has never seen anyone crying so bitterly. Not just her mouth and her eyes, her whole body cries. Mother goes to her, gives her something to drink.

She puts her fork on her plate ... ridiculous sight, a bunch of brown beans in a puddle ... She sits with her hand cradling her forehead ... her fingers press into the depression in her temples. Mother stands over there with Mrs Snoek ... she sits here ... with the table between them. People are further apart from one another than the stars.

'Well ... what did you say, Mother?'

'The money is the worst thing.'

'He shouldn't have sent it to us. He shouldn't have put temptation our way. He knew just how dreadfully short we were. A hundred guilders ... oh, a hundred guilder note!'

'He did it for his daughter ... for Mietje ... because of the great disgrace. A Jewish girl ... you get it with the others, but not us! Not even once, for as long as the congregation has existed.'

'But doesn't something like that come out later on? And why couldn't they wait anyway?'

Silence. Mother wipes her eyes with her handkerchief. Outside, the splashing is growing louder ... more raindrops, bigger raindrops, raindrops more uneven than before. You know the kinds of rain by their sound as they fall on the water in the ditch.

All of a sudden, the kettle on the stove lets rip. You will find the following words in a book ... in one, in ten, in twenty books: 'The kettle sang gently.' Oh, what fools, to call that gentle. It is a red hell full of black devils ... it is an unlit fair in a downpour where murderers sing drunkenly ... witches ... a hurricane ... a boiling sea ... pitch-black night, screams of sailors on the verge of drowning … it is the long, low wail of people being tortured on the rack … death rattles … martyrs' groans … all complaint and all despair … all fear and all desperation blast into the room from the tin whistle.

'And Mrs Martens had said: she decided not to come this time. And who can blame her, with a husband who drinks it all away. She got the money for little Karel and the money for little Rose … And now here we are again … scarcely another three months and here we are yet again … Oh the torment, the eternal torment …' The words form a lament, the voice wails against the kettle. Hammer blows … hailstones … Mrs Martens is the midwife … In three months Mrs Snoek will need her again. The tiny pale Rose can't walk yet.

'Aren't you going to eat your beans? Aren't you hungry this evening?'

People are further apart than the stars. She leans back in her chair, lets the lamplight hurt her eyes. Pain that numbs.

Heaven and earth … heaven and earth … is that all there is? Is Andy right … is that all there is? Why is Mrs Martens needed again in three months' time at Mrs Snoek's, who calls it 'eternal torment'? Why couldn't … Mietje Weil … why couldn't she wait? Heaven and earth … Heaven and earth … heaven and earth …

'What are you doing sitting staring into the lamp? Don't do that, stop it now, it's bad for your eyes.'

I want to extinguish, to deaden one pain with the other …

'I was looking to see if it needed some more oil …'

'Oh, if big Boasson can persuade your husband. Then we would have a majority, then we would be saved. And we wouldn't rest until all the money was paid back, right down to the last cent.'

'Yes … the money … because the money is what's so bad.'

The sound of the kettle is more high-pitched, more hellish. You couldn't bear it, if you always understood what it was saying … you could bear life, if you always understood everything. Most of it passes you by … One thing at a time, and then only half of it. Voice of water … voice of wind …

What do you call it, what did Mrs Koeman call it that day? She yelled it out over the bottom half of her door to deaf Breg … A Barren Bride … that's what it's called. And she meant Kaatje Punt, and now it's Mietje Weil. Words from dreams, chilling, red-hot words: Perrol with the Red Hand -, the man in the Iron Mask … a Barren Bride.

'But Mother, does it depend on Father now?'

'Yes, on Father …'

'Yes, on your father …'

But then there's no need for Mrs Snoek to be afraid. No-one is that cruel, and certainly not Father. They regret it, and the money will be given back. Who could do more?

'Mrs Snoek, then there's no need …'

'Nathan has many obligations towards his Father who has passed on.'

In Remembrance of Grandfather. Remembrance.

Oh, as if the door had opened and Remembrance had walked in … even the kettle's shrilling has softened to a lament … deeply saddened, but no longer raging. Before Remembrance entered, there was this one certainty: 'Father must do it, Father must save him' ·, and now there is this other certainty: 'Father may not do it. Father must report him.'

Yes, he must be reported! There is only one word for what he did, a word that you will never say in front of Mrs Snoek … Mr Snoek was bribed! They were so bitterly poor, Grandfather was poor too, sometimes there was no fuel in the house, there were unpaid bills in the drawer. And yet Grandfather did not take the money. A mistake had been made at the cheesemaker's and Grandfather was the Guardian of the ritual laws … the losses could be enormous ·, it was the cheese for the Passover celebration. Then towards evening, one of the gentlemen came to Grandfather's house and talked of this and that, and eventually produced two hundred guilders from a black wallet. Two hundred guilders! And Grandfather said: 'You should be glad if I keep it to myself that you have had the effrontery to do this.' And the other put his two hundred guilders back where it came from and went away. And of course Grandfather did not tell it any further, that is the best part of this best of deeds. Intractability without nobility is too little, nobility without intractability is not enough, but together …! Intractable and noble … The best of the three deeds of Grandfather's that they know about.

First of all, there was a big fight in the village horse market, the policeman lay on his back on the cobblestones, underneath the drunken Belgian, who was much stronger than him. The farmers stood round them yelling, but there was no-one who dared do anything, the Belgian had pulled out his large, sharp knife. Grandfather was passing and grabbed him by the wrists and wrested the knife from him and held him down with one arm and his legs … and with the others' help tied him up … because, well, those farmers had found their courage, and while all that was happening Grandfather did not make a sound, did not speak a word. But a woman fainted, because Grandfather's face looked so pale above his black beard. And from then on in that village Grandfather was called: the strong Jew.

And a small child had been blown into a sluice … a gust of wind on a stormy day had blown it in from several feet above … and from several feet above Grandfather jumped after it, into the dark sluice … and Grandfather was given a big gold medal for that, but later on he had to sell it …

But the third deed is the best deed, and Grandfather's portrait hangs in the front room … To think of something … is to send part of yourself out to the thing you are thinking of. Thinking of Grandfather's portrait, in the front room, in the dark … is to be there, and here, simultaneously. Oh, the wonder that sometimes suddenly attaches to very ordinary things … And everyone says that she resembles Grandfather. 'You with a beard would be a replica of your Grandfather.' One eye slightly wider open than the other -, one pointy eyebrow, one straight … but Grandfather could subdue dogs with his eyes. Even so, you must first be put to the test …

Mrs Snoek has left the room for a moment.

'Mother, what can happen if the men report Mr Snoek to the Rabbinate?'

'They can lose their income because of it … it is a very serious thing … it's the money … you see … the money. The Senior Rabbi is strict.'

Oh yes … the Senior Rabbi is strict. You were a child still, once a year he came to inspect the school … he was collected by carriage from the station and there was no other day in the year when you heard the dripping tap in the turf cupboard so distinctly, you sat motionless and your fingers were cold, and your heart was thumping above your churning stomach and because of that churning inside the words you would soon have to say were getting all mixed up … the 'Song of Praise on Beholding the Wise Man'. And one of the gentlemen of the school board kept going to the outer door … his boots creaked in the corridor … he was tiptoeing, and you didn't understand why, but you would have done it yourself … and you tried to listen with him for the sound of hooves approaching in the distance, for the rattle of trundling wheels … at last one of them came in from the corridor, pale … 'The carriage is nearly here.' And you grew cold and hot … for the moment was here … now you would see him, and stand up from the long bench and all together say the 'Song of Praise on Beholding the Wise Man'.

And poor Mr Snoek might be being denounced at this moment in front of this strict man with his grey old eyes, seated there on high … and what can a Senior Rabbi understand of poverty, of money owing to the baker, the shoemaker, the dairy … and Father must take the decision, and Father does understand what poverty is, but Father is also Grandfather's eldest son!

Yes, this really is a weighty, serious matter … and yet at the same time these are the light things you cling to, to ward off the other, that hidden, luring thing. O, Andy, it cannot be that you might be right …

But what decision will Father take …?

Quiet, after her last bout of crying, Mrs Snoek is sitting slumped like a sack. Her eyes have been cried away, deep into her head, her mouth has been cried slack, her threadbare, old, rust-coloured bandeau sits askew on her yellow forehead that shines as though she had washed and forgotten to dry herself. How unspeakably wretched you must be, to sit like that, slumped like that, so motionless, hapless. Penniless … hapless … the one word brings the other in its wake, like in a poem. To be poor is hard … but penniless. Oh, pity … sudden pity colliding with you … gust of wind that knocks you over on a street corner … I'd rather you burst into tears again, Mrs Snoek … oh, don't sit there as though you'd still be sitting there if the house caught fire.

Mother has gently placed a fresh cup of coffee in front of her on the table cloth. She quickly picks it up, drinks greedily from it, it does her good … you can see her retreating from her prison of suffering. And now Mother even dares to talk about something else for a moment, and she herself speaks … No, she hasn't heard anything from that Headmaster, that nice gentleman who said so emphatically 'You will be hearing from me,' but at the moment there is a better chance that she will be able to stay where she is 'temporarily,' because Klein is on the official list of candidates for Head, and then a position will fall vacant.

'And then I won't have to leave!'

'Then you won't be able to travel up and down?'

'No, they won't allow that then, it will have to stop.'

'And have you already looked for lodgings?'

Oh, poor thing … poor thing … it's such a struggle … she fights free of the panic that is crushing her, but only just, you can hear it in her voice. Beneath her clammy, yellow pallor a fierce glow begins to grow … she listens … her ears strain … or can you only say that of eyes … And Mother sees, Mother senses and, so as to help her, Mother talks of the family she will lodge with … a warm family, relatives of 'uncle' Zeelik. It seems so jolly there, they sing, eat delicious meals, there are girls, daughters of her own age, who like going out. Oh, she will have a fine time there … Mother is happy to let her go.

'And David has also fallen on his feet …'

'David … yes. That is true. Look … this letter came from David this morning.'

Oh, Mother give it here! Let me read David's letter right now.

Yes, he is doing well, he is content. Early in the morning he arrives at the big house … along a sandy path … the morning sun sets the windows on fire … it is still so quiet everywhere at that time … in the fields, in the lanes, in the large garden. Nowadays this is where he himself wheels Berthold in his invalid carriage … and he listens to him repeating his lessons and explains everything to him. At first the servant pushed, and David walked alongside the little carriage, but Berthold did not want it that way any longer. He is sitting by his window in the mornings when David comes … that is why David has to take the sandy path, not the avenue of beeches … so he can see him coming in the distance. He sits … at his window … how did the poem go again … how did it go?

At his window he stands gazing
In his white shirt all alone.

Is this Berthold then? But surely David didn't know him then … He sits at his window … and every day he asks the same thing: David must come and live in the house. But David cannot do that, David may not do that, Father would not want to allow him to do that. But David doesn't want to either. In their childhood he observed the ritual Laws more strictly than she did. He cannot live in with Berthold, Berthold mustn't keep asking him every day. The entire letter is about Berthold … that name everywhere, like a miniature portrait. He has just had his eleventh birthday … so lovely … so blonde … He will do for David what no doctor has managed to get him to do … the endlessly repeated exercises … Before David came, he struck out at the doctor with his fists … he didn't believe that he would ever walk again … he didn't want to make the effort … now he believes, now he wants to … later on he wants to work for all the exams that David is working for now … and David must stay with him for ever …

'Don't you believe it too, Mother? That David will stay with Berthold for ever?'

How very strange … what on earth is happening? She could see a sandy path among broad avenues, a window glowing in the morning sun … Berthold is sitting at the window; in the distance, over the sandy path, David is approaching … but here sits Mrs Snoek. Just like that, as though she had returned from a distant journey … one minute I am there, the next I am here … and I am in two places at once again … and the rain splashes in the canal … it is evening … This splashing, this evening … the round, brass lamp … all those winters … all those evenings … now it could be any evening in any winter … Time … Time … a gilded pendulum figure, a funny little old man … and you are suddenly full of this thing called: memory. How easily satisfied you are with a few words … and how little purchase they have on what is hidden. No, not these words … no, this isn't what I mean either … What I really mean: there are fish, but they won't take the bait …

Have Mother and Mrs Snoek already heard voices? Yes, you can see it from their faces. Voices and footsteps had already made them sit up and listen, out of the splashing, out of the distance, but it is only now that she hears them. 'Mother … they are coming …'

The decision … the Decision … is now very close.

Are there two of them … or are there … three …?

Three … Because the front door opened …

It is as though they came from a distant journey, as though they were exhausted. Father … Father … what did you decide … which of the two claimed you … Pity or Remembrance?

Before she, before Mother has grasped it … before one word has been spoken … Mrs Snoek is standing by her husband and they are embracing one another … Peace. This is how it was meant to be. Peace … but Remembrance creeps out of the room. O, Remembrance, you are frequently honoured … this time the other had to count for more.

Mrs Snoek stands crying over Father's hand … and something is flapping: big Boasson's large, red handkerchief.

'Hurry up with the coffee cups, you there …'

'Yes, of course, big Boasson … I mean … Mr Boasson.'

In his large, fat hand he holds up a large, greasy paper bag.

'The best cups, Mother, the Sabbath cups … is that all right?' Andy, Andy, now I know for sure … that you are wrong! This is life! We are born for these burdensome things, they are light things at the same time, light you escape into … strong, white, radiant light … for working together like this … being there for one another like this … overflowing …. flowing together … for this we are born … each of us anew, each of us in our turn.

'Shall I pour straight away, Mother?'

They are sitting hand-in-hand, Mr Snoek and his wife … they look at one another like happy children. Doesn't he see how ugly she is, with that threadbare, sagging bandeau and that fat, purple nose … doesn't she see that his mouth is full of broken, brown teeth …?

They look at one another like happy children …

Now big Boasson tells us about the discussions. When Father had finally settled matters with himself, Father then convinced Mr Wolfsthal also. This is what he said. 'This once …' Literally, this is what he said, 'This once I shall allow Grace to count for as much as Law.' Yes, thus spoke Mr Wolfsthal, in his grand seat, in his grand room. Big Boasson had held those words as though in a little box and now they are on the table among the cups and everyone is looking at them. 'People should do that more often, people should always do that.'

Father shakes his head.

'If only it were always possible. But it won't get you very far. It must not be done always, may not be done always. Because where will it take you? Grace is beautiful … but you won't get far without Law …'

Father … Father … don't let them hear. They are looking at one another like happy children. Forget it for a moment, put it aside, the fact that you are Grandfather's son. Remembrance already knows it … Let this moment of now, our sitting here together, round the table and the lamp like a sun in the middle, big Boasson there and Mother here and you and I and both of them … o, let it be perfect. I sense it too … it isn't as simple as Boasson says … I sense it surrounding our lives … rising … arising … mysteries … questions … just like when I was a child and I could sense the sea beyond the wall of dunes, once the schoolmaster had told us that we live lower than the sea … but the master also said that we can sleep peacefully in our deep hollow … in this way I sense it surrounding our lives like the sea, dark, unfathomable … this mystery of Mercy and Law … of Pity and Remembrance … and the thing … that Andy talks about … and everything … time and memory and where we come from, where we are going to, what our … our … task is … and wind and rain … but let this be perfect just for a moment …

Big Boasson laughs out loud because Mother cannot divide the last cake into six … he wants the knife, he wants to do it himself.

… and how did it go, what did it say …

- But now for that pinpoint of joy
   At midnight and in those surging billows …

Ah, but, this is De Genestet, it is from 'Poor Fishermen'. 'Pinpoint of joy' is really quite beautiful … 'surging billows' too. Pinpoint of joy … the bright interior of a small, lone boat … it races over the waves … in the middle of the night, the middle of the sea … and so is this here, this moment of now, of ours … Pinpoint of joy, and out there in the dark the mysteries murmur and the questions clamour …

3
Voices

The autumn evening is like a summer night, the shop smells of ginger and roses. Inside the shiny white walls, it is so white and so light and so hot, it felt like you were sitting inside a giant light-bulb, though the whining sound is only the small blue flame emerging from a small iron tube on the counter next to the woman serving, and the woman is also in white. Her eyes stare, she is tired, her taut cheeks glow, her large bosom heaves, her hand seems to move by itself, a dull, subservient hand that grabs baking tins from the black heap, tilts them towards the flame, shakes them empty, flings them away … and the fruit buns fall into the bag … four, five, six …

'Here you are miss. And you sir?'

The door stays open. A group of three or four makes a rowdy entrance singing as they make their way in out of the darkness. Playfully they jostle one another so as to be served first, they are keen to be off again … in the enclosed, white heat they long for the sweet, open darkness, where uncurtained windows glow orange and red in the grey facades … girls and boys lean out as far as they dare … their heads and shoulders reaching out towards girls and boys down in the street … there is a warm, gentle breeze and high above it all, a vast starry sky.

She is sitting on a packing case against the back wall opposite the open door and she looks at the posters and looks at the woman and looks into the lamp again and outside again and at the faces of people coming into the shop … all human beings … human beings like herself … fellow human beings … and she missed her turn long ago … but this is a sweet imprisonment. This was how it felt when you used to lean your chest against a gate, above ground ivy and speedwell, by the sparkling water of a wide ditch … and your eyes travelled out over the spring countryside …

and there were bees … and you were in a trance … everything expanded … you too, you opened out, you managed to hold on to that sensation that felt so wonderful … standing in the sun like that and opening out like that so you could touch the horizon … But how busy it is here this evening. The whole neighbourhood has come out for buns … the baker's men downstairs can't make enough, they are short of baking tins, they send the boy upstairs for every handful of empty ones … The day before yesterday was the Day of Atonement, they still don't seem to have recovered from the fast. Any minute now the woman will call out again, and she knows it makes no difference …

'Father, father … come on father … come and give me a hand.'

At the top of the green staircase is an open office, even more brightly lit than the shop and a heavy man sits there with his nodding head of red hair bent over his thick books, and he doesn't even answer, he waves his hand dismissively behind him, he grinds his heavy feet across the sandy floor in irritation. He is a cruel, strange man, his mouth is thin, sucked tightly shut, and her mother is dead … and she lives alone with him … and her breast rises and falls underneath the tight, white apron.

Look - out there, right in front of the door, there is a large ball of crumpled paper, dazzlingly white, blown against the pavement edge. It rustles, it struggles … as though caught under a hand … tries to move on … past the shop … you can clearly see this happening … you would like to release it, help it on its way … It is as though it is alive … you might almost say: it has an active will, when you see it striving so insistently. And why shouldn't you say that it is alive? A breakaway breath of wind that has entered its folds … this has become its soul, its will, its striving. A breakaway breath of wind … and a human being, then …? Yes, but there is so very much going on inside a human being …

The roses in the earthenware container behind the bascule bridge scent the air. Before she knows it, she has jumped up from the packing case -, why now? She used to do this as a child … she used to run along all the gardens and then suddenly dip into one, there were hyacinths, in a bed beyond the grass, damp and cool. Each scent leads through another gateway to another dream … and there are so many … and that is only scent. The scent of hyacinths is nothing less than heavenly peace … but roses make you into a concertina … you are pulled wide open and sounds come out, such strange and deep noises.

She is back sitting on the case against the wall … she has just missed her turn. Her thumping heart sends the blood to her head. Bertha and Saar have come in and seen what happened and they make fun of her, they mock her together with a boy, the boy who is chasing after Bertha. Was standing over a container of roses so very silly? How difficult it is, not to do silly things here. It doesn't seem to be that easy to learn to behave like the others. She has been doing her best for this last half year. From the first day she has done her best. They said: you must grow your hair, you look like an idiot with your boys' hair, and she did it. Andy would never have approved, but Andy has gone, she has run away with a married man, he was waiting by the sluice gate, he had a shining, flowing beard. She went away without saying goodbye … there were days beforehand when she scarcely said hello … it tore something out of her leaving a bleeding hole, but she couldn't be Andy's boy anyway, she wants to be a girl. On Sunday she wears the red velvet hat, Bertha and Saar bought it with her, it took hours, a whole afternoon … 'We're never going out with such a dope again' … some ten, twenty hats were put on and taken off again, the mirrored doors opened and closed … oh it was torture … and they press the brims over your ears … and they blow their breath into your face … and the hat is always askew.

She is sitting with the sisters and friends in Bertha's little room, she takes a piece of sleeve material, she grabs a fold of skirt between her fingers, she says: what lovely material, - how much did you pay for this material, - like she sees and hears others doing, - it looks simple, but … you need to know what you are doing. Same with the fashion pictures. She says: this would look good on me - but the others laugh. She knows all their songs, she knows 'Brave Bard Sosthène', she knows the song about 'Trinquart, that jolly captain …' she knows 'Sail sailor-boy …' and even so it's not the same. Somewhere in the neighbourhood lives a singer, who they all adore, they say so to each other when they meet him on the street. He smiled at Bertha, and she immediately bought his picture, in a frame of orange plush and he is called Philippeau and now his portrait stands among those of the sisters and friends on the cupboard in Bertha's room, and all those portraits are the same: shoulders half bare, head and neck turned backwards, eyes wide open, mouths taut. This is: 'modern' and 'chic'.

'Modern' and 'chic' is what everything must be. Clothes: 'the latest thing' or 'something a bit different'. It's anything but easy, you can't make sense of it, you have literally always got something wrong. She is sitting on the packing case again and calms down, they've stopped paying any attention to her. Tall Joppe came barging into the shop … and all the girls are crowding round him and all the boys are slapping him on the back. He can do conjuring, he can imitate animals, he tells endless jokes and even the woman behind the counter gives her hands a moment's rest, her eyes brighten, she smiles, her bosom quietens under the tight apron. And against the kerb the lonely paper ball still lies dazzling in the dark, and struggles to move on ... and feels like a new friend ... Yes, there is something about that crumpled ball that makes up for the mockery, but what ... it is inexplicable.

Unexpectedly a human foot has liberated it, the slow foot of a bent old man, - it has been released ... and off it goes ... have a good journey, paper ball, with your soul and your will from a breakaway breath of wind ... and what will happen to it now ... oh strange, this small anguish, as though this was a parting, and that same old foolish pity, as it sets out on its way, alone, in the evening ...

'Good evening, Mr Balloski ...'

It sounds too high-pitched, too bold, too much ...

Hesitantly, suspiciously, the old man pauses. His eyes blink at the light and the bustle, he shrinks back, he would rather go away again ... but Joppe has already grabbed him, with his resounding, reverberating voice he grabs him, pulls him towards him.

'Good evening, Mr Balloski, good evening! And how has Mr Balloski been keeping since last week? And how did Mr Balloski spend the Day of Atonement? I want to know: did Mr Balloski have a pleasant fast? If Mr Balloski had as pleasant a fast as the person standing in front of him - as me - his humble servant, - then Mr Balloski has had an exceedingly pleasant fast ...'

Saar and Bertha and Rachel and Selien bounce against one another like rubber balls, push each other against the wall, against the counter, with helpless laughter ... but Kaatje and Rose look serious, they disapprove. Everyone in the entire neighbourhood knows how Joppe 'fasted' -, and she knows it too, she was there herself, she joined in. They were all together in Joppe's house where he bosses his half-blind father around, his well-meaning mother, the sisters who have spoilt him since he was little, - and they ate forbidden things on the Day of Atonement! 'Are you so childish ... do you think that God cares about what we eat ...?' yes ... no ... but something wasn't quite right. Your argument can be solid and you can still be wrong.

'And Herman Melhado is coming too! He is coming! You holier than thou little thing ... not quite that holy after all ...'

Yes, he was there too. He is tall, pale, his teeth gleam. He throws his head back when he laughs ... it makes you shiver suddenly ... he laughs a lot. And he had brought along his guitar -, but surely they wouldn't stand for that, playing the guitar on the Day of Atonement! Opposite Joppe's house is a little neighbourhood synagogue ... she stood by the window and just happened to look down on its courtyard ... and now and again an old gentleman appeared or a fat lady in black, with a large white handkerchief in her hand ... or a small boy, or a girl ... they each came for a few minutes' break ... you could imagine how stifling it must be inside, all the candles burning, the curtains closed, people in sackcloth ... and she in Joppe's room, the windows wide open, the table full of forbidden food ... and all the world in a glowing golden sun, because this autumn is like a summer ... She stood by the window ... she heard him behind her ... sensed him coming ... a shiver in the space between her shoulder blades ... and there he was, next to her, and his arm was around her. And they stood together like that ... the warmth of his hand on her hip, though he was a stranger. Oh don't stay there next to me, you strange stranger, your presence is senseless, is unbearable ... oh stay on my hip, you warm hand. And then a little old lady came out of the synagogue ... she hurried into the courtyard, needing air ... and yes, it was the same little old lady standing there now behind Yitzak Balloski, and she signals to Joppe with her eyes to leave the old man alone. But Joppe seems crazy ... the girls make him drunk with their attention ... yes indeed, it was the same little old lady and Herman said:

'What do you think of such idiots?'

Then one feeling killed the other ...

You, stranger, your nearness is unbearable ... and the warm hand became repellent, an insult.

'No, no ... they aren't idiots.'

The wind rushes past the open door, is louder than a moment ago ... a sweet smell wafts in from the hairdresser's, wafts past .... He walked back to the table, he said something to Selien, he laughed, threw his head back ... o, she shivered ... his white teeth, his red lips. No, no, no ... don't think about them.

Joppe, o silly, feeble joker ... Joppe, you still make me laugh ... laugh with tears in my eyes ...

'You aren't answering, Mr Balloski. I reckon all you can think about is cakes and shortbread. Did you or didn't you spend the Day of Atonement pleasantly fasting?'

The little old lady can't stand it any longer.

'You pour scorn ... do you think the entire neighbourhood doesn't know ... godless boy ... eating and drinking you were, the whole day ...'

The lady behind the counter looks up the stairs in fear and dread, into the little office. For a moment Joppe is shamed into silence, but it doesn't last long.

'Since you heard what she said, I may not deny it any longer. But you, Mr Balloski ... as a learned man, as a knowledgeable man ... do you believe in a God who demands of us that we torture ourselves for whole days with fasting ...? In all conscience, Mr Balloski, do you consider eating on the Day of Atonement a bad sin?'

'Yes ... it is bad ... bad the way you youngsters violate all the laws. Because the question is: what will you do without them?'

Now Joppe loses his equilibrium for a second ... the old, fierce eyes bore into his so unwaveringly ... what will he say ...? He laughs ... like water flowing over a stone his laugh closes over that one moment.

The girls turn away, this is beginning to bore them ... they hum, rearrange their ribbons in front of the mirror, pat their hair, replace a hairpin ... is this what you need to learn ... how to sway, humming ... to rearrange ribbons ... replace hairpins ... but how do you learn it, to be always thinking of your ribbons and hairpins ...

Saar has her goodies and wants to leave, but Joppe suddenly takes hold of her, pulls her into his arms, so that she squeals with laughter and fright. 'Saar ... no ... don't go ... Mr Balloski wants to know something. He wants to know: what will you do without them?'

She throws herself back against Joppe's arm ... she laughs, stamping her feet ... and all the other girls surround her again and they toss the following words to each other: 'Mr Balloski wants to know something, he wants to know: what will you do without them! Saar, what will you do without them?' They whisper ... mouths to ears ... mouths to mouths ... and they laugh. Oh, this is scandalous, scandalous! But old Balloski doesn't notice. Two young men have come in, red-haired, pale, serious brothers, and he is talking to these two now, and to her, yes, to her. And Joppe chases the girls from the shop, pushes and shoves them along, running after them ... you can hear their laughter fading into the evening ... 'No, it is not a question of doing or not doing something. But you must make things difficult for yourself. It is something they often ask me ... they think a lot of things are childish, but that's not what it's about. They ask: does God want us to do this or does God want us to do that ... God wants only one thing: that we make things difficult for ourselves.'

This is a breakthrough, a dawning light. She is standing beside the red-haired, pale brothers ... the dawning light reaches them too, and all four of them look at one another, forming a circle of eyes.

'The socialists make things difficult for themselves ... they fight the police ... they lose their jobs ... they get their noses bloodied ... they eat dry bread ... and that is what it is all about. Not what you do or what you believe or what you think, but whether you are prepared to act on your thoughts and on what you believe in. And the socialists are.'

'Shh, Mr Balloski, for god's sake, shush, Mr Balloski.'

The little old lady warns him in a beseeching whisper.

The steps of the green staircase creak ... he's coming downstairs, he is like an animal, with his threatening stare ... silently his pursed lips tauten.

'You were saying, Mr Balloski?'

'I didn't go so far as to say that they are good people ...'

'No, as I live and breathe, Constant, he didn't say that they are good people!' The old dear just blurts it out.

'And I don't say that they are not good people either. I don't say that they are good people and I don't say that they are not good people.'

He turns and is gone.

'Your shortbread, Mr Balloski ...'

He doesn't hear.

The little old lady shakes her head, the red-haired brothers smile briefly at one another, embarrassed, dejected, they approach the counter. The gleam has already gone from their eyes.

'Are you perhaps going the same way as me down the street ...?'

The old voice sings, they had involuntarily caught one another's eye.

'Yes I am ...' Oh, friendship, warmth ... human hearts, close to your own heart ... suddenly this little old lady is dear to her.

And they walk beside one another, in the shifting breeze that seems cool but can't be, or you wouldn't have to keep wiping your damp face.

Upstairs, downstairs, the lamps glowing red, orange ... and everywhere voices singing, as though the houses themselves were singing out into the evening, with wide open glowing mouths. Complaining, the little old lady walks beside her in the dark.

'Why does he do that ... he should keep his mouth shut. He mustn't get a name in the neighbourhood for being a socialist ... and he needs whatever anybody can give, he needs cents and small change.'

'Is he so poor ...?'

'Yes ... poor ... and all alone.'

She tells his story and his life is revealed. Torn from his family, cast destitute out of Russia. O, accursed country ... You can't run a bookshop in a damp cellar. No you can't. And if he would just hold his tongue ...

Laughter and song cut like knives through this picture of a life. 'Chantez, Chantez, ma belle ...' A print: Port Said, a steamer sailing away

… a sea, grey-black, with light from a tower poured over surface like milk.

Now she is alone, the old lady went into her little alleyway. Alone with the wind, with the smells, the singing houses … Was that the smell of grass, from far outside the city, where water and meadows lie breathing in the dark, in their sleep … and is that white thing over there not her friend the ball of crumpled paper, struggling to make its way through the long street? Where to …? Why …? And what is this new feeling …? Oh yes, here it comes, here he comes … it is the shivering sigh, that brings release … and now the soft pressure on her throat … it is the new Friend, it is Wonderment … and there is no friend more timid than this one …, nor one that is more demanding. Because he demands all and scarcely touches you … never closer than the silvery tingle that flickered next to your eye when you pressed your finger on your eyeball in play when you were small … always next to your head, next to your eye … You must give yourself consciously to him … you must be quiet as a mouse … undress, strip away everything … listen. And then Wonderment says: This is Life. And suddenly you breathe the breath of Wonderment. You can say it yourself - 'this is life' - but this way it doesn't mean anything, it isn't anything … only when he says it first for you to repeat: This is Life. The wind that winds around me, the stars that stare … I who am 'I' and who says 'I' … I-in-I … and quieter now, even quieter … because this is at the heart of it … 'I' perished, 'I' is nothing … this is a precious knowledge, an uncertain, fragile, insecure knowledge … but be careful that your thoughts keep on flowing gradually and evenly past everything … that they don't attach themselves to anything, and don't solidify around anything … because each separate thing that you think about brings 'I' in its wake … and 'I' returns, 'I' grows bigger, swells like an approaching boat, a train thundering towards you, and all there is left is 'I' with its things and the Friend has gone …

Oh, he flees from the slightest thing … even these thoughts can easily send you into a daze, you wake out of it with a jolt and you have been abandoned … You must have dozed while wide awake, you must think of nothing and of everything … then the Wonderment comes, then the Friend is there … you are hardly allowed to welcome him before he tears himself away … and most times you plunge into emptiness … but this time there is something that catches hold of me, that supports me … Yitzak Balloski … and his words.

Yes, old man, I have you to thank … because you said it exactly … as I felt it, that day, by the window: God does not demand this or that, only 'something', only that we should make things difficult for ourselves.

And you learned about islands, thrust out of the ocean by a great force ... and this is one of those islands ... the more difficult I can make things for myself, the happier I shall be.

But Ebner, yesterday at school ... No, it was Bauk Boomsma first, who has just got engaged to Arjen Brand ... 'You and your constant giving ... your constant running to the children ... your sentimental fussing ... you're only doing it for your own pleasure anyway ...' Before she could answer, Ebner was there, standing by the tall window on the upper landing, where the water's shimmer shines through, against the white walls, against the white ceiling.

'Yes, Bauk, you are right -, and why do you think you became a socialist?'

Bauk:

'Out of academic insight ... out of a sense of duty.'

Ebner's pale mouth formed a smile inside his beard.

'No, Bauk, for your own pleasure, just like her. There is only the pleasure you seek, the pain you avoid.'

Blushing, she - Bauk - stared, she seemed breathless and then Arjen Brand came down the stairs sending his harsh voice ahead of him.

He is younger than Bauk, all he knows is rights, he talks about rights, stands up for his rights, unflinching.

'Is our worthy cynic holding forth again?'

Bauk coloured a deep red: 'O, it's a disgrace! Arjen, let's go!'

Ernestine was walking past, with a pile of exercise books, little, fat, ugly, dear Ernestien, the new friend ... she gave a quick smile as she passed, shook her head, she doesn't think it any of her business.

And she remained alone with Ebner for a moment, the school echoed around them in full voice, children's laughter and water shimmer and all the doors are open, and all the windows wide ...

'Ebner, is it true?'

'Yes ... it is true ... but there are many desires. Desires we respect and desires we despise. But a thing is never worth less because it makes us happy ...'

Making things difficult ... following desires ... why is everything always in conflict with everything else? Or is 'making things difficult' ... also ... following a desire ...?

And so a door shuts, and you can't hear the voices any longer, and frightened sparrows fly up in all directions, they hide ... not a sound ...

Yitzak Balloski ... gone ... all gone ... and the island sank, disappeared ...

Oh, he is whistling, he is whistling out of the red window …

No … no … no … I am not going to look up, I don't want you to whistle …

But a strong hand could not have lifted her chin up more imperiously.

No … no … no … I am not coming, I am not coming into your small, dark garden this evening.

But she has already signalled yes with her eyes.

The little garden, dark, enclosed in rustling ivy, … even darker the gateway through which she slipped.

Her heart is beating a song of bitter-sweet surrender … there is only one thing: this. One thing to want: this. To long for, to pursue -, this. To have come into the world for, this … To forget everything, to cast everything aside … for this. If he doesn't come, if it doesn't come, then life no longer has any meaning.

'Eva … Evie … are you there … have you come?'

'Yes, I am here … I came …'

From the gloom he sends his little laugh to meet her: I whistle and you come … you always come. His hands reach out, they float white between dark earth and dark sky … and her eyes search him out, search above him, find the sky, the sky comes alive. They are standing by the gate, in the rustlings of the ivy.

No … no … no … not that … not laughter … not so reckless … not like tall Joppe with Saar in the shop a moment ago … Let's … o my dear … let us … From the sky, from the staring stars, the word she is looking for drops down to her … let us be noble. Place them softly, your lips, on my lips, and your hands … place them on my shoulders, or give them to me to hold in mine, but don't let them move burning … so shamelessly … all over … all over … Let this thing of ours be one-and-the-same thing with all the rest, in total peace. Because the breathless whisperings drive me to you, I seek you for the hidden rustling, the gusty wind shoved me through the gateway … and now here I am … now all must flow together in total peace … She utters none of this inner questioning, this complaint to him, not a word, nothing … she only says: No, no, no … and struggles free of him in the dark.

'But what are you doing here … if you don't want this, if you don't want anything?'

Oh, is that what you think … oh, do you think that I desire this … is that what girls come for … And you dare, my boy …. You dare to say that to me, to Me …! A burning pillar shot up and as if before her own eyes, she saw written:

Me with a capital letter! Like in the Ten Commandments: 'Thou shalt not take My name in vain.' And she shivers with the shock, - for what was this feeling, that filled her like a flame and then shrivelled …?

Her lips are wet from his, she can't shut them, she wears them like stains, carries them with the burns from his shameless hands through the gateway of whispers … and this is the garden of her own house and she throws herself against the fence and plunges and presses herself into the ivy and rubs her lips in it and sinks on to the damp grass and throws herself on her back and in her eyes, burning eyes, she catches thousands of stars, all the stars …

Sky, high, staring Sky … is that why I am here … did I succumb to this? Never again … never, oh, it's one thing to say it!

Upstairs in the house, in the small room where she sleeps, with the casement window wide open onto the back alleyway. And a sudden joy, - at what she knew and then forgot, - Ernestien's books, *Johannes Viator* by Van Eeden and Gorter's poem 'May'. She takes first the one and then the other … but the one she has put down always attracts her most strongly … and she swaps … puts both down … it is this urgency with new books that brings on such panic. You can't absorb it all in one go anyway. She used to be like this at the weekly market standing in front of a bookstall and the wind riffled the pages as though with fluttering fingers and your eye kept snatching an odd word from between two pages … and every word grabbed you in one of your many selves … as different smells do.

No … this is making me too tired … and I am already so tired … oh, this day is endless … endless … and yet again she is unable to leave the book lying there and sits with it resting on her knees, on the edge of her bed …

And now a word grabs her … a word that she always thought was shameful … but it is by the great Poet … and this … this … oh, this … she has to read.

'And in the things of the Body, which cause such trouble and distress, there is a law that all can know. All know it, and it is so very simple.

Only Love in the highest degree, stronger than the whole soul, renders bodily desire good.

Love, utterly unique, entirely perfect, of human being for human being, but also, in a deeper understanding, Love for the Child, the Unborn. This, and this alone renders bodily sin good.

And where it is not present, complete, perfect, unique, self-aware - there all bodily sin is dirty, despicable: debauchery, adultery. All, all. Whether out of pity, whether out of obedience, whether out of hunger.

It matters not. All equally dirty, equally loathsome, debauchery, adultery …'

Debauchery … adultery … all the rest …

This is a sudden, deep silence. She is sitting on the edge of the bed, her eyes escape the small, dark room, through the window, into the night, through the spaces, towards the sky. Oh, the restlessness, the stirred-up, red-hot, restlessness in all those houses, all those people, sending calls and laughter to one another from open rooms, across the deep, brooding-black gardens, from veranda to balcony, house to house. An occasional one among them dark and closed or lit up by the green light of a study … and above it all, the laughing and singing, the sleeping children, the laboured breathing of the sick, the solemnity of the earnest, and above herself the great heavenly peace.

All the rest … what happened just now, in his garden … well, the Poet has spoken. Never again … But her staring contemplation seeps into the almost-done day, dismantles the day - wall built high, oh, endless day! - and it is morning again, and the school has water-shimmer playing through it, young noise echoing through it, children in the new day.

And she walks along the corridor, and he comes towards her, lets her past at first, then turns round and looks at her, and she sees, and it cuts right through her … every day the lines in his face grow sharper … every day the old eyes sink deeper … and it is Arjen Brand's doing, made worse by Bauk, since they got engaged. Oh, Arjen, let us be merciful, of course I am in favour of the Republican School, but can't we wait until he has gone? Bauk, face flaming red in an instant as always: You do not understand matters of principle, because you are a girl, a truly old-fashioned woman, solely an emotional being. You wind him around your finger, the silly old boy, and that satisfies you …

But straight away Ebner … yes … when Bauk has a go at her like that, Ebner always seems to be around … Oh, but this is the wrong track … this is wandering off the path … No, he stood there and looked at his watch and said: 'Can you come with me to the staffroom for a moment?'

And she followed him and they sat opposite each other, among the lockers, the piles of exercise books, textbooks, pencils, surrounded by a dusty, musty smell.

'Well … it's a bit difficult, what I have to say to you, because you do it in all innocence …'

Why did she immediately know what he meant … what was it in her that responded immediately, while she remained silent, while she gave him a questioning look … Not in innocence … not in innocence … How … do you know everything?

'Wim is too old … you don't realize … it's not good, you must not engage in rough and tumble with him … I think it's a pity that I have to say such a thing to you …' And then: 'Because you do it in all innocence.'

They sat together for a moment without speaking; around them, beyond the chink of the door, the school began to quieten down.

'Do you understand what I mean …?'

If you could only say calmly and honestly: 'No, Sir.' But you have to admit: 'Yes, Sir.' And he goes over to the window, presses his face against it, firmly … so that he has to push back his cap … peering down from his erect position his eyes seek the street … they detect the waiting boy … and he brings out his rattling bunch of keys … he taps … he gestures … he utters the words that can't be heard down there … like people do when greeting someone on the other side of the street … 'Go home, Wim … home … don't wait any longer …'

And she sits on the hard chair, feels herself sitting there, looks around past all the open lockers … hundreds of small blue exercise books … piles of five … five, ten, fifteen … alternately with their spines or their pages to the front … with every breath her throat catches. He walks past her, out of the door, into the corridor -, she must wait, she must not 'regard the conversation as at an end'. Pedlars screech at the side of the building, - the hoarse chair-caner … the half-mad scissor-sharpener … he makes his cry into a drunk's singing … a boat blows its horn … oh, home … the harbour … breaking waves … David-and-her … a motor-barge is chugging its way through the water … down there Wim was waiting, he was waiting for her … the dear boy … He is part of school and yet is outside it, he has his table set apart in the back of Arjen Brand's class, he is working for an exam, for a free place. Ebner is not so good at arithmetic - he comes to Wim with difficult sums - Miss Korff sometimes spells a word wrong -, the children rush to Wim for a judgement! Arjen Brand can't tell stories -, he says: it is not a school 'subject', it's nonsense, he hates doing it; now they've swapped - she goes and tells stories in Arjen Brand's class -, Arjen Brand teaches mental arithmetic in hers. She would like to swap with everyone, so as to tell stories in all the classes. Oh, the warmth, the intimacy, sparkling pools of eyes lifted towards you. She goes into the classroom and Arjen leaves. 'And remember, all of you: Order!' She has to laugh at this, the children too. She is already in the teacher's chair. 'Hello, Wim' -, only with her eyes, across all the rows, to his small table.

He smiles, he blushes. One of the oldest girls looks round at Wim, looks back at her … a vague, dwindling smile, a dawning understanding? Oh no, for she is the one in the teacher's chair, she is 'Miss.' And Wim closes his books, turns his chair to the front, to her. He has black hair, grey eyes, his hands are always clean, his mother does her best to dress him reasonably well.

'Miss, what story are you going to tell today?'

'You will hear that soon enough, Jantje Drost, you inquisitive little thing.'

'Tell the story of "Beauty and the Beast" again.'

'Haven't we just had that …?'

They count. Yes, you are right, it's already longer ago than I thought. We can have it again … 'But then you must give me a minute to think.' Words … thoughts … ideas, new ones and ones from last time, gather in her from all directions, like clouds on the horizon, they arrange themselves, take shape; at the foot of her high teacher's chair an expectant silence. Outside on the quay life in the open, barrels rolling, boats chugging …

'So, children … I'll begin …'

Now the utter contentedness that finds expression in sighs and vague smiles, but will not yet tolerate movement, until she herself steps on to the floor, from the high chair.

Racing up and down the stairs, Wim has brought up her coat, her woollen hat, from downstairs, from her own classroom. This is the third floor -, Arjen's classroom and the empty half-dark evening art room and the attics and the grey corridor, abandoned, shadowy. The water shimmer does not reach this far.

'I am bigger than you.'

'You are indeed …'

'I'm stronger too …'

'That remains … to be seen …'

Laughing, he has gripped her in his arms, so tight and powerful that her feet lift off the wooden floor.

'See … See …?'

'Wim … Wim … don't drop me …'

'No, I won't drop you …'

Laughing eyes that glow … glowing eyes that laugh …

'Did you really think I would drop you …?'

Oh … where did he suddenly find that voice?

'Yes … I thought …'

He pulls her up, she leans momentarily against him, her back to him, and she shuts her eyes … and his hands glide over her breast … and they press … so softly … and for a moment … each small hand of his against each small breast of hers.

Oh, all the roundness and softness of all that is round and soft in the world for the pleasure of those small, those small, those young boy's hands ...

'Your storytelling was so beautiful again.'

'Did you really think so ...?'

'A whole week in Mr Brand's class is not much fun. That grimacing face to start with ...'

'O, Wim ... are you allowed to say that outright?'

He laughs.

You are very strong, Wim. How old are you again?'

'Fourteen. And you?'

'I am going to be twenty in the winter! I could be your mother.'

'I wish you were my mother ...'

'But what would you do with two mothers?'

'I would ... be able ... to sit on your lap ...'

And they go down the stairs, broad, grey steps with a dull sheen, they descend to the regions of water shimmer and outside noise. The whole school echoes, fathers and mothers walk in and out. Arjen Brand and Bauk watch, with disdainful smiles.

'Disorderly racket ... eternal messiness ... if only the school assembly had been set up.'

'Yes, the Republican School, and the old ...' Bauk interrupts herself, she nudges Arjen, she indicates Wim and her. Arjen glances across, but it leaves him cold, everything leaves him cold. Now Ebner, Ernestien, Penning who teaches gym and sings German songs loudly in the corridors ... and everywhere noise and echo ... shimmer and reflection ... cry and reply ...

'But my dear girl, have you been sitting there waiting all this time?'

'Sitting waiting ...? Yes, Sir ... sitting waiting ...'

'Did I perhaps ... upset you? You see ... much is done in innocence, that is nevertheless not good ...'

A flood of questions wells up, suddenly, from inside her, to her lips ... but she keeps her lips closed around them, like a tap holding back the pressured water. If the tap is opened, this question emerges:

'What is ... innocence ... Sir?'

But she did not ask. And now she has the answer.

Because to feel that a ... boy ... a lad ... o little Wim ... where did you get that voice ... and what glowed like that in the depths of your eyes ... to feel it ... to want it ... no, not in innocence on my part. 'Pity'? ... 'Obedience'? ... 'Hunger'? ... One of the three ... or none of the three ... or all three ...? Oh, I don't know, I don't know ... I only know this: Debauchery … adultery … debauchery … adultery … It ticks like a clock, it beats like a heart.

And she goes to the window. The voice of the wind is deeper now, - its breath is cooler, it seems to come from higher up, from further away. Everywhere the open houses are pulled shut, pushed to, the lamps blown out, turned down. At last this everlasting day is also coming to an end. Detached from everything, as though floating in space, she feels herself standing at the high skylight, conscious only of her own existence. Just as 'I' had left her before, had evaded her, so as to evaporate in wind and world and in the stars … sink without trace … up, down … the same thing … oh wondrous … but now it has come back to her and has gathered around her, has solidified around her and she is all alone in herself …

I am. This is me … this is my Body. Inside my body I carry my Conscience, I am my Conscience. There are the Things of the Body, and there are the Things of the Conscience … and I am alone. I am quite alone. My body is the body of the whole world … and my conscience is the conscience of the whole world … and I am as alone as the ball of crumpled paper on its way through the dark, through the endlessly long street. Who will help me, who comfort me? Best of all, perhaps, that wondrous Friend called Wonderment.

4
Encounter

In the soft warm silence of the empty classroom where she sits alone at her table in front of the empty rows, a voice flies across to her and snatches her away from her book. Ebner stands in the doorway.

'Did you ask me something?'

'Whether you were walking home the same way as me.'

'No, I can't leave yet. I have to wait for Ernestien. She hasn't given me the concert ticket yet. But she isn't alone. Mrs Brom is with her in the classroom.'

'Yes, I know. I saw her arrive.'

She has stood up, has put down her book and walked over to him, - together they stand in the doorway. They look at each other. They are thinking about the 'scandal', how its sudden revelation spread through the school like an insurrection, like a fever, which had them all in its grip to such an extent that they all forgot the disputes over Power, - all of them except Arjen Brand.

All the life in him seems to be focused on that one thing, - his face is angrier and crosser every day. Getting engaged has made a big difference! Engaged to Bauk ... They look at one another, she and Ebner, each of them leaning on a doorpost. She knows that, as far as possible, he prefers not to discuss what is occupying them all, but she can see in his face that he would like to talk to her about it, to return to this morning's conversation with Penning and Miss Korff.

But he doesn't, he strokes his pale red beard and remains silent for a moment. And then out of the blue:

'Ernestien told me about her offer ... that she has invited you to live with her and Dora. And about the milieu, the people, where you are now. She said: Eva doesn't belong there. I just don't understand why you haven't jumped at the chance.'

There you stand in sudden dismay, - you seem to have lost the power of speech. He waits, - she is silent, - the seconds stretch out, each second lingers ... like a heavy, wet rope, with each of them holding an end, so that the silence hangs in between them ... growing heavier for your arm, more difficult to lift.

'You went over there, didn't you? Didn't you have tea there?'

'Yes, last Thursday.'

'And you still couldn't make up your mind ...?'

Can he see it ... can he guess it ...? What lies hidden, the secret passageway, suddenly seems laid bare by his piercing eyes. But that can't be so, because he doesn't know anything.

The high window makes a muffled, soft rattling sound in the wind. It cannot deflect the wind, neither can walls or doors, it blows through the whole school. The rain is thrown against the windows in great handfuls, the sound of sweets being strewn for the children on St Nicholas' Eve. It is autumn: October, past its sun-wreathed and damp-enveloped peak, slips into the gloomy valley on its way towards dark November. The white dahlias on the window sill stand out - a halo of shining white rosettes of light around the green pot. In the distance the tower pulls its mantle of mist closer.

'Mrs Brom is taking a long time.' He looks at his watch. 'I have to go. I still have three hours of extra lessons today.'

He leaves, and she goes back into the classroom, to her chair, to her book, but she can't get down to the book any more. For a moment it managed to divert her from what fills her so she can hardly breathe, something that concerns her and something that concerns someone else, someone she scarcely knows, and who she suddenly cares about ...

Ebner touched on both with his few words and now she has to give herself up to them again, now she cannot escape them any longer. Yes, Ernestien told her everything -, she knew before it had got to the point where everyone knows, where the children in the top classes, in this school, in his own school, laugh and whisper about it.

Mr Brom is Head of the school that stands at an angle to the quay, facing the side street. Until recently he occasionally came into their school to consult 'the old master'. You saw him in the corridors -, a dark, respectable, unapproachable man. Sometimes he walked past people and children without recognizing them, left their greetings unanswered, but he stopped for the smallest little pot, the tiniest plant, gave advice on how to look after it, pointed out what was wrong, freely offered his help. He lends out books on the subject to all and sundry -, he has shelves of them, he devotes himself to them, he seems to live for nothing else. He has a gentle, pale, kind wife and three grown-up children, two sons and a daughter -, who all look like him, the eldest son most of all: dark, respectable, unapproachable. He has a good position with a large bank, the second son wants to become a vet, the daughter gives piano lessons. Ernestien knows them well, she goes to the house, Mrs Brom and she come from the same village. What she cannot remember because they are much older was told her by her parents: in the beginning the Broms were hard up, they had difficult times -, the two sons, now so hefty, so strong, were sickly little boys -, Mr Brom spent his evenings teaching, his nights studying … this way they struggled together through the years … like fighting your way through undergrowth … until at last things began to be good and light and airy and free around them, until now at last they were able to start thinking about peace and quiet -, he and his gentle, pale, kind wife.

Next year is their twenty-fifth wedding anniversary … and at his school they had been saving up for a great celebration for over a year, for a beautiful present … and now, and now … once when she was a child, she came out of school and met Jans Dorpema hurtling down the street and he shouted: 'Have you heard about Pastor Boeke? He's dead.' And she had seen him walking around the day before. You never know what's around the corner. Six months ago a new cleaner was taken on by the school, to replace old Mrs Slop, who couldn't go on any longer. On Wednesday afternoons and Saturday afternoons, the cleaners have to scrub stairs, mop floors, clean windows. Mr Brom is in the habit of going back to school on free afternoons for the plants that he grows in the school garden under cloches, in small frames -, he also does an hour's studying -, and he fell in love with the new cleaner. She is young, she is called Joop … she has red cheeks and teeth so large that she can hardly close her lips over them, so that you can always see them. And her red hair is so long and so heavy, it works loose while she is scrubbing, and wherever she has been, there are hairpins on the ground. And they say … they've seen it themselves … that he sat in the room with Joop on his knee, that he … kissed Joop … they say that Joop called him 'Martijn' while two girls from the top form were standing there … they say that he wants to divorce his wife and marry Joop … they say that she will only kiss him if he gives her money … she buys silk blouses with it. She bought a purple one, and a red-and-green striped one with it … A cleaner … a woman … who sits on a man's knee for money … But is it all right to believe such horrors, even though you have only been told them, but shouldn't you rather insist, even to those who saw what happened, that they are wrong, and do so against your better judgement, because you need to be able to live, because you need to be able to breathe. For there is no comfort anywhere, if this is real.

In his own school no-one greets him any more. Ernestien says: some people are using the situation to take revenge, because they thought him too strict and too orderly. The big boys shout in the street: 'Martijn, Joop is on her way.' Boys, who once would quake in front of him if they saw him coming round the corner towards them, are full of daring … and everyone wonders: will he be able to stay there, is his position tenable there? His sons despise him, his daughter avoids him … his wife does nothing but cry day and night … he is silent.

Apparently at home he no longer gives an answer to anything, to anyone, he says: 'I have said all there is to say, so now you know. I have nothing to say for myself …' Ernestien knows this from his wife. 'The old master' is completely thrown by it, but he doesn't want to talk about it, doesn't want to hear about it, he said to Penning: 'I'd rather you didn't tell me, Penning, keep quiet about it, if you don't mind.' Bauk blames everything on Joop. Her cheeks are aflame. They should lock up such a … hussey … such a creature … such a wretch … beat her … Men don't know any better … but a woman must be made to understand that she must leave married men alone … she should be … she should be …

'Bauk, remember you are a free woman …' Now she flares up even more fiercely. She begins to hate Ebner. Ebner only talks about the subject if it can't be avoided. He says: Every human being must carry his own burden … Arjen growls: 'The fellow leaves me completely cold and you all with your gossip, your old wives' chat: I'm sick of you.' Then Bauk makes a huge effort, and talks about nothing but the Republican School all day long, but if one of the others comes with a story about something that is supposed to have just happened, to have been seen, to have come out … then she can't hold it in any longer … and she flares up … they should do this to her, they should do that … Penning pronounces:

'I do not understand what you actually want. Can the man do anything about it? Each individual is what he is. What he has to be, what he has to do. Can I help it that I'm going bald? Can Arjen Brand help it that Bauk has hooked him? Ebner might have preferred to have a wife and seven defenceless babes rather than a landlady who pinches his butter and smuggles margarine into his butter dish. What do you all want of this man? He is what he has to be and he does what he has to do.' He calls this determinism. You learnt something like that at school: determining, identifying plants. 'Certainty out of randomness.' Because one characteristic is lacking and another is present, this explains why he has no choice in the matter …

Miss Korff pressed her hands against her ears. 'Cynic … cynic … that is what happens when you have no faith.' She is actually Roman Catholic. She says: 'Brom is in the Devil's power, the Devil has got the better of him.'

'But Miss Korff … only yesterday you said: a man like that belongs in prison … But if the Devil has got him … then it isn't his fault any more …'

'Oh, no …? And should you not resist the Devil then?'

'Should …? Should …? If you can! But if the Devil is stronger …? If you fight someone stronger than yourself, is it your fault when the other one wins?'

'That makes things jolly easy … if you're allowed to use that kind of argument.'

'But you brought up the Devil! Not me.'

Penning interjects: 'And can you also tell me, Miss Korff, what God is busy doing all the while?'

'I'm not talking to you, you make fun of everything. You, a cynic … and her … a frivolous child …' And she walks off angrily and Penning goes on his way laughing.

Frivolous child … me? It didn't occur to me to make fun. This is a matter of the very greatest seriousness. This is a question of the very greatest import … But people like Miss Korff make you … dizzy … in the same way that the 'solutions' to mathematical problems of children who can't think for themselves, and who can't grasp explanations, sometimes make you dizzy. How can you say one day: he belongs in prison -, and the next day: the Devil has got hold of him? Whoever speaks of Guilt must not speak of the Devil -, whoever brings the Devil into it has done with Guilt. Guilt lies in the self. Does she not see that …? How do you live with such a … in such a … in such a muddle, such inner disorder? You couldn't even put up with it in a 'maths problem'. Sometimes - for days on end - you couldn't overcome your dislike of learning off by heart something that you didn't care about -, your geography book lay unopened, when you were supposed to be learning your lesson. But one of those maths solutions kept you awake at night with worry … because you couldn't go to sleep with it in a muddle, because you would be stifled by the inner disorder! …

'There isn't a mistake in the question, is there, Sir?'

No the question is fine. Then there must be an answer. Then there must … be a Solution. 'And even if there's a mistake in the question you should be able to detect it.' 'Yes, Sir, but that doesn't help me at all … to work out where Mr Versluys has made the error.'

You pondered the why and wherefore on the way home. And you thought: only that which is generally applicable is interesting. Ernestien walks away when she sees the others standing together. Everyone knows that she knows the Broms. She does not want to be questioned.

She saw the house being built … now she must watch it fall into ruins. This is how she herself puts it, and it is a hard thing to do, often she can't sleep because of it. Lettie, the daughter, has fled the house, is staying with friends … the two sons only stay for their mother. Almost twenty-five years … but you never know what is round the corner.

'I don't want to reproach him … I must not reproach him … I can see all too well how it's making him suffer. It is like seeing a man set fire to his own house …'

'A man who does that is described as mad … you would say he was mad … isn't that right, Ernestien …?'

'Yes … of course. But God … you do expect a bit more wisdom. All those years … and the way they struggled through them together … Lettie will never get over it … she revered him … she has torn up the photographs of him … burnt them. He should have understood all that …'

Should … should … well, even Ernestien is talking like Miss Korff: you should resist the Devil …

Yes, you should … you should …

She gets up from her table again, goes to the door, listens out in the softly-whispered, wind-rustled silence. Two gentle voices from a distant classroom … Ernestien and Mrs Brom … you could fall asleep standing there like that … in that whispering … the muffled, soft rattle of the big window … and those voices. She tiptoes across … there is the big window with a silver cloth of rain spread tautly across it -, it no longer lets even a shadow of the tower through. But the little corner window, protected by a jutting wall, is clear, almost dry.

Dark with damp, tall, gloomy - the back wall of the school opposite. The colour and grain of heavy grey drawing paper. Large windows with grey-on-grey striped curtains, small ones with little pieces of green and lilac coloured glass that you know are there, but can't see. And here is his room, 'senior school master's room', and there he is … standing with his legs apart, hands in pockets and eyes following the low clouds racing past, you can tell from the movements of his head. And still, almost a week later, that glass of milk is still there, half emptied and then forgotten … he, for whom no-one could be neat and tidy enough …! Did someone call him …? He turned so suddenly, tore himself away from the window. Is he listening out for her arrival in school ... Joop with her big teeth, her red hair that comes loose while she is scrubbing, scattering hairpins which he picked up and kept ...

If he were suddenly to look at this little window, he might see her standing there ... their eyes would meet ... perhaps they would acknowledge one another ... but he would not guess that of all of them, she is the only one who understands him ... Because she alone knows, she alone experiences, undergoes, along with him this strong force that renders you powerless ... and is all that remains of everything else ... of everything that the others speak of that seems so strong: a sense of duty, willpower, dignity ... things you spoke of yourself when you were still free and did not understand. O, desire ... desire, irresistible and undignified desire ... Just as once you hung on to your rope, and were one with your rope, in the tug-of-war in the gym class. You did not want to cross the line, you had decided that for yourself. You would clamp your feet on to the floorboards, you would screw them into the floor. And your whole body, your brain, your heart, flew to the assistance of your arms and hands ... and you felt your back stiffen ... you were nothing but one taut body, a taut will, not to ... not to cross the chalk line. But when the other proved stronger, you were over that line, instantly and absolutely ... That's how it goes.

What you considered to be the best of all was: dignity. Better than: duty. Dignity is purely of yourself and unto yourself. That is why you found that song so beautiful at school -, it was a dialogue between people, who agree how they will live. Not six hundred and thirteen command-ments and prohibitions. Not 'thou shalt do this ...' and 'thou shalt do that ...' These people made a pact with one another ...

'Seek truth, act with kindness
Love God, go the way of fairness.
All the days of our life on earth ...'

You thought: If they had asked me to join them, I certainly would have done. It must be better to act together than alone. And then suddenly it all fades into dull, powerless words ... and what seemed to be rock solid in you, something to cling to in times of need, turns out to be as insecure as poles in boggy ground. Oh, the gusts of desire, irresistible and undignified desire! And so your little clog-boat capsized ... No, you would never have thought it.

Ernestien has asked whether she will come and live with her and Dora, on the other side of town, where they have rented a floor in a quiet, airy house. Ernestien worked in a school in that neighbourhood, but she prefers working-class children and this is why she came back to this neighbourhood. She is ugly and little and sprightly and fat, she is an ugly, little, fat, sprightly bundle of pure benevolence. She and Dora do not have to live on what they earn alone, they have inherited money, they own a piano, their own furniture, they can buy books … they don't spend their money on clothes … They won't spend every long, precious day talking about dresses. Oh to be able to live in a quiet, airy house, in a little room with a window on the park, with people who are not for ever pulling at you and tweaking and fiddling and finding fault, where you would be able to kick your red velvet hat into a corner, where you would not be made nauseous by the fashion pictures and dress patterns and swatches and lace and whalebone and ribbons and artificial flowers and scent … where you would not live with the constant oppression of being thought crazy and not being able to work out why.

Ernestien came to visit one evening last week. They drank tea in Bertha's room, the four of them sat at the round table, but the table top could have been an ocean, a ravine. They say everything differently, they mean everything differently. Ernestien says of people: they are nice people. She means: the way they behave. Whether you can trust them, whether they are reasonable people. Saar and Bertha say: they are nice people. They mean their hats, their dresses, their houses. They say: 'We couldn't decide.' Ernestien says: A book by Couperus. A book by Tolstoy. She says the same. The main thing about a book is surely who has written it. Saar and Bertha ask: 'Have you read 'The Ruby Necklace?' If you ask the name of the writer, they don't know. 'What has that got to do with it?'

Rachel came in, she pulled a face in the mirror, behind Ernestien's back, to Bertha and Saar. They have another way of talking about you, of making fun of you, while you are sitting there, without you realizing: they look straight at one another and then start humming … At least they didn't do that this evening, didn't dare.

And then suddenly … there stood Herman in the doorway, with his guitar, with his new songs. They flattered him: 'You must sing your new songs, Herman.' He said: 'If I may make so bold.' But Ernestien did not move a muscle. He went and stood by the cupboard with the photographs, placed one foot out in front, the knee bent … strumming away, he formed a circle with his mouth. Bertha, Saar, Rachel looked up at him with eyes swimming in adoration, Ernestien dazed, subdued … In her a poisonous turmoil: Now look, listen, take it all in … draw from it the strength to stay away, to evade, to refuse. This is him! 'If I may make so bold.' And immediately the rush of pity … he is defenceless, and I am handing him over - oh, I am betraying him … ahh, he doesn't know any better … Ernestien sat so still, sat so mute … not just still and mute like someone listening, but stilled and muted in a daze.

He didn't stop after the new songs -, the girls didn't want him to. He strummed, he sang, one song after the other. And then Ernestien suddenly looked at her. Yes, Ernestien … I know, I understand, this chorus has a hidden meaning … it has an unspeakably low hidden meaning.

The next morning at school Ernestien said: 'They are good people, I have nothing against them, but you don't belong there …' Ernestien, go on, say it now, ask it now, then the secret will be in the past. She asked: 'And who was that young man?' She mentioned his name -, 'a neighbour'. She couldn't say: that young man lures me with a whistle into his garden … that same young man, who stood there, his knee bent, against the cupboard with the peacock feathers and the photographs. And: 'If I may make so bold.' He kisses me on the lips … he touches me, wherever he wants … and above our heads are the stars, they stare down on us, and around us is the hidden whisper … the wind stirs through the ivy like the stag beetles whirring over the canal in spring … and my heart thumps in me: debauchery, adultery - debauchery, adultery … Never do I feel that peaceful flowing together of all the rest with our togetherness, I must hide everything of myself from him and now I say nothing … if after that one evening I had been able, if I had been able to leave his eyes, his laugh, his letters unanswered … but I went to him … and now the same thing cannot go on repeating itself … and now I say nothing, and the longer I go on, the deeper I sink … he doesn't want to know who I am … I wish that I did not know who he is … O, gust of desire, of irresistible, undignified desire. And so our little clog-boat capsized, as we sailed it, David and I, in the blue harbour, in the breeze coming from the brown-plumed reeds …

And if I were to come to live with you in the light, airy house, without fashion plates and lace trimmings, and 'make your selection' and 'this is very popular at the moment' and those portraits with the necks turning and the mouths pursed that make me feel sick … then I won't see him again, and then he will forget me, he will forget me for Selien, and my life will become empty like a home after its inhabitants have moved house, like the school after four … As a child I used to stand there … mother would roll out the pastry … I watched the ball spreading out into an endless yellowy white surface … my days will be endless like that … I have already been through it … when we argued and neither could give way to the other … and the moments roll over me like wagon wheels, and each moment, snatched from the others, is itself perceptible … and each hour contains thousands of them, more than there are seeds in a rosehip … they roll, roll, I lie underneath the rolling moments, and there is no end to the day.

Oh, restless man over there at the window … growing more restless every second … he, too, lies underneath the rolling moments … which I alone understand … he pulled out his watch ten times, twenty times in one minute. He went away, and came back again … stood for a brief time and went away again … and now he is there again … And now … now she has come … she must have come … he listens … his hand reaches upwards … the grey blind drops right down to the window sill … the half empty glass of milk tumbles from the sill.

Here, where she now stands alone in the silence, warm from the heating, chill from the draught, here is where they stood yesterday in the clamour of the dispute. Miss Korff pressed her hands over her ears. 'Cynic, cynic.' Penning grinned: 'And what is God doing, meanwhile?' The Devil has got him - and yet, and yet he is still to blame. 'Or else it would be easy …'

Oh yes, he's got it easy. Oh yes, if he does all the things they say, if everything happens as they predict -, if he lashes out, his house in flames, his wife destroyed, his children fleeing from him …, all for the red-haired Joop … and the scandal … the boys in the street who used to respect and fear him. 'Martijn, Joop is on her way …' yes, he's got it easy, nice and easy! All that is needed now is for Blame to be heaped upon him. Oh folly, blind, cruel folly … But Penning with his determining … determinism … 'Everyone is what he is, everyone does what he has to do. No-one can be otherwise, can do otherwise …' No. Yes. One or the other. Either will and guilt -, or no will and no guilt. No. Stop. Lean motionless against the rainy window, stand still in the stillness … and wait … for … it will come … to you … It wheels in circles around you … it is looking for you … it is looking for your heart … now it is aimed at you like an arrow out of the endless distance. Lean against the window … you have it … it has you … it could fell you.

There is no Guilt -, but there is a Sense of Guilt.

No-one is guilty -, but without a Sense of Guilt, all are lost. The arrow has struck me where the hidden divide resides … it is as though I am cloven in two … I am split in two … I am two … I am two bound together in one, I am two face-to-face, I am one turned against itself. You must absolve everyone, and therefore you must also absolve yourself … if you don't want to go to sleep with chaos, if you don't want to suffocate in the mess inside you … but for every absolution applied to yourself, you must appeal to a higher authority, to the other half of yourself … you must allow judgement to be pronounced by the other, by the second you ... and that judgement is your support and guide ... and if you don't hold on to it ... then you are lost ... lost ... lost ...

Everything becomes clear, mists lift, and once more language makes all clear: to guide is to judge, Judge is Guide, gives direction.

Oh clarity ... clarity ... stay near me, stay in me, stay around me ... let me think this for the rest of my days ... There is something else: you cannot apply your own sense of guilt to others ... it is purely your own salvation, your own counterweight, each person guides only themselves by it, against the grain of rational knowledge, but turns that rational knowledge towards their fellow human beings and absolves them using that knowledge ... and so things will become clear of their own accord ... as Ernestien once said, having learnt it from her father -, that virtuous people judge themselves harshly and others leniently.

Until now I had not understood this ... at least, I had not understood that it had to be this way. 'In the nature of things', - as Mr De Veer used to say -, routine phrase, it made you laugh. And yet not so silly: in the nature of things. You must always pay more attention to what everything means. A brisk step crossing the floorboards. Ernestien, with tears in her eyes.

'Here, the ticket ... poor dear ... I had forgotten all about you. Will you call in this afternoon, and tell us what it was like?'

'Yes ... I promise. Are you very sad, Ernestien? Is she very sad?'

'Oh, it is all so dreadful -, it's getting worse. Her entire family ... a gang of rogues ... they have latched on to him ... they are bleeding him dry ... sometimes he doesn't have a cent ... he is cutting down on everything ... and now he had asked Coen, his eldest son, for money ... supposedly his book bill had been higher than expected ... but it was for her ... for her again ...'

'Oh ... Ernestien ...'

'Well ... you go along now. I must get back to her.'

Out of the noisy morning the afternoon has been born, quiet and peaceful ... the low-lying water gleams beneath the swirling mist, the faintest breath of chrysanthemums lingers in the damp air, along with the smell of leaves rotting in the mist ... O city, overwhelming, overabundant city ... I wanted to be able to close myself off for a moment from your plenitude and multiplicity, but I am in their grip, they beat against me like waves, so that I stumble ... but I can't go on, because I can't go without breathing, and every breath I take fills me to my heart with your breath ... and your breath is the breath of eternal ebb and flow ... leaves, flowers, mists, sounds ... October ... and your soul is the soul of what remains eternally … the grey houses, the grey bridges, the grey water … and all this penetrates me, pushes its way into me, and wants … and wants … it always wants the same thing, it wants to be fathomed again, wants to be understood. Halfway across this bridge, where I stop as though restrained, it surrounds me, binds me, and stares at me and stares down on me and stares up at me … the large, blank window-eyes in the buildings … the dull trees … the shadowy water … I am the centre of everything. As small as I am, insignificant and small, under the eternal sky, it nevertheless sends out its entreaty to me alone.

It all wants to become one, united in my comprehending mind, through my powers of understanding … each thing presses me, it pleads with me that I should, in my comprehension, connect it to all other things, unite it with all other things, that I should release it from its loneliness … bridges and flowers … houses and sounds, all of heaven and all of earth … but I cannot … I cannot connect it all in my comprehension since my mind has not yet fathomed it … Why does it have to be me in particular? Why do I always have to be the one? I don't want this, it is destroying me. I want to stand in front of shop windows, I want to look at shoes, stoves, books, lace collars … I want to go to a cake shop, I want to buy toffees. If I go to a cake shop, I will choose a cream bun with chocolate icing, if I buy toffees … no, red-and-white sweets, which are cheaper. And almost as nice. So there. And remember how you used to look round the corner out of Loerie Bitter's alley … has it gone, Mr Heyl the butcher's nasty, black dog? Yes - David says - it has gone, we can go home … How afraid we always were of black dogs.

But I really and truly am going to a concert -, I am going to my first concert! Ernestien said, it's a nice programme, but I won't follow it all. The symphony probably least of all -, the composer is called: Gustav Mahler -, but at the end there is a solo, a blind girl will sing it. Ernestien knows that girl. I must listen carefully to the violin concerto above all. A violin concerto has four movements, a symphony also has four movements … 'Andante' means slowly … 'presto' means fast … Ernestien has written it in pencil for me. There are also 'sonatas' and 'suites' … eventually I will learn. Ernestien said recently: 'You seem musical to me' -, she said that one day we would also go together, she, Dora and I.

A soft wind heavy with moisture rustles in the young, brown trees in the square … the recessed doors are still locked shut … people are waiting. There are mainly ladies and girls waiting, an occasional young man -, a few more older gentlemen. And these people are all your fellow human beings, your unknown fellow human beings, and there are almost as many kinds of people, as there are people. How is it that you can always immediately read from two eyes and one mouth whether someone is hard or good, stupid or sensible? Why would you like to stroke one face and slap another? But you mustn't look at them so concentratedly, it embarrasses them, it makes them angry even -, the others don't do it, no, not one of them. Everyone looks ahead of themselves, or talks or says hello. You must be like the others ... remember to be like the others ...

Twilit warmth, solemn noises, reminiscent of a church ... high up silvery light coming through recessed half-moon windows. Hanging in the huge space the sparkling clusters of white-shining chandeliers, and deep in the twilight the red-velvet seats, like toy bricks, like a postcard parade ... like guardsmen. She looks down into it over the balustrade. Ernestien said that she should choose a seat up here, in the curve against the wall, behind the people.

Peaceful now ... peaceful ... none of this raises pressing questions ... all is peacefulness and expectation ... though expectation is never wholly without fear ... it feels like being under water.

But the sounds are growing louder ... and that feverishly fast sound, that seems desperate and urgent, is the violins being tuned, it makes your heart suddenly impatient to join in ... people are talking quietly and quickly, they all have things to say at the last minute, before they must be silent. But something happened that she missed ... and all the lips close over the unuttered words, and all the noise subsides and for a moment it is so terrifyingly quiet ... you are suspended ... you hang there ...

But that is how it used to be ... The lamp was lit and shone right into all four corners of the room, and the room was filled, suddenly, with something spreading out from that fierce, that golden light inside the lamp glass ... And you always asked, always wondered: what could it be ... O, incomprehensibility, everlasting incomprehensibility ... this is invisible light, and yet it is 'something' and it is more than light, and the whole space is filled with it and your head is in its midst, it finds the gateways of your ears and you yourself are now filled with it. If not now, then never; the light fills you.

But Ernestien spoke of 'understanding music' and I want to ask her this afternoon -, what she means by 'understanding music'. Who can have the powers to understand this? Can you understand light ... or stillness ...?

'Understanding' -, that is: being able to explain in words. No ... actually understanding is: comparing with something else. Can you do that? How can you grasp something that brushes past you like wind ... something that penetrates you as well ... as when you see white tulips in the sun, in a garden ... they wave about, it is the Easter holiday ... or a summer's night in bed ... you can't sleep ... frogs croak ... there are night-time whisperings ... but you surely don't understand them? And this is everything all-together ... it is all the rest in one ... Yes, if you could double yourself ... one to listen, one to simultaneously comprehend ... or, if you could catch ... could hold on to this illuminating light, this tenuous, elusive light ... like people who take photographs ... another light on a sensitive plate ... it is called: fixing ... carry it with you ... every day ... in everlasting reflection ... constantly contemplate it ... until you have reached an uninterrupted and deeper understanding ... but you can't think at the same time as listening ... can't listen at the same time as thinking ... and your desire for thought clashes with your desire to listen ... and soon you will no longer be able to do either of them ... Oh, forget about the need to 'comprehend' ... now you have this one divine certainty: for as long as the violin is playing ... for as long as the sound rising from the depths fills the spaces as it spreads out, right up to the silver niches and sparkling chandeliers ... and if that could always stay with you ... you would never desire anything more, and all would be good and you would be at peace with everything, and there would be no more mysteries -, you would know them all simultaneously ... and no longer seek to know them ... you would find everything possible ... you would want to take everything upon yourself ... then you would be released from yourself for ever and you would be given to yourself for ever ...

And it stops playing ... and it disappears ... that's what it was like when the lamp was extinguished and the light died. A person has a memory, and can repeat something, she herself actually has a good memory ... and can repeat many stories ... but memory is no use here. This, like light, passes through you, pervades you. And you must return to those white tulips, to that garden, to those smells, to that sweet morning, to that southerly wind ... you must have patience until night falls again ... from afar, through silences, the sound comes ... you lie back in bed, in the dark, and your mouth is open, but you cannot give it a name ... I discerned hundreds of wonderful things. I saw the reedy pool too, that I went past in the train. I called out to it, that day ... Reedy pool, one day I will come to you ... I did not come ... but now it has come to me ... and has reminded me of my promise, of my broken promise ...

But what does it mean, to understand music? For it is surely unfathomable ... As empty of light as a room where the lamp no longer burns, blown away leaving an immense empty space where the chandeliers sparkle ... Isn't it so ... isn't it so ... isn't it the way I think it is ...?

Yes ... it is so ... everything is just as you think it is ... Dark eyes ... soft, deep eyes ... dark eyes, soft deep eyes have replied to my eyes ... my eyes looked up to dark deep eyes. For he is standing and I am sitting ... and he is leaning against the balustrade ... But he is moving ... and he is a man ... and you yourself are a girl ... he is a man and you do not know him at all ... he is much older that you-yourself ... a gentleman in grey clothes ... But his eyes and your own eyes -, he was only eyes, you yourself were only eyes, but now he is a man, a gentleman, whom you do not know at all -, and you simply don't look at a strange man like that. It is not respectable ... it is unseemly, and it is just as well you are on your own ...

But our eyes have spoken to one another and I was not a girl and he was not a man, and we have confided to one another, what we both know, that music is incomprehensible.

Down stairs, round corners - the doors are wide open - the notices on the walls flutter against you and at the bottom you plunge into a sea of people ... which carries you into the rain and dusk of the wide square, with the little brown trees dripping with moisture and ruffled by the wind ... with the breath of chrysanthemums ... on the opposite side, as though across water, the lamps glowing orange, red, shine out from the large, dark houses.

Deep, soft eyes ... dark eyes ... which I lost in the sea of people ... I was not a girl and he was not a man ... we were eyes, which, independently of everything and above everything, met like dark birds under a large, yellow-flushed evening sky ... and the two-of-them alone ... confiding to each other in full confidence: music is unfathomable ... mystery of mysteries, the unfathomable of all that is unfathomable, and all is unfathomable. But this tugs you far away, to the limits ... you will never reach the farthest limits this way ... the limits where the vistas are. Vistas of what you call 'I'. Endless and limitless I, in the endlessness and limitlessness of distant vistas, of constantly shifting vistas. -, and at the same time, here walking through the gloom, here across the square, so small in its boundedness ... past the stocking shop ... past the almond pastry bakery ... making way for the tram so as not ... with its vistas ... *With* its vistas ...? With or without its vistas ...? And Moses went up from the plains of Moab to Mount Nebo ... facing Jericho ... and Moses saw the endless vistas of the land where he was not allowed to live. I have today stood high up on the Nebo ... and I did not stand there alone ... deep, soft eyes ... dark eyes ... together we stared across the Land ... from Jericho to Zoar ... but no-one may live there, no-one has a home there ... Oh, Moses is not the only banished one ...

In the last of the daylight the ponds gleam, brilliant-cut precious stones, set in multi-colours and green and golden brown ... the paths fold around them, grey with damp ... and everything is so heavy with silence ... as though with water, so heavy ... Autumn hush, Autumn droop ... the other silence is not this silent ... The few people walking about are caught in this silence ... held ... captured. The ponds reflect their pale faces, their dark clothes, the ponds reflect the stippled colours and the green and the golden brown ... Sometimes they stand still ... and move again, but slowly ... so this silence, this autumn hush seems to weigh on them ... And that lone man there ... the multi-coloured flower bed has caught him ... he is staring down into it ... he can't move away from it ... Oh, the breathless showiness, the hushed brilliance ... in the autumn shadows ... no words for it, no words for anything ... and open to everything. Oh, lonely man there, I know so well ... But he looks up ... he looks towards the sound of my feet ... and it is those eyes ... it is the dark, soft, deep eyes. Together we stared into the same vistas ... And now ... what shall we be? Shall we again be only eyes, or shall we be man and girl? If we are man and girl, then in half a minute, we will have passed each other, and may not even look round at one another, because we do not know one another. To me he is an unknown gentleman ·, to him I am an unknown girl ... you meet hundreds of strangers every day, and thousands in a year, like this, in trains and on boats, at the post office, in the street, in a crowd ... and pass them for ever, as if they were leaves, as if they were stones ... Shall we pass one another like that ... because we are not 'relatives', 'friends', 'acquaint-ances', don't even know each other's name, or which house the other lives in, have not been introduced to one another. Or birds ... two birds flying straight for one another in complete trust, free of everything, above everything, between yellow-grey rippling water and a yellow-flushed evening sky? No ... we remained a man and a girl ... and passed each other ... yet there was one brief moment, in which neither of us knew which to be, in which we hesitated in each other's direction and a thread was spun, but we pulled and it broke and each one was left with their own half ... But I ... I am released ... But I ... I am liberated ... And my honour is restored. Deep eyes, dark soft eyes have released me, liberated me, restored my honour.

The fences are firmly in place in stiff, clammy earth. Dignity ... I can be dignified again ... I will be dignified again, I will resist. His eyes swept me up to the heights, accompanied me on to the Nebo ... Gusts of desire ... unworthy ... no longer irresistible ... you besiege me in vain ... oh you no longer even besiege me ...

Man at the window, oh restless one, growing more restless with each moment, as the moments roll over … I no longer share your fate … I let go of you, I can no longer be with you … poor man … ah, poor man … I leave you on your own … And Ernestien … I am coming … I am coming home to you … no more empty days, no more long days. I could, if I want to, stay there, because what was irresistible yesterday would today find me unapproachable … because I am released … I do not come in fear … I come because I love you and because it is good to be with you … because I belong with you and not with the others, over there. In the quiet side street, the street lamps shed such a humble, trusty light, and here is the house. Her finger pressed … the bell delivers its message behind the closed door. A chestnut tree shot through with golden light in the dusk … luminous dome … self-illuminating, and over there the ponds … and here the lamp … and a breath of wind … and on the ground a skipping leaf … oh, unforgettable moment …

'Ah … is it you? And did you enjoy …? Was it beautiful? Did you walk through the rain? Or did you get so wet from the moisture in the air? And where did you sit …? Do take off your hat and coat. You really will have to buy an umbrella one day. You will have to take the plunge. Come, child … we have a fire. Dora is making tea … and Emilie has come to play for us. But if you don't feel the need for music for the time being, feel free to say so! Yes … and another thing. You will have to make up your mind fairly quickly about the empty room … because Emilie knows a girl … a cousin, I think …'

'I've already decided, Ernestien. I'm coming, I'm coming! I would rather come today than tomorrow.'

5
May Day

Now there is a May wind blowing, now the May green flutters in the breeze, the May sun glitters … it is a day like an open yellow tulip, so fresh and so lovely, and yesterday it was still April, last night it was April until midnight. She heard the clock strike, it was a moonless night, and everyone was asleep and in the dome of silence the flower opened … it is the First of May, it is the Day. She is sitting in the empty classroom on the smooth surface of one of the benches and David's letter is in her lap and Berthold's picture in her hands. He is fourteen now -, David and she are twenty-two - he is tall and blond and splendid, he seems grown up: his withered legs are hidden in long trousers -, his recovery has come to a standstill.

For two years now David has been living in the house with many windows, with the large lawn, where sandy paths and avenues of beech come together from all directions. David does not often come home any more -, he has been to the coast with Berthold a few times, staying at home with Berthold in the house on their return, and once they all went away together …

Ebner comes in, he has his thin, grey summer coat over his arm. Yesterday he was still wearing his blue winter coat.

'Can we go?'

'No, not now we're all supposed to be waiting for one another … Bauk and Arjen are with the old master.'

She doesn't ask with words, only briefly with her eyes.

'Well, I don't understand either. In six months he'll be gone … why on earth can't they leave him in peace for the short time that's left?'

But he sees David's letter and goes to read the newspaper. Now it's quiet … distant, closed voices … more distant, open sounds

... dreamy ... dozy ... Distant lands ... distant seas ... strange names you learned ... years ago ... but they attached themselves, they chained themselves to the moments ... and return again with those moments, year in, year out ... the inflexible regularity of a calendar ...

But Bauk and Arjen ... yes, the dispute is flaring up again. Mr Brom is no longer the subject of conversation. He has been transferred to a smaller school at the other side of town, and he has been forgotten.

Joop with the red hair, with the teeth she can hardly close her lips over, Joop now scrubs the stairs, washes the floors, cleans the windows of other municipal buildings. They are not married. He begged his wife to hold him back, to hold on to him, and she is trying to achieve this. But how can it be achieved? He wants to be simultaneously held back and released, he wants to be thwarted, and he wants to get his way. Evening after evening he slips out of his house to go to Joop ... and if he stays away, as a punishment, he has to ... clean her shoes. They really shouldn't tell you these things ... they stay with you ...

A human being can descend to all sorts of things ... a human being can very easily descend to many things! Miss Korff lives in constant fear of diseases ... but just think for a moment of the temptations, of the trials ... Will you withstand them? And if you don't withstand them, what will your life be like?

How unsafe life can be ... unsafe. Lettie fled the house, the city, Ernestien hasn't heard another thing from her in months. She only writes to her mother. 'I am doing fine, I am well.' The last thing she wrote to Ernestien was, on a postcard: 'What did I tell you!' She broke off her engagement because of her father - 'ugh, men ...' - and the boy was distraught. He lay sobbing with his head on Ernestien's lap ... and a year later he went off to Indonesia a married man. That was when Lettie wrote the postcard to Ernestien: 'What did I tell you!'

How shockingly unsafe life is. You should just do what she and David did, when they were children, if there was a row at drunken Bol's ... you put your fingers in your ears ... or if you bumped into 'Mrs Death's Head', who had an open hole, with a tip of flesh sticking up, in the middle of her face. 'It might be us one day ...'

No ... no, look the other way ...

But suddenly I am sitting right in the sun ... I am sitting with one side right in the sun ... that side of my white dress is warm ... that side of my body, my shoulder and my hip, is all warm. And my face ... oh, I only have to raise it slightly to the window, and now my whole face is in the sun. And the sun caresses me ... no, the sun kisses me ... sun-kisses ... sun-kisses ... sun-kisses on your closed eyelids ... sun-kisses on your cheeks … sun-kisses on your lips … and you open your lips and they leap into your mouth, and you breathe sun-kisses …

'Ebner … just look …'

'What …?'

She had wanted to say: 'Ebner, my whole face is covered with sun-kisses, right into my mouth.' She thought he was reading his newspaper. But he started, because he wasn't reading, he was looking at her … at the sun-kisses on her lips … and his own lips are thin and pale … they are … oh, what are they … I know, they are starved lips. Oh, Ebner, don't you want … don't you want to kiss the sun-kisses from my lips … wouldn't you love it if I stood up now, and came over to you, and gave you my lips … I would be none the poorer for it, you would become much richer … I can spare a hundred kisses for your lips … your poor starved lips.

You are not supposed to do such a thing, and you don't do it. Ebner reads the paper … But a word has come into her head.

It was the big evening, Seder Evening, and Father gave the signal. And David stood up, or she stood up herself, if it was her turn that year, and she walked through the narrow passage to the front door and opened the front door as wide as it would go. Outside it was dark, damp and dark -, and strange noises emanated from the tall elm tree on the other side, small voices of newborn leaves … and you stood, you stared … behind you was the quiet glimmer of the oil lamp against the shiny yellow wall, and out in front of you the wide, hushed darkness … and you stood, you waited … your heart was beating with hope: they'll be here any minute now …

This is what was said, all together, with solemn emphasis, and father's voice had sounded the loudest, to be heard above all the others: the righteous voice! *'Kol dichfin yasei uyachal.'* All who are hungry, let them come and eat, all who are in need, let them sit down with us and celebrate Passover …'

This is what is said and afterwards you open the door to the living room … and you wait … and you listen … but it is quiet … and there is a dripping noise … something splashes … it is the rain of the day gone by, caught in the elm … but any minute now you really will hear footsteps … now they are approaching, the Strangers from memories and from dreams, and from pictures … the dark ones, small ones, crippled ones, with kaftan, beard and tall hat … rushing, rushing and busy, talking feverishly to themselves with hurried movements, and stumbling in their haste … and the silent, limping and disfigured ones, that are as pale as ghosts, their unfocused eyes burning … and they are coming to us … they are hurrying to us ... for we are free and for this one evening we are rich and there is enough food for everyone ... so that your heart beat with hope, because it would be so wonderful. And once that Russian came home with Father from the synagogue, and his lips ... thin, pale lips, hungry lips, oh, Ebner's lips ... And he trembled, waiting for the food was torture to him, and you would certainly have given him your portion, but it wasn't necessary, because Mother always had enough for everybody ...

This is not allowed. Ebner, poor man, lonely man, old man, come to my lips. They are like warm cherries ... I give them to you, you may take them. But Ebner is a respectable man, you are a respectable girl yourself -, a respectable girl is what you must be. You must always fear 'disrespect' in a man ... 'disrespect' is one of those words of mother's, that sometimes make you smile suddenly. Men don't know any better, men must be kept on a short rein, Bauk says.

If Ebner were to want to kiss me now ... then I would have to box his ears! Wasn't it the story of 'Kobus and Agnietje'? And there is one about a 'little widow' too. And one in Staring's work. Yes -, and Justus van Effen's. Everywhere. You read nothing else. There were always 'impertinent suitors' wanting to 'steal kisses.' And all the respectable girls are poised ready to box their ears. But the impertinent suitors are not angry. Quite the opposite! Because when Agnietje ... it was Agnietje, wasn't it ... when she forgot to box his ears, and when she said: 'Steal as many kisses as you desire, Kobus ...', that is the last she sees of Kobus. But the firmer the boxing of the ears, the sooner the wedding. Because she really wants to marry him, even if she gives him a box on the ears in exchange for a kiss. *'Kol dichfin yasei uyachal'* - but a box on the ears for a kiss. And this is a wonderful world, and this is a complicated story ... and you don't understand it, but you must join in anyway. Or they would despise you and you don't want to be despised. You can't bear the idea of someone despising you.

But it's like blowing dandelion puffs in all directions ... leaving the empty, flat, pale green silky pad ... Yes, Ebner heard it too ... He looks up, he looks happy, above their heads Hugo came into his classroom and tuned his violin ... for so long that the violin grew impatient and like a child you finally release -, 'Do your coat up properly first, put your hat straight, and here, let me do up your shoelace or you'll break your leg' - off it races, with a shout, it tears itself free and you stand there laughing, bewildered ... this was how the violin finally broke free, burst out into a song of jubilation ...

'Come, proletarians, keep your courage up,
Victory still awaits us ...'

Listen, just listen … the gay violin, the vibrant violin! And do you notice, Ebner, how the other sounds hurry, how they rush towards us from all sides, how every murmur strains to flow together, and how everything, everything now becomes a murmur …? In the same way sometimes, everything becomes colour … if there is one strong colour … that bright orange African marigold … and I didn't know that there was so much orange hidden in my flowered dress … Miracles, miracles, miracles everywhere … life lives in everything …. Oh, and everything calls to everything …

'Ebner, Ebner … can you hear it … can you feel it?'

This is the Awe, the holy Awe. Like riding on high in Elias' Chariot of Fire when he ascended to Heaven. And the white flames wreathe you round, the white flames encircle you so tightly that you cannot breathe …

'Do you understand how there can still be people who don't join in with us, who won't, who don't believe, don't understand …?'

He laughs.

'How old are you ….?'

'Twenty-two. Not a child any more, if that's what you meant …'

He looks at her.

'Are you sure …?'

Ebner, how soft your eyes are. Ebner, do you want my lips …?

These are waves, momentary waves, waves that scarcely form thoughts, let alone words. They both lift their heads to the bright white ceiling and Ebner says: 'How young that boy is …'

'Join us in throngs of thousands

No power can us withstand.'

Throngs of thousands … throngs of thousands … surging throngs … how did it go? There was something white at the bottom of the glass … the throngs surged up like bubbles … throngs of thousands, sparkling tiny bubbles, welling … it was deep down in the glass, and the glass sparkled with clear brightness, it stood in splashes on a green iron table, you were looking out across water … it was on the terrace of the coaching inn. And uncle Elie had taken you out for a walk … and uncle had ordered coffee for himself … and suddenly a sugar lump tumbled over the rim of your glass into your soda water. And there was a sudden fizzing, not one big fizz, but hundreds, thousands of sparkling tiny bubbles rising from the bottom … and this is how you feel now, the expectation bubbling up from the depths of yourself, sparkling tiny bubbles, pressing against the sides, from the inside out, and they would push you apart if they could …

'Ebner, why aren't they coming ... where have they got to?'

The day is running out ... the day is a candle ... it was lit last night at twelve and is burning down to its end ... every minute ... so why aren't they coming?

'What is the matter with them?'

'Oh, it's bound to be about Maartje - you know who I mean. It all went horribly wrong as soon as she was in Arjen Brand's class. I had told him: give the child some freedom, it's what she's used to, she's always been treated differently by everyone -, or rather, all the children from that family have been. Before long she says: 'Sir, I'm feeling so shut in.' And then she is allowed to leave the class for a minute, to walk around the yard. The children are used to it. 'No,' says Arjen Brand. 'Nonsense. Equal treatment for all. Equal rights. I'm not having that silliness.' But he made it worse and worse. He fails like all the others have -, and she is a poisonous little creature if she is thwarted. She is frightened of Arjen ... but their home life is wretched ... and then the mother came to school a few days ago and the old master spoke with her, he didn't refer her to Arjen, she wouldn't have gone anyway. She creeps into her cellar if she sees him, she's scared to death of him. She's got a screw loose as well. Only the old master can get on with her. She has placed all her children here with him ... first Elbert, the eldest, he has done reasonably well for himself ... and Mientje and the twins who are both dead and now Maartje, the last one, the craziest of the whole lot ... she has always sorted things with the old master. Now try and get someone like that to understand something of a Republican School, of decisions taken by the school meeting that "only and exclusively the class teacher may consult with the parents of pupils." But I think I can hear them coming ...'

Yes, there they are. They are talking in the corridors, angry words, furious footsteps. Loud voices, loud heels, loud echoes. Anger makes Arjen pale, his cheeks collapse in folds, his face looks thinner and greyer -, but Bauk's face gets red and wide, expands and swells. She is already talking to Ebner from the corridor.

'So, now he knows what's what. And from now on he will not let his heart influence him. It is, in a word, disgraceful ... disgraceful ... First bringing your so-called discussion items to the school meeting and then simply going your own way, against the decisions ...'

Ebner is silent. Upstairs Hugo tunes his violin briefly ... fine, light, tentative sounds ... the violin is still tame, not impatient ... little birds in midday contemplation. But any minute it will be off again ... hold yourself in readiness ... any minute now, here it comes ... you can be sure of it

'You know as well as I do that the woman isn't right in the head. That she's afraid of Arjen.'

'And why in the world should she be afraid of Arjen? What nonsense.'

'The old man is leaving in November.'

'Even if he was leaving tomorrow. It's the principle of the thing. Such a mean, old creep.'

Oh, be quiet ... be quiet ...

Come Socialists, close your ranks
The Red Flag we will follow ...

'They followed the pillar of cloud by day, the pillar of fire by night.'

Closing ranks ... following flags. It creates images. Thinking and listening are transformed into warmths ... movements ... surges, they rise up, evaporate and condense simultaneously.

Ebner points to upstairs.

'And he allows that as well. Neither Noordhoek nor Cramer nor Van der Wielen allows such a thing ...'

'Because he doesn't care about us.'

'Exactly! Looks down on us.'

'Doesn't even think we are quite all there.'

'Worth bothering about.'

'And he's too feeble to have his own point of view.'

'No inner core, like a true bourgeois.'

'But shouldn't we be going now? Isn't it time?'

'Bauk isn't quite sure whether she's coming with us.'

Huh, why wouldn't Bauk be coming with us ...?

'Bauk, why wouldn't you be coming with us?'

'I've been feeling a bit floppy recently. I really do think now that I'm pregnant.'

This is to Ebner. And Ebner says nothing. But to you it's a blow to the back of your head, or from walking head first into an open cupboard door, so unexpected ... Oh - a word that you hardly even think ... It hangs in the air, between Ebner and Bauk.

'We've been married for nearly a year. And I've missed now for two months running.'

Bauk ... no. No. Ebner stands there relaxed, Arjen hasn't even heard. He is staring into the sun, but he sees no sun, his forehead is deeply wrinkled ... he is brooding over his trampled Rights. I heard wrong. I heard right. Bauk ... what you said first was bad enough, but this is not allowed … Ebner and I, we were here alone a moment ago. And the sun came wandering across the sky to me and the sun gave me kisses, my lips opened and my mouth filled with sun kisses. He looked at my dress … he looked at my lips … creamy gold, my skirt was … in my lap was a large puddle of golden cream … my white dress … And my lips red. O Bauk ,,, Ebner has never been married … perhaps he doesn't even know what you mean … though Andy once told me that even unmarried men know these secret things … He looked at my lips. It is the first time I am wearing this white dress that Dora made for me, because it is the great Day … My white dress. My red lips. You mustn't say that, Bauk. You have no right to. It is not only your secret, it is the wretched secret of us all. If he knows this about you, then he also knows it about me. I do not want a man to know this about me, at least I do not want him to think about it when he sees me.

Oh, but here comes Hugo … Hugo with his eyes full of golden laughter, his white teeth. How his violin exulted. He plays out of happiness, out of the fullness of his only happiness: Socialism. Hugo -, make her fall silent with your presence, you are a boy, and as young as I am, she will be ashamed in front of you. But Hugo stays in the corridor with Ernestien … who came from the other direction, they bumped into one another, and Ernestien tells him something that makes him laugh. 'So it would be getting on for autumn … and my leave could start straight after the summer holidays. But I don't know exactly. I've been rather irregular recently …'

Ebner, why aren't you saying anything …? You have always defended me against her … are you abandoning me now …?

'Even before I married I was always …'

'Stop, Bauk … shut up … I don't want to hear. I do not … I do not …'

She falls silent, she stares, blazing, breathless. Arjen turned round.

'What has got into you …?'

Ebner stands still as though all this was lost on him. All you can do now is flee, flee with your blazing face buried in the skirt of your white dress … and sob.

'What is the matter with you …?'

Ebner answers …

'Perhaps she's not used … to people speaking … so openly about these things …'

'Her …?!' This is how someone might fling a knife at you. 'Her?! She may well play the prim one. That man-chaser … that flirt … that boy-chaser … not even trusted with the boys in the top class. I wouldn't want to leave her alone with my own husband for an hour …'

'Are you listening, Arjen …'

Arjen doesn't speak. Is that Hugo and Ernestien coming in?

'What's the matter with Eva, Bauk? Why is she crying like that?'

'The child is crazy. You're not even supposed to talk about every-day, natural things to Ebner, a man of his age … Sexual matters …' Oh, here we go … here we go … go on then … more blows … more punches … I have already retreated …

'With her musty romanticism … bourgeois holier-than-thou … but I call it dirty … yes, I call it dirty … We had hoped to be rid of it at last … as honest, modern people …'

Arjen suddenly perks up, as though he has clutched at something in Bauk's last few words, as though he had doubted at first … and now is certain … that Bauk is right.

'Hey you … are you actually a party member … have you joined …?'

'Yes … yes … and what does it … what do you mean … why do you ask …?'

She turned her glowing face, wet with tears, to him, she doesn't care.

'Because you … because you appear to have gone mad. No need to bite …'

Oh, the old spectre. Not like everyone else … always different from how they want. Who is right? Ebner, who is right …? Which one of us ought to be ashamed …?

'Come … come …'

They are alone. Slowly he allows his large white handkerchief to unfold, he is much taller than her. He dries her eyes carefully, he wipes the tears from her cheeks hushing her.

'Come … come …'

And she leans against him, and she whispers:

'Ebner … I am not a boy-chaser … Or … am I a boy-chaser …? Who can tell me what I really am …? Can you tell me …? Ebner, who am I …?'

Listen to that tiny, racing, that muffled … shy, fearful sound … that is his watch … but the deeper one … heavy … so heavy … thumping against my temple … that is his heart … his heart is beating against the hollow of my temple … How is it beating … why is it beating like that? What is it your heart wants, Ebner … what does it desire … why is it beating like that … what is it after … racing after … what is it so desperate for …? Heart locked up in darkness … desperate heart … knocking against my temple. Beating, beating heart … heart of the whole world … Do I know … can I … may I …?

'Let's go. The others are waiting.'

Yes. But take my hand for a moment. To where the world ends … take my hand! And now let me go … hand me over to this. For it will carry me further … and all is well. The May green flutters … the May blooms are fragrant … the May red glows … the Mayday burns like a candle … flickering, white flame, flame of Happiness. Oh, the day is filled with Happiness … the day, the city, filled with Happiness. Hundreds of eyes radiate it, beam it to each other, hundreds of mouths exhale it, breathe it to each other … faces glow it in each other's direction. Oh, flickering, white flame of Happiness. Quivering hearts, unable to bear, to contain their own fullness, singing, singing mouths …

'This is our Sacred Ideal …'

This is how a lamp throws out its light … this is how they sing out what they have in them, sing it into the air, flame to flame … the city is aflame, the sky is flame. Each one carries it before him, all carry it together … it carries them all:

'This is our Sacred Ideal …'

Who was it who once made sacred echo in 'sacrosanct'? Sacred … Sacrosanct … the poet Vondel!

Without God nowhere is sacrosanct …

Yes, sacred is sacrosanct. The Sacred Ideal surrounds you like a wall … it arches over your head like a tent. It is a house built round you. From now on you will no longer wander in darkness and uncertainty -, there is a Light that has lightened the darkness. There is: the Party. There are: the Leaders. Hugo Mols says: 'Tak …' the way you once used to say: 'Father.' Twice Hugo has sat in a breathless circle of listeners and heard him speak, the Leader, the Father who knows, - he knows all there is to know of then, now and whatever is next. Everything has now become very clear, very light, very simple, there is no more chaos. I remember as a child I once sat in front of the jumbled pieces of a jig-saw map … it was a big box full of pieces. Father had brought it home from an auction … you had never seen it complete … you took a piece in your hand, you put it down again - you thought: in all of those pieces one Image is hidden … but what must I do to summon it up, so that it comes to life … what do I tackle first … what do I begin with … and you felt panicky. And that's how it was later … there was always the enticing, hidden, single

Image ... and that frightening jumble of individual pieces ... and now the Image is alive ... the Image of the World ... no more fear, no more panic, no more uncertainty -, the greatest of all has revealed the eternal truth and the Leaders, the Fathers, transmit it to us. There are no more mysteries, there is no more doubt, no more despair.

Hugo Mols desires nothing more. This is his first and last desire since he left the orphanage, this is his first and last happiness. He says -, be true once and for all and in all and your life lies before you. Just give yourself over to this, follow where the Fathers point. You may hope that one day you will also be allowed to act - you may attempt to make yourself worthy of being given a task. But if it falls to others, you must still be content, still keep on serving faithfully and honestly. You must decide on this once and for all your life - Hugo has decided ...

Sacred. Sacrosanct. Once, years and years ago I had a bad dream, about the man with split fingers. And the next morning Mother said: 'Why do you always race through your night-time prayer so disrespect-fully? That's why you get bad dreams.' But the night-time prayer was long and you had to repeat the Shema three times, and you were sometimes so sleepy. But the day after the dream she said it very deliberately, she called them all to her, the Protectors, against the man with split fingers, and placed them round her: Michael in front of me, Gabriel behind me, Uriel to my left, Gamliel to my right ... 'and above my head the omnipres-ence of God.' And what you had repeated on so many evenings for so many years ... though it had not come alive before ... was suddenly with you, - the Awe, the Fiery Chariot ...

And above my head the omnipresence of God ...

And it stayed for days. You went to school ... you sat on the swing ... you stood fishing for sticklebacks ... 'And above my head the omni-presence of God ...' like eternally echoing music. Sacred. Sacrosanct. Now this ... the Party. The Sacred Ideal. And above my head the omni-presence of God ... Utterly sacrosanct ...

She joined a great, jolly gang with Dora and with Ernestien and with Ebner and with Hugo ... all friends ... all trusty hands, pressing your own hands, eyes, surrendered to your eyes, laughing mouths speaking warm words. She hears names, catches them, repeats them ... mixes them up, and laughter follows ... now and then she hears her own name ... 'This is Eva ...' 'Yes, she's called Eva.' The way Ebner says her name ... oh, I want you, I must give you my lips, because of the way you say my name, so that it is a caress ... I would like to be a small child and you would hand me from one pair of arms to another and they would all kiss me, men and women would kiss me. This is Love. This is Happiness … You are not a 'mister' or 'missus,' not a miss this or that … you are Dries and Ben and Jaap and Willy, Dora, Eva, Ernestien … A fat woman has kissed her. 'Eva, I think you are a darling. You must call me Aunt Line. And you'll come and see us one day? We don't have any children. Will you come for coffee …? For a meal …?'

Oh yes … I'll come … oh, yes … oh, yes … and a laughing man said to Ebner … 'What a nice girl …' He said it softly, but I heard it anyway. A large man with a large moustache. And Ebner laughed as well. 'Yes, she is nice … she's called Eva …' Oh, all those eyes, all those hands, make you want to … but there are so many, whole processions of them pass you … with an occasional laugh, a backwards wave of the hand, a shining glance … a short, triumphant cry, like the sound birds leave behind them in the air as they fly … And your heart aches with the pressure of love … love for all those who share the Ideal with you. It is a field of daisies … you pick more and more … your apron is full, but still you haven't picked them all …

The day burns like a candle, burns down to its end, collapses, burning … into the cool, clear evening. Now comes the fullness of gratification … walking slowly, talking calmly, as they make their way home … suddenly you become aware that the others are still there … the enemies, the mockers, the unwilling, rude, and unreceptive. They stand to one side, they grin, point, stare … How hard you must be not to want this, how dim-witted not to understand it, cowardly not to dare. So hard, so dim, so cowardly … and then daring to show yourself, here, where the silver-white bird-cherry scatters its small, oval leaves from swaying branches in the clear light, in the descending cool, in the stirring wind, across the shivering grass, across the blond wrinkled water. Hey you there, standing there, your fat stomach shaking with mocking laughter, you think you're so fashionable and we're so ridiculous … or you, you slanderous, scraggy, urban oaf with your bargeman's beard … if I were to grab you by your arms, by your legs, drag you into our midst … after a quarter of an hour, you wouldn't want to leave us …

But over there, beside that gaily coloured, round bed of tulips, red tulips, yellow tulips, striped tulips … all day long they have drunk the sun and now they give back the sheen of their excess … Look, Ernestien, isn't that Arjen Brand and Bauk? Yes, it's them, they've seen us too.

Oh Bauk … Bauk … let us be all right, let everything be all right again. Perhaps I was wrong -, definitely I was wrong. We must be true and honest in all things, and as human beings, we should be ashamed of nothing.

Yes indeed … now they are all coming with us … they may all come with us, mayn't they, Ernestien … and we throw the windows open and we leave the lamps unlit … for we want the last of the day, of the Day … we are not yet ready to surrender to the night, by any means, for then the day will be past … we want the distant murmur from the warm heart of the city … this is the Celebration, the May Day celebration … we want the nearby whisperings of satin green in pale blue evening cool … newborn green, May green, celebratory green … we want the smells, the voices, the gleams … we do not want to miss a sigh, a rustling of the Day, of this day. Now all sit down … round the table … by the window … Aunt Line and Uncle Daan and Arjen, Bauk, and Ben and Jaap, and Willy and Walter and you too … awkward Frisian … I've forgotten what you're called … even though you're grumpy … even though you won't meet my eyes. Well, I expect he's tired … Ben is tired too … you can see it when you look at him …

'He's not strong and he's sitting a difficult exam. German B - imagine! And he's a good learner but not a fast one.' This is what Aunty Line whispers, she is his upstairs neighbour.

'Ben, please don't sit so close to the window, the evenings are still cool, at this time of year.'

Obediently he pulls his chair up to the table. And Rebecca stands unexpectedly in the doorway.

'Hah, Rebecca, where did you come from? Like a ghost, through the keyhole? Because no-one heard you ring the doorbell.'

'I've been here for a while. I was sitting in the kitchen with Tonia …'

She hesitates in the doorway. She doesn't know most of them, she's not a party member either. She is not one of the mockers, the rude, cowardly, narrow-minded … and that is why she will eventually come in. Her father was a Rabbi and she is wholeheartedly committed to traditional Jewish Law. She doesn't talk about it, she feels it -, in the Ghetto, where the poor Jews live, she fights against faithlessness and indifference, she goes among the poorest, she gives her time and her money to these very poor people. Ernestien once wanted to know, when they had just got to know one another, whether she might be a Zionist, if she can't be one of the socialists. But she is not a Zionist either. She says: I don't want to hear about all those things. I know my work, I know the way I must take. She is thin and yellow, with a large nose and deep, urgent eyes.

'Here, I fetched the newspaper from the letterbox as soon as it arrived.' Ernestien holds out her hand, but Arjen snatches it, and she gives in laughing. He has gone to the window with the paper, has spread it open, trembling with impatience, it hangs rustling from his two hands. In the cool, late light, his face has turned grey, but his eyes have lightened to an almost transparent water-blue. Restlessly they strain, peering, searching along the long columns, up, down, up, down, as though they were running up and down tall stairs.

'How did I guess? Here is the old bourgeois claptrap again. Here ... here ... You really should read it ...'

'Read it out! Read it!'

He gabbles the words, mangles the sounds, stammering with indignation.

'Veldman, too, spoke as usual with persuasive eloquence. But we must disclose that every time we hear him thunder on about 'social injustice', 'exploitation', 'oppressed proletariat', we cannot help but think of his large villa, and of his paintings and of his library ... And then ...'

'Oh, throw the useless rag in the waste paper basket. Get your wife to light the fire with it in the morning.'

'Take no notice. Don't let it get to you ...'

'What low tactics. They can live however they like. And then they expect us ... As if that has anything to do with it ... And they know that perfectly well themselves. They do it just to spread mistrust among the proletariat ...'

'Pathetic tactics ... playing the little Tolstoy ...'

'Tolstoy didn't do that anyway. Tittle tattle ...'

'And even if he did ... the sentimentality. Pointless humbug. I wouldn't give two cents a copy.'

'If you still wanted one. More like one cent - between three of you.'

'Rebecca! I say Rebecca! Are you drunk? Wake up! You're holding the tray at an angle and all the cups are sliding to one side.'

'Here, here ... take it!' She thrust the tray into Ernestien's hands ... she is trembling, she turns to Arjen.

'So, that is what Sir says ... and that's the way it is ... that in your party it doesn't matter, it doesn't count, who you are, as a human being, and how you live, as a human being ... But if it's right, sir, that this Veldman lives in a large villa with paintings ... and all that stuff ... then the man who wrote that in the paper is quite right ... Then, I tell you, that the man who wrote that ...'

' ... is no better himself ... Just stirring it up. Mean tactics ...'

'It doesn't matter whether he is any better … and I quite believe you that his motives are not noble ones … Most people's motives are not noble.'

'Here, Eva … go round with the tea.' Ernestien speaks quietly, she is flushed, she is embarrassed, but smiles a little …, she probably doesn't think it altogether wrong, that Rebecca should say these things. The others sit there, their faces frozen with indignation, stupid with amazement. Arjen shrugs his shoulders, he growls -, this is beneath him, this is not worth the effort of answering.

'Here, Ben … without milk for you … Aunt Line … a lot of both for you … and Walter as it comes … Arjen … Willy … Rebecca … take a cup, take this one, it's the weakest …'

'Thanks … thanks … but I'm not staying here another minute.' And she is gone.

And so a hailstorm is unleashed behind you. They are all talking on top of one another, Bauk louder than all of them. But Ernestien says nothing.

And Bileam went out in order to curse, and uttered a blessing because he had to. You can't keep silent if you have to speak.

'But wouldn't it be better if you could live that way yourself …?'

'What is she saying …?'

'What do you mean …?'

'What is it you are trying to say, child …?'

'Well … I mean: living like that …'

'Living like what …?'

'The way you want it to be one day …'

'But you're raving, you're rambling, you're talking like the bourgeois newspapers …'

'Come, child … at the moment it would be completely pointless.'

'Senseless … in a society, which is not yet ready for any of this.'

How neatly Aunt Line puts it.

'Well, you don't do it for others, you do it for yourself …' And deep down, the wide echo of oft-repeated, long-known words, the ever-recurring cautionary summary of the food laws. 'They shall be an abomination unto you.' Doing wrong and standing by while wrong is done … cheating and … unclean things … even as a child you hated this, in others, in yourself, for yourself, for your own sake … the world was no better for it … no purer, no richer … but there are things, that you can't do, for your own sake. Take inequality … there he was standing in the sun, high up above the hundreds who were listening, listening … and his outstretched hands … and his triumphant voice … 'They shall be an abomination unto you.'

But what if you can't hate it so deeply yourself, can't hate it so fiercely that it would be impossible for you to live with it, where will you get the strength from to bring about change …?

'It's all very easy to make demands if you have nothing so they don't apply to you …'

Make demands …? No, of course not, you mustn't make demands. Let us at least acknowledge powerlessness … Bauk wants it too … frankness. We must not deny all that is lowly. Let us then not deny lowliness in a single thing …

'And who would be the first to ridicule Veldman if he did give things up? Those same bourgeois … who now scorn him.'

'Not worth discussing. Leave that child to talk rubbish …'

Oh … Bauk! One day I'll murder you, I will. Because I don't believe that we two can live long in the same world. It will come to it - that I will kill you. Do you know, Bauk … that there is a murderer in me? Old Salomon Beer once suddenly took hold of my right hand, when I was a child, he bent my thumb down … he said … You ought to be careful that you don't commit murder. It is in your hand and your grandfather was an irascible man. A noble human being … a man mad with anger … and you resemble him … said old Salomon Beer … and he would have said more, but Mother forbade him. Bauk … there are moments, in which I know that I could be noble … but I could also murder you … And no-one need speak in my defence. 'Diminished responsibility …' No. None of your diminished responsibility. It was me! Me! No tears. No regrets. Why did you do it, actually? She got in the way of my life. And I will walk calmly into the prison …

Dizzy … dizzy … white froth in your head … and here sits Ben. And he is talking, he has been talking for a while. Say it again, Ben … I didn't hear you … I didn't understand you … all I heard was noises …

'I said: they are all atavisms of old ideologies.'

Atavisms … ideologies … but … what is this all, exactly? This is how you dream about an exam. One question follows another and you know absolutely nothing, and suddenly you shout out: But Sir, I haven't studied for this paper at all!

'It's all individualism … individual morality … all outdated … out of the old box. Concerns that bothered the eighteenth century. The Enlightenment … Lessing … even Kant with his Categorical Imperative … thoroughly bourgeois … bourgeois individualism …

Schiller too … and Schleiermacher just as much … each with their very own morality … bourgeois morality … fine for those days. Fine for those people. But if we haven't got any further by now …'

'Pastors talking rubbish …'

'Girls talking nonsense …'

'Mouldy old romanticism …'

The hailstorm, the rattling hailstorm, like a moment ago with Rebecca.

But Aunt Line battles against it.

'Leave him be … leave him to explain it all to her properly. She is still only a child.'

The hailstorm abates.

'And now, Ben …?'

'Now we no longer waste time on the business of individual morality … now there is only what we know for certain … the great System … with its purely scientific basis … and its expression: the Party. The Class Struggle … and that you must be on the right side, on this side … on our side …'

'If you've finished lecturing, Ben … may we have your valued advice over here? You see, the question is: Walter and Willy think … that something must be done about that chap … that newspaper oaf …'

'I'm coming. Do you mind, Eva …? We'll talk about it another time.'

Eighteenth-century concerns! That means I must be more than a hundred years behind … so it is high time that I catch up! Schiller … And Kant. But he was a great philosopher, wasn't he? Outdated … all outdated. Who else did Ben mention …? We'll talk about it another time …

And Hugo, last week … near the school a canal was being filled in, for the creation of a square. Barrowloads of sand … barrowloads of sand … and we were standing by. I said: 'They aren't making much progress. How much sand does it take, before you can see progress?' 'Oh, hundreds of those barrowloads …' And we were silent for a moment, and then Hugo spoke again: 'You see, Eva, this is the way to be! For your own sake this should be enough for you: one barrowload of sand. And one day the square will be there … You must be able to efface yourself like this. You must realize that you are nothing …' And he looked very pale and his voice … you simply looked in another direction. How good, how beautiful … if you can efface yourself in this way. A barrowload of sand … see it tumble into the water, a thick, brown-yellow cascade that disappears … smothered on the bottom in the dark … this should be enough for you …

It doesn't matter what happens to you.

This is what Hugo says.

Hugo, you are right …

It doesn't matter what you do. This is what the others say, this is what Ben says.

Ben, you are wrong …

There is a difference … but where …? Here's a fortunate thing: you always know unshakeably that there is a difference somewhere, before you know what the difference is -, so you can seek it until you find it, until you have it before you in words.

You seek in silence, you seek the silence. Here is the silence, I am as good as alone … they are conferring, animatedly, and they are arguing … And if I now follow this sense on the inside, cautiously feeling my way, inch by inch, this sense that there is a difference, moving towards that difference … then I first arrive at something I already know … and I believe that there is a link … but I couldn't say so for certain … oh, you have to be so careful with these things, for all too often … appearances deceive … and it is just like it was with the jigsaw map … it must all be broken up again. And started from the beginning.

But … could Miss Korff actually be in love with Penning, and could that be why she is always calling him names …? Always the same: 'Cynic, cynic … that is what happens when you lose your belief …' It was a crazy story, a horrible story -, you didn't know at first whether to laugh or cry. Penning had heard it from his doctor. There was a porter in the hospital, who had too small a thyroid, or not enough of one … And anyone without a thyroid, or without enough of one, apparently cannot fall in love … and this porter never looked at a girl. And then they … well now, Penning wasn't able to say what they did … but it came down to this … that later on he had too much or too large a thyroid, and from then on he couldn't leave the girls alone … Yes, when Penning roars like that and Miss Korff acts so strange -, well you laugh along, even though you feel more like crying … because a story like that is not cheerful. And here come Arjen and Bauk …

'Hello, you … turtle doves … honeymooners … do you actually know where the seat of love is?' They stood still and for the third time he repeated the story of the hospital porter … Arjen shrugged his shoulders, he didn't even laugh, but Bauk had her answer ready.

'Do you really think that you can get at me, at us with that one? Do you think that we are afraid of the naked, natural truth? It'll work with her … the romantic idiot … Treat her to your delightful story, that you've just dreamt up of course.' But that wasn't true. And a few days later the three of them were walking home at four o' clock, Penning, Ebner, and her.

'Now I'll show you the violin that I have been eyeing up for months, the one I'm going to save up for, if only I can keep my money in my pocket.'

And they came to the shop -, there were pianos, and violins.

'It's that one … the one hanging there … oh, what a glorious instrument.'

'A thyroid gland,' said Ebner …

'A thyroid gland … how do you mean?'

'Where the seat of love is … where the seat of music is. That hospital porter couldn't fall in love, when he had no thyroid gland, and he couldn't stop falling in love when he had one. And this is why you jeer at love! And if I spoil the violin by cutting its strings or throw the whole thing into the fire -, you won't be able to make music on it. But this doesn't mean that I jeer at music …'

'I don't see … that it's … the same thing …' But oh dear, how small-minded it all sounded, And Ebner didn't say any more, he just laughed.

But I won't get where I want to be this way. You walk in the countryside and you come to a ditch … you are in the wrong place … the plank across is further up. But I do believe I needed to go that way. I went home … I thought … if there is a fire, tonight in the shop … in the storeroom … and all the pianos and violins are burnt … will there be less music in the world …? No, there will not be less music … because Music is like Light, is like Love … Something … that cannot diminish … But I also wondered: if there were suddenly no musical instruments left at all … whether there would still be music … No … there must be instruments … and there will always be instruments … you could not get rid of them all, or imagine them gone, you would always think them up and make them. Telephone wires … leaves on the trees … and a thin string between your teeth … after all, these are musical instruments of a kind.

But this won't get me there … What happened next …? Where do I jump over the ditch? Now here it is, and this is the crossing … now I have it, now it has me … The shop with the instruments *and* the barrowloads of sand … It doesn't matter a jot what happens to you. Hugo, you are right … this surrender of yourself is the greatest, the most beautiful, the highest …

But if the instruments are no good, what then …? Oh Hugo, look at the way you tune your violin, so carefully, for so long, listening so acutely, just this morning … before you started playing … Smash it, and nothing is lost. Neglect it … and all is lost … We may die … but we may never decay! We can surrender ourselves to the former, but never to the latter.

Oh Ben … and all of you others … you are wrong … It is of no consequence what happens to us -, but what we are is of great consequence … And if that wasn't the case … then nothing else would matter - then everything might as well go to hell ... to blazes ... to damnation ... the whole world ... and here it is again: dividedness ... that each of us is Nothing and Everything simultaneously ... the least important and the supremely important ... like that one violin ... It can be lost at any time ... but as long as it exists, it must be good, or it will help to spoil the world ... And what can we improve in a world that we will only spoil again ...?

Ben ... I know ... I think I know ... No ... Ben, I don't know ... where shall I find the courage ...? I am more than a century behind! Could it be that simple actually ...? But Ernestien lit the lamp -, they all stand up ready to leave.

Oh ... are you going away already, Ben ... and I was about to tell you ...

Past Aunt Line their eyes meet, in a reciprocal question.

'How strangely our conversation came to halt, just now ...'

'Yes ...'

He looks at his watch.

'I can stay for a minute, if I may. Ernestien, Eva and I were interrupted mid-conversation. If you don't think it unsociable of me, Aunt Line.'

'No -, but don't be too late, young man. And wear your scarf, when you leave. Ernestien, will you make sure he doesn't forget his woollen scarf?'

And they stand together by the window, and each one waits for the other to start speaking.

'You can see through the whole park, right to the other side. But when the foliage is dense again, which won't be long, then you can't any more ...'

'Yes ...'

Purple tulips, white tulips. Purple ones grow darker, white ones lighter, in the dusk. The sweet breeze opens your lips, wants to enter your throat ... but the wind is not alone in that ... gentle laughter does that too ... whispering ... shuffling feet. All is quiet again, all is different ... The Day past.

'Well ... we were saying ... and you thought ... you maintained ... and then I said ...'

'Well, Ben ... and I have been sitting thinking ... about everything you said ... and I think ...' Well, what do I think ...? I don't know ... and it doesn't matter ... because he wasn't listening .... He was looking at me and he wasn't listening ... Were you perhaps looking at the little curl against my temple, that sometimes creeps into my ear? Yes, Ben, it

sometimes creeps into my ear. Everyone thinks it is a funny little curl …
it is almost perfectly round, it shines in sun.

'Really you ought to read a lot more first, know a lot more.'

'Yes, of course.'

Oh, of course I need to read a lot more, know a lot more … Or
were you looking at the curve of my cheek? I have a pretty chin, I have
a soft neck … my chin and my neck really come into their own in this
white dress, in this new white dress. The white dress is actually a bit too
thin, for such a cool evening, and I was thinking of putting on my blue
woollen school dress … but how fortunate that I didn't. How fortunate,
how fortunate, that I didn't! Because just imagine if I had. The seamstress
has altered the sleeves and that makes the shoulders so ugly, and you
can't see anything of my neck …

'I could lend you all kinds of books …'

'That would be wonderful. You really must …'

He will lend me all kinds of books! And this was such a lucky
chance, that I should be standing on his left. Because otherwise he would
now be able to see that disfiguring red spot by my nose. Ernestien said
yesterday: 'You will have to pay a double fine if I hear one more word
about that silly little spot.' But today I hadn't thought about it at all
… except for this morning, briefly … and a moment ago I was sitting
alone, I was sitting as good as alone, because the others were debating,
arguing, I was alone with myself behind my closed eyelids … and then
I didn't exist. None of me existed. My dress, my shoulders, my neck and
my cheek, and the disfiguring spot by my nose, and the little curl at my
temple … and now suddenly there is nothing else. It's like when you turn
the telescope round for fun and what was big and close recedes into the
distance and is little … They were big things and they were so important
to me … I myself was little and distant … now everything is the other way
round … I wanted to say: 'Ben … that's what I thought …' But he wasn't
listening … I saw that, felt that … and amazing … amazing … what was
close by, what was important to me, receded into the distance and was
little … and I-myself came to the fore, and only I-myself am now up close,
and I am so big, I am bigger than all the rest of the entire world. And I am
now close only to me-myself, only this is important: that I did not put on
my threadbare, blue school dress, that makes my shoulders ugly, that
covers up my neck, instead of this white one and that I went and stood
on his left …

6
The Night

This sensation of being propelled upwards out of a dreamless deep sleep, - when have I had it before? What was it? Was it the lift, rising up out of rainy gloom towards the high, silver light? No -, it was when you dived for the first time from the diving board, you plunged into the darkness, the water held you … and expelled you again and your eyes caught sight of the sun and the blue and the green. Security and joy -, experienced afresh each time. Yes, it's true … two weeks ago it happened, and as often as sleep carries me away, so I return to myself and the knowledge is there afresh, and he is mine, and as once they had dwelt on the sun, on green and on blue, so my eyes dwell on this quiet, white thing beside my bed - his crib.

He sleeps inside the little draped enclosure; behind the half-open dark door sleeps the kindly old woman, in contentedness. She says: it's been years since I slept like I do here, now. And upstairs sleeps Ben -, my husband, his father. This is how 'doctor Jaap' arranged it. Ben needs a good night's sleep. All three are asleep. Only I have been suddenly deserted by sleep, only I returned to myself, and outside the wind keeps watch. It rattles, dull and deep, it lisps behind the closed doors, the life of the night is lived out in darkness, hidden, intense. Wind and rain pervade the world -, and infuse the whole with sound.

That is what it was like on the island, that cool August day the year before last. The sky hung low, the dune hollows were fragrant, each scent called to me, but I walked past. Dora walked ahead and behind her Ernestien -, I followed; we walked laughing along the springy boards, over the narrow single-plank path that mounts the dunes, drops down into the hollows, from the grey Wadden Sea to the blue North Sea … where there were no more plants, there was just the blue and the sparkling white, this is where the man waited by the sea. Ernestien had said: 'He wants to show us the wild ducks' cage, we can tell the children at school about it.' And we followed him through rough patches and dips of dune grass and sand, we followed him wordlessly, to the sound of crashing seas, screeching gulls. Once houses stood here, people lived here -, the sea chased them inland -, all that stands here now is a hedge of whale ribs, bleached, porous things that belong under the ground or in an ossuary -, and the centuries make their weight felt. The knowledge of the uncounted, the unmeasured centuries makes its weight felt. And you thought … what is Time without people to measure it …? And this question rose from your eyes, up into the clouds, away with the seagulls -, and one day I will return there and my question will come back to me -, seagulls and clouds will have kept it for me.

But Ernestien pulled me by the arm. 'Look, over there … that's where the duck decoy pool with its wicker cage begins.' Oh, it was a paradise -, a pale, blond mirror, framed in yellow and brown. Ridges of dune shelter it from the storms … it is so safe there and it is so still there. The free birds are wheeling high up, the captive ones are swimming down below, gold and green in the pale mirror, and they lure the free ones down from the air … they come …. they swim in ever smaller spirals … 'Can they ever go back …?' The man laughed at this. They will never go back. Would they … Ernestien, would they soon forget sea and sky, would they soon forget endlessness, limitlessness? What do we know about ducks and whether they soon forget …? And you stood there and it was as though you had stood like that for centuries -, for centuries the same cool August day by the sea, no other world than this small one, no other sound than sea crashing and gulls screeching, flapping, clapping … From the heights and open spaces they wing in, descend and swim in ever narrower spirals … and this is my room, mine and Ben's bedroom. I lie here alone in our bed … I am still rather feeble, I lost a lot of blood, and in my breasts the milk swells, the day after tomorrow Ben will come back into this bed. When I shut my eyes, I still see everything that is around me, I know it from so many days, so many nights. Chairs and a table, and a big cupboard, and a little one, and a washstand, and the shiny black clock. A calendar hangs by the mantelpiece, with birthdays marked on it. David and I are at the end -, on 31st December. Everyone takes their turn at having their birthday -, the day that they arrived.

Today Ben said: 'Will you remind me that I must write to the tailor? I am not at all happy with my coat.' 'Yes -, and the chimneys need sweeping.' The ducks fly out of the wide spaces, into the ever narrower funnels … It's right, people would get lost in the wide open spaces, they need rooms with chairs and cupboards, they need to be able to flee into calendars with years and days. Walls and weeks between them and the wide open spaces. When I was a child, didn't I run home, fleeing from the voices of water and wind - to the wild duck cage? And the door closed and we were all there together and David and I flew at each other over the crust of the fresh loaf. Yes, Ben , I agree with you, that the coat is not right. O look, Mother, five, six blighted potatoes today ... And Mother ... Miss Drukker gave me a fig ... But it really was like this: the voices of water and wind tormented me too much ... The voice of the water comes out of the grey-yellow horizon ... it comes to me across the white wave tops ... and it whispers to me, something I can't understand. The voice of the wind rushes up behind me and rapidly lisps something in my ear, but I don't know what ... and is ahead of me, and turns back again, and catches up with me again, and I can't stand it ... and Miss Drukker gave me a fig, and it is my turn for the fresh crust and if David won't stop it, I'll hit him.

And Ben came to fetch us from the island ... I will never forget the island, I return to it, to the cool August day, to the wild duck cage, to my questions. It was a Sunday. He came from the other side, with the flat countryside and the little church towers, sailing across the Wadden Sea ... He emerged from a fog. I was wearing a brighly flowered dress. He said: 'How brown you are.'

You are ... you are ... Were they all his words, or my own desires? Summer dreams ... word dreams rising from the dune hollows ... at night between the sound of the two seas, fragrant small island surrounded by singing seas ... And from the window you saw 'the romantic house'. Every morning it became a sturdy 'bourgeois house', every evening it became 'the romantic house'. Only from that one window.

Four months since that evening, the first of May. Ernestien lit the lamp and the light shone through my closed eyelids, so that I was transported into a solitude with only Hugo's words and my own: Nothing matters, because we will be lost. Everything matters, although we will be lost. And there stood Ben and joined me by the window, and that is why I am lying here now, and why I have him, I have it, in the little white wicker basket, and everything that happened to me flowed from that evening ...

Very soon he was: the first thought on waking. And in the evening he came for you and you talked to each other, in the park ... and you found large open spaces in yourself, where he and others had knowledge -, books, studies, exams, diplomas. Not empty spaces, but flat countryside and lakes, flowing together from manifold musings.

'And you've got a good head, you grasp everything straight away.' Together on a bench by the pond. And the pond gleams. And the clock in the clock tower strikes.

'Extraordinary boy ... did you think I was stupid? Why would I be stupid ...? Do I look more stupid than I am? Am I more stupid than I look ...?'

A feeble joke from a book for girls.

'So why didn't you ... qualify to be a headteacher ... or to teach secondary level Dutch ..., or something ...?'

'It didn't even ... occur to me.'

'And your future?'

'I never think about my future, I think about my past, and I know that I am alive, now.'

'And don't you care about money, then?'

'No, I don't care about money.' And suddenly, with a laugh ... a 'pop-up' thought: '"Some verses and some love" ... that's what I care about.'

'Kloos ...?'

'Yes, Kloos.'

They laugh, but Ben continues the thought.

'You've got a good memory.'

'No. They explained a compression pump to me twenty times and I still don't know what it is. I can't remember anything. What I understand, I automatically know. Once when I was a child I was sent out of class. First an hour in the corridor and then writing out the line: "I can do it if I want to." And I had a sudden thought, I went back into the classroom. Sir, you must turn it round: "I want to when I can do it." He said: "You just turn round and get back in the corridor."'

'So you could think logically?'

'But later on I didn't understand perspective at all. And the teacher said: "because you can't think logically."'

And you are both silent ... and you think ... it is all different, different ... everything has the wrong name ... everything has the wrong concept attached to it ... you ought to be able to throw it all up in air ... and build it up again ... not according to an example ... but according to your own insight ... but Oh God, where do you find insight ...

'Once when I was at school, Ben ... I was in the sixth year, I wasn't even twelve years old. We were given words to fill in. "If you take something that doesn't belong to you, how should you describe that?" And the master said: "Wrong." And I said: "No, Sir, it is: illegal." And when I went home ... I was thinking constantly of Russia ... on the Volga

... of Nizhny Novgorod and I asked myself that day: "How did I know that?" Don't you think that everything you need to know comes to you, by itself? When I was bigger I found that idea in a newspaper report of a lecture on Plato: Plato said that all wisdom comes from wonder. And it stayed with me. And at the same time I was reading about all kinds of wonders ... the boy Woutertje Pieterse in Multatuli's novel ... and Newton with the apple. I read them because I knew them. They came to me ...'

But then I caught the scent of roses ... and roses make you like a concertina ... you are pulled open and sounds emerge ... sounds that are thoughts, that are scents ... and all of it was in me, and it was all one. Except for Ben ... sitting next to me. Really you too Ben, together with all of this, should be in me, be part of me ... This is how it should be, this is how I want it to be. And I took his hand, and I laid my head against his shoulder ... and he played with my ear. He said ... child, little one ... And then I said it ... yes, I said it, that big, sweet word. I said 'darling'. Because I wanted him to be my darling. But it bothered me -, even the night did not bring forgetfulness. It was still with me when I awoke. Oh, thou shalt not ... My Name ... The very same, not in vain.

And the next evening 'doctor Jaap' came. He said: 'Ben's not right, again ... the old story: malaria. And now I'm going to insist, right now, I am going to prescribe a rest-cure.' Ernestien gave you packages to take. 'If you go to Ben this afternoon, give him ... here ... this Hauptmann play ... and here, he's so fond of salty aniseed balls ... perhaps they'll give him a bit of a thirst for his milk.' You bought peaches yourself ... and you didn't go out for cakes. Never again would you go out for cakes ... Never again would you bring flowers home for your little room. That was something wonderful indeed, something stable in your life. For now there was never a day, never an hour -, when you didn't think: mis-understanding attaches itself to everything, and we say everything wrong and we see everything wrong ... everything we think we know about influences and characteristics ... and what we need to know ... and how we must learn ... and what we ought to do ... And you couldn't listen to anything, to anyone any more, without asking yourself: But is it really, is it really the way you say it is? And if it isn't, what is it really like? You couldn't read another page without putting down the book, because you felt you couldn't breathe from the suppressed panic. Once there was a glass bell jar, the teacher pumped the air out, all the air ... the air bag stiffened, expanded, swelled ... and collapsed ... That was: a vacuum, or airlessness. And so you find yourself in the midst of a vacuum with your head surrounded by airlessness - by thinking about everything: the way we say it, the way we see it, the way we teach it to one another, the way we repeat it after one another … that's not the way it is in eternity, but how is it then …? And you thought: this is too much, and I can't go back -, it's devastating me, but I can't stop it … I am burning my boats, I am destroying my world, I am consuming myself … oh - no - if only that was all: a Burning Bush. But there is this: I buy peaches for Ben, flowers for Ben, sweets for Ben … each and every day. Each and every day I am happy, because I am not eating cakes. Now I always know where I shall return when all of this weighs too heavily on me, where I shall flee when the vacuum suffocates me. It will all fall away from me …. as a child I was peeling an onion and I thought: these are its 'skirts' and where is the onion itself then? They have wrapped me in two layers, three layers, ten layers and where am 'I', who am 'I'? But this will remain standing, in the vacuum, in the naked light that penetrates the brain through the skull, the senselessness, airlessness of all things …

Love … friendship …. human heartbeats against your own heart … things that are unassailable, indestructable, unshakeably beyond doubt and despair … beyond the despair of doubt.

'You won't be waiting much longer to get married, I expect, now Sir is doing so well?'

There were flowers on the table, flowers in the window, flowers on the floor, at the foot of the bed … from Ernestien, from Ebner … from Jaap. Now we are here … and such a fortunate and beneficial appointment! Miss Rika … she was so poor and she was already getting old … her furniture was falling apart. First she brought up her brother's seven unruly children, then her sister's five and then they made her feel she was superfluous, so she moved to the city and …

'Now I shall lose Sir as well.'

'But come and live with us when we get married, come to us to look after us.'

O Ben you are sweet …

'You don't mean it, I am fifty-seven years old.' But she was trembling, tears shone in her eyes, at this solution. She has a child's round eyes.

'Yes, you must come to us.'

'Then you musn't wait too long to marry.'

Ben put out his hand, he pulled her beside his bed. His eyes were dark and deep in his thin face.

'Ben … dear.'

May I say it now … may I say darling now? You mayn't say it: it is too sweet and too big … it should make you tremble, you don't tremble … not like you did in some of those nights, when you whispered it to a man you don't know. The word flew out … like the dove flying from Noah's ark across the waters … and found no place to set her foot … and did not return …

It was autumn, you were walking home. Now I'm going to get married.

Now there will be no more secrets. I'm getting married and I'll have a child. It will be Ben's … I really want to have it. This child is the only thing you are supposed to think of … the other things, the secrets, are connected to it. Like in Van Eeden's *Johannes Viator. The Book of Love*, or Perk's 'Mathilde'. 'How I sometimes long for the permitted and inevitable outcome. So that I - let me kiss you again - will see you in my children.' No. Not beautiful. Painful, enough to make you shudder … 'Permitted'. 'Inevitable outcome.' Not beautiful, not loving, not sweet … 'Night song' from Van Eeden's *Ellen*: 'mellow, mellow, mellow is my love's soft hair. Upon my pillow it lay spread wide, and fair.'

She had left the book at school. Miss Korff had found it. 'This is immoral.' 'What … is immoral?' You didn't even understand what she was getting at. Is that what the poet was thinking about? Yes, that is what he was thinking about, you holier-than-thou hypocrite … You can't fool me. I know you. I've known you long enough. In which case you're ahead of me. I don't know myself … But just imagine that you really said that to Miss Korff!

The doors rattle gently … somewhere in the north lies the island, between the North Sea and the Wadden Sea, and in the dark the same wind is now besieging the hollows, the rough patches by a duck decoy pool … We rented the upper floors of this house … we bought furniture … Miss Rika sewed the curtains … so-much-by-so-much … and she sold her own things, and she came … and now it has all come to pass. See them come in from the wide spaces … from horizons, across the heavy, blue waves … just like the song: 'Sur les beaux flots bleus …' Why am I so wide awake tonight, why is it opening up to me tonight? The doors might open wide, the doors to the balcony … and imagine if he were to enter: Johannes Viator.

You would want to ask him … want to tell him.

I was a girl and you came. You know yourself only too well when that was, you must remember that evening. You laid down the law to me. You must know. Tell me, Johannes Viator -, is this what you meant …? Are these 'the Things of the Body' …? And the 'bodily desire' that you spoke of …?

You can tell when Ben wants it, because he gets so ... embarrassed. Bodily desire. He says: ' .... or would you rather go to sleep?' You would frequently 'rather go to sleep', but you don't say so, never say so ... and then sometimes there is an expectation, like on that evening. There was a ring of dancing children ... and each one had a ribbon in its hand ... and all the ribbons led to the centre ... to Something ... Someone ... radiating, binding ... All ribbons, all eyes, all joys uniting in the act of radiating, binding, connecting. Thus everything organizes itself, thoughts organize themselves, all knowledge organizes itself round one idea ... thus the world organizes itself to form a circle dance when the sounds of the organ rise from the dark little chapel below ... with the old organist sitting there, all alone, by a single lamp ... thus, that evening, everything pointed towards what was still to come ... what must come about ...

The flowers had been so fragrant ... and together you lingered ... and: 'Listen to the birds this evening, Ben, listen to the birds ...' and every breath was a descending mist ... did the pools ever gleam so deeply ...? Shimmering, golden light ... 'Let's just stand here a moment, for I know that song ...'

'Es war, als hätt' der Himmel
Die Erde still geküsst
Das sie im Blüthenschimmer
Von ihm nur träumen müsst ...'

And everything arranged itself, all is arrangement. Order. Wasn't that amazing, years ago ...? A pile of iron filings on the table ... the Magnet approaches and they arrange themselves. And there is no heat that can meld them so that they do not arrange themselves ... the Magnet approaches. One day the children will find the One, the Oneness in their ring o' roses ... the One, the Oneness that gathers all the silver ribbons together, that is all these children together ... around which all these children arrange themselves. All those flowers and all those birds, and every breath a descending mist ... shimmering, golden gleams on water ... 'Es war, als hätte der Himmel ...' hand-in-hand ... waiting for the One ... one who wears the heavenly Smile on his lips and unutterable Gravity in his eyes ... and life will overflow its banks.

'No, Ben, I don't want to go to sleep ... I want ... what you want ...' The silver ribbons hang limp ... the oneness, the bonding has not come about ... the children do not know each other ... all together they know the one, the Oneness, and it knows all of them ... but more than ever, they are estranged from one another. Go home … everyone for themselves … your dancing ring is no longer a ring o' roses, cannot be a ring without the one, the One …

And Ben says: 'Are you lying comfortably?'

Yes, Ben, I'm lying comfortably.

The walls of the room contract, it becomes a narrow shaft, a cage, a tall, narrow cage. You ought to be able to get up … go out. Where to? Oh: into the water, for example. Or: into a cafe, for example. Right in the middle of a fight. Knives. Screams. Someone being stabbed to death. But don't you come too close to me … o bloody hell … Like a thousand iron rings tugged along a brass rod … how can you be so coarse, so mean, as to think of a fight … and for such a curse to well up inside you!

And Ben says: 'Shall I tuck you in?'

'No, thanks … go to bed, go on, it's late …' So these are 'the Bodily Things.' Now you can face Johannes Viator. There is nothing for us to be ashamed about. We are married, we have bought chairs and tables and this big bed. We are very affectionate to one another. We would do anything for each other. Ben says: 'You are pale; shouldn't you rest for a while?' I say: 'No - you, you should work much harder.' And there was also this precept: ' … in a deeper understanding, love for the child, the unborn'. We acted in accordance with this. This is our justification.

'Oh, mastery over the desire for pleasure

Resounds like a hammer blow through my proud body …'

Did you find *that* beautiful? No. Ugly, false … you didn't even believe it … This isn't it. He doesn't know … and the others don't … none of them knows, only she knows. Colette's Claudine, She and he know. *'Il ne me demande rien que la liberté de me donner autant de caresses qu'il en faut pour que je dorme, au petit jour, sur le lit toujours fermé …'*

Oh … *toujours fermé* … they forgot all about it, all night long …

Helberg saw the book lying on the table.

'Do you read that rubbish? It's pure pornography.'

'No, it is not pornography.'

'But child … Jacques ought to know. He knows these things.' She put the book away and silently gave her reply.

'No, Ben, he doesn't know. I know. There are two minds in this book. And one of them has taken away the other's freedom. The one who is not free is the woman. And she will liberate herself. Colette … Claudine. She knows everything that I do not. I cannot follow her yet. She embraces me, but she is more than me … more mature than me, stronger than me. Beside her I am a mere child … perhaps I shall one day be her equal. She knows the spaces above the wild bird cage ... she wheels in across the heavy, blue waves ... "*sur les beaux flots bleus* ... " she knows the One, that connects everything, around which everything organizes itself ... within which life overflows its banks, heavenly smile, serious calm. She has come to me ... I will be without her no longer ...'

But that morning in the bathroom ... oh, unmistakeable, roundness where there was no roundness before. It is mine, it is my own, I will now carry it with me every day, co-being, co-life.

'And wasn't it wonderful, when they put it into your arms?'

Yes, Ernestien ... dearest Ernestien, loyal, ugly ... it really was wonderful. They gave it to me and I was not allowed to move, I was allowed to put out my arms to take hold of it. And at last I saw it ... for so long I had felt it ... and now at last I could see it. Soft ... warm ... smelling of soap ... it was mine. And do you know what was funny? That I knew its little clothes. I had known the little clothes for some time, of course. Before I knew him, I knew his clothes. That's not something you experience very often ... And the pain was gone ... it was all over ... the misery of the shame ...

'The shame?'

'Not for one moment did the shame leave me ... I covered myself.'

'In front of Ben ...?'

'No, not in front of Ben. In front of the doctor ... in front of Jaap, you know, Ben's friend. He ... Ernestien ... he likes me, I know it ... we have talked about so many things. And then he had to see me like that.'

'That you should have thought of that ...'

'The thought never left me for a moment. I can't ever forget that I'm a girl. I mean 'a woman' now, of course. But Ben was sweet .... He was trembling, he shook. He sat by me just where you are sitting now. He said: you must go on, you have to get through it. And then I fell back into the boiling oil ... it was something from a picture, and everything had a name, the things had names, the window had a face ... And there was something else that was strange, the pain slid away and I was sitting on the swing, my head against the rope and it was ... do you know what it was? It was the Andante from Schubert's 'Unfinished'. And do you know what that is, Ernestien? All the suffering and all the joy in the whole world ... it falls onto your shoulders like a cloak ...'

But Ernestien was already gone ... the very first day! It was the thoughts, recurring thoughts, and the hours constantly forcing themselves upon me, the long hours that were still to come.

And there stood Ben, and Jaap, two men in their dignity, upright, clothed, and me, I, me, I who is also me ... oh, just-as-good as you two, except that you are men and I have to suffer this, me, myself, I must get through this. But suddenly I fell into the boiling oil, *so* deep … I'll never come out of it again … and then I pushed it out … it left me … it departed from me … and I died … lying on my back I was dying, and raised my head and saw it lying there … so pitiful, so adorable. It lay there naked in a stream of blood … pushed out … and then I loved it … I loved it with such heartrending pity … the whole world's suffering, a cloak which falls around you, weighs you down … and I was dying, but not dead … Schubert's Andante led me on, accompanied me. And when I woke … I knew this: A moment ago there was someone here, whom I pitied searingly. He lay there naked in a stream of blood.

They gave him to me, he lay against me, and I hold him against me, and I will never let go of him. There was a cord which they cut, which they knotted -, they cut him loose from me, but he is still joined to me. An hour ago I did not know him and now I have given him my life … he can't talk … he is like a small animal … me with my distaste for low things, bodily things … he weighs seven pounds. And the way I have always experienced new things and will always experience them … islands rising out of the sea, pushed up out of the seabed, and here to stay … that is how it was then, and is now.

Jaap kissed me … he said: 'I'm going to keep kissing you until you dare to look at me again …' 'Is it allowed, Jaap?'

'It … is … allowed.' 'But I daren't look at you, you who saw me like that.' 'But you must … or I won't stop kissing you.' He kissed my lips.

'Is that allowed, Jaap?' 'It … is … allowed.' And he moved to my ear. 'Never more …' Perhaps I dreamt that. So be it.

The doors are rattling, a deep, dull sound, the wind moves round like a weary sigh … quiet … quiet … he is stirring in his little white basket. Here I am … I'm here … but I've never seen your eyes like *that* before. How quietly you lie there waiting … stay like that a moment … I'm coming … I fetch the candle and the low chair and I'm back … did I talk too much, wasn't I quick as a flash? And now I lift you up and cradle you in my arm … you weigh seven pounds and you can't talk … and you rule my life and all my happiness rests with you. My lap is your home, the crook of my arm is for your little head … never before have I been in so confined a shaft, alone with you. You have learnt since this morning, you didn't cry, you know me already, you trust me, you know I'm always here, and that I will always be here from now on. And now I put down the candle, there! So I can see you, without it bothering you, and we are together in one chair … oh, you are forcing me into a corner and I like it there … and now I give myself to you, you may take me … with your round little head and your hair fine as the March grass …

The doors are rattling, a soft, dull sound … the wind moves round like a weary sigh … space calls to me, but I don't go … you forced me into the corner and I like it there. Oh, so greedy … so greedy … you're almost hurting me. You were too greedy, now you can't take any more … milk spills from your little mouth. Are your eyes really going to be like mine? Yes, the eloquent, vivacious brown has almost filled the murky greyblue emptiness. Do you yourself know this? Is that why you're looking at me like that? You never looked at me like that before tonight. Are you grateful - because you could take me when you wanted? I'm grateful too, because I can give myself when I want. And we look at one another. And I have never looked at your father like that. He took me and I gave myself … is that how it was? It must have been like that, or you wouldn't be here now with me, in my lap. We didn't look at one another … and we didn't recall it … we pushed it away from us … because we were ashamed. Worlds … worlds turning … each in its atmosphere of shame …

Never more estranged, never further away than in union.

People are further apart than the stars … we didn't get close to one another … You little mouth is pursed … you haven't had enough yet. How greedy … how greedy … your little throat undulates, *so* greedy … greedily and steadily you drink me empty. And I've only got one hand for you, for I cover my eyes with the other, because of what I suddenly know: this must be it, to be taken while giving like this … my heart is beating like never ever before … and the fire spreads through me, so that my own hand can feel it and it is there … where the secret feelings live … there where I received you … and that is how I know for sure. And you may never be taken from me … because the cord that they cut, that they knotted … it binds me to you and you pull me along by it …

Agatha … Agatha … oh you poor thing, you poor, poor thing, only now do I understand.

She came this afternoon. She said: 'It was three years ago. This is the first baby I can bear to see.'

She doesn't want to have another child. It had a tiny wound like a pinprick … it lived for eight days, it had been expected for nine months … all that was left were the little clothes and the little white basket, empty.

'Agatha, you are still so young.'

'No, never. No, never. Never again will I get attached to something. Not to people, not to any animal. I am so happy that I don't have any parents any more. Now I have to separate myself from my husband.'

Because we're crazy, we human beings, with death everywhere, everywhere … a little wound like a pinprick … and Death crept in, and then you're supposed to form attachments.'

'Because we have to, Agatha.'

'I don't, I'm free, I am cutting loose from everything … I don't want a child, or any animal, I don't want a husband. I want to laugh in his face … you know who I mean.'

'Yes … you mean Death.'

'I didn't have to spell it out to you …'

'No, you didn't have to spell it out. You mustn't summon him.'

And I closed the drapes of the basket around him. Now He won't find him so easily. I close the drapes of the basket. Now He won't find him so easily.

'Is it not cruelty, that we have to become attached like this? People die all the time. Ought we not to have learned how to console ourselves in the face of death long ago?'

Tall and thin, she sat bolt upright, in her black clothes. She has dark blue eyes framed by dark lashes … like Andy had … Andy … who wanted … to make a boy of me …

'Ought we not to have learned how to console ourselves in the face of death long ago? I could forgive Him everything … you know who I mean now?'

'Yes, Agatha, I know who you mean now.'

'Everything … everything … crime, and illness and the evil that he spreads … if only we were able to find consolation in the face of death, or did not have to become attached like this. But these two together are unbearable.'

The doors bang, rattling in their frames, the wind will not die down. Yes … now I really must go … now I really must go back and experience the spaces … above the narrow shafts. Now I will leave the golden, brightly wreathed paradise.

Damp … damp and dark … the dawn raises itself hesitantly out of the night … between the four shivering poplars the light begins to lighten. Softly … soft, closing the doors behind me … it was a little wound like a pinprick … And now I stand here all alone, shivering in the darkness, in the whispering dampness and if only I could fathom fully this small thing … If I could only fathom the true essence of this alone, this: four trembling poplars in the night … damp roofs above sleeping people, deep hollows of gardens, night-black inside wet fences. And thin clouds, restless, feverish, three layers one above another, seeking one another, avoiding one another, mingling, separating. And all of this together: *one* unrelenting puzzle, *one* impenetrable secret. This is what it is like to stare up at mountain tops from deep valleys. There is only one enchantment that leads to the top of mount Nebo … music … music … and the vistas lie before you, like in the picture of Moses … 'stretching from Jericho to Zoar.'

There was a brick wall, which gave off the heat of the previous hot day, in the cool of evening -, it struck your hand like the air from an oven … I remember when I stood there and was carried away by the music I had savoured … Schubert's 'Unfinished', the Andante … it impels me upwards, up mount Nebo, to where the vistas, the ever-changing vistas can be seen. Who knows the vistas of his own soul, if he does not know music? But the mystery does not stare him in the face … for he is unaware that there is such a mystery.

Trembling, whispering poplars, febrile clouds … I do know that I cannot escape the question.

Why are we inconsolable in the face of death, when we have known him for so long … Ernestien because of her mother, Agatha because of her child … destroyed, torn apart, damaged for ever. Why may we not be consoled in the face of death?

Agatha, the answer is this, and it is so bewilderingly simple, so amazingly straightforward: it is not given to us to be consoled for eternity in the face of Death … because we create life, we keep life going … we must love life … because we must hold on to it, must depend on it, flying in the face of suffering, in the face of reason, of everything …

Of everything? No.

This is the turning point, this is the beginning of the road that leads to the rest. The rain beat down, branches snapped in the storm, old Vermei was reading out loud in the history lesson. He was reading about Jerome of Prague, about his 'beautiful and fearless death.'

'When the executioner was about to light the fire behind him, so that he would not see it, Jerome said: "Light it, so that I can see it, because if I had been afraid of it, I would not be in this place now."'

The rain beat down, branches snapped … the kite tugs at its string. Long-drawn-out moans of pain inside you … I wanted to be able to do this, but I can't. So this is Life, rattling its chain, its heavy thousand-linked chain. No, no, we do not always love life. There is always the glow from the Chariot of Fire. Later the Most-Exalted, Socrates, appeared. To follow Him. 'They followed the pillar of cloud by day, the pillar of fire by night.'

'And why do you find him more exalted than the other, the one in the Gospels …?'

'Oh Jaap ... because his end was accomplished so ... so soberly and so quietly. The conclusion of his *Apologia*: "The hour of departure has arrived, and we go our separate ways, I to die, and you to live. Which of these two is better only God knows." Without drama ... so soberly and so quietly ... that it knocks you flat ... flattens you completely. He went ... his own way! That is all.'

Tomorrow I will go to Agatha. I will tell her what happened to Mr Brom. One year before his Silver Wedding he fell in love with the young cleaning woman, Joop ... who had such abundant hair that it came loose while she was scrubbing and she lost her hairpins which he picked up and kept ... and his daughter fled the house ... and his sons despised him and he demanded of his wife that she should release him and hold on to him ... and we spoke about his Guilt. I stood by the window that was criss-crossed by the rain ... there were white dahlias too ... there was a tower shrouded in mist ... and I felt the arrow ... which headed for me from somewhere unknown, and cleft me in two halves, one which confesses while denying -, one which denies while confessing. We are: two-bound-as-one, we are: one-turned-against-itself.

Agatha ... you have a balcony, a balcony like this one where I now stand and see the shivering poplars. Go outside on a night like this. Then you will feel the pendulum swing. Then you will be at one with everything, caught in the pendulum swing. And if the pendulum takes you to the left, then you despise life and tug on your chain, and you want to follow the Most-Exalted ... and all is filled with the glow from the Chariot of Fire. And if the pendulum takes you to the right, then you hate death and cling to life, as animals do, blindly. With the animals ... and the stars ... you are caught in the pendulum swing ... and outside the pendulum swing there is nothing. Nothing. You will find it difficult to grasp this, to understand ... it will merely be words ... until one day ... the Word becomes Spirit ... and you will know ... for ever, no, for a moment ... Word becomes word anew, devoid of meaning. But you *have* grasped it. And then you must flee, into the wild ducks' cage. To tables and chairs, to your husband's new coat, to the milkman, who is watering down the cream, to the calendar with the birthdays. You should not be afraid: it won't follow you, you have to look for it, chase after it, catch up with it, Know it. Forgetfulness is found in the smallest thing, and this forgetting is: Mercy, for it is so ... merciful ...

Tomorrow I will go, to Agatha. Tomorrow? But tomorrow is today, the dawn no longer hesitates ... I will go in. Softly ... softly ... here it is still dark ... the little white wicker basket light. The chairs ... the table ... my big bed ... but *this* is not flight! No, this is not flight, but I am cold, and I am unutterably tired, and I want to go to sleep. But this is not flight. I want to know that I am in the pendulum swing, and go on knowing it … without willing it, without a goal, without a destination in the unfathomable pendulum swing … I do not think that a human being can reach further, or become freer. Is this … is this then that Truth of which it is written, that it will set us free? Renounce all, give up everything. But I want to sleep now … I am cold and tired … I burrow deeply into my blankets … And wasn't there a book … a play … no, it's a game: Who loses wins … Who loses wins … who loses wins …

Now I sail away, now sleep comes …

7
David

The wind drives the snow ahead of itself -, it rushes through the grey streets, round corners, as though in hasty, focused flight, down the sloping path, through open gates, into the park, but finds no rest in those spaces either. The solid ground deflects it, the dry shrubs shake it off, it cannot settle anywhere, the frost has dried it out and it has lost its sense of direction. She walks with the children on the hard paths, their footsteps clatter, the ponds gleam -, glassy eyes in an expressionless, leaden grey face. The bare trees crack and snap. These are the days between Saint Nicholas's Day and Christmas - short stumpy days, helpless days, aborted days - days in which you no longer miss the sun, as though you had never known it, but in the inner city warmth wells up from red lamps and all day long, the door to evening stands ajar, and a dozy winter sleepiness hangs in the air - you give yourself over to it, you feel yourself to be contained and bounded, like the earth contained and bounded between horizon and sky - numbed and comforted by it. But this is like waking from a dreamless sleep.

She arrived home with the children -, every afternoon she first goes to collect Claartje and together with Claartje she goes to meet Eddy from school, and with both of them, with each one holding one of her hands, a warm hand shut tight, she then walks back under the tall, bare trees and she crosses the square, they cross the square, three-in-one, and hand-in-hand, and side-by-side … firmly resisting the biting wind which shakes the iron pot 'For the Poor People's Christmas' in its stand, and makes the old Salvation Army woman stamp her feet … and they enter the streets and penetrate to the rosy heart of the wintry city and walk among strangers, look at them, brush against them, and remain, hand-in-hand, just the three of them, three-in-one.

And they arrived home and Ben said: 'I have to speak to you alone for a moment.' And she stood with him in the cold room and waited, and spectral fears appeared, as though from behind the horizon, shadows of possibilities were cast, and she thought, 'How grey his beard is getting' -, and then Ben said: 'Prepare for the worst. David is dead. David died in the night.' And then suddenly it was as though through all those years -, no matter how close you were to the children as you walked, and Ben is there as well, you never betray him ... and father-and-mother over there in the little town ... though they weren't strictly speaking fully present any more ... they lived beyond the horizon, pushed back behind the children, behind Ben, behind the big events, the growth and the pain ... but through all those years David was beside you, even though there were years among those years, in which you hardly saw each other, he was fully present and then Ben said: 'David is dead - he died in the night,' and he was no longer standing there beside her, he sank down to the ground -, in the cold room, by the grey window, he sank in a heap on the ground. And there was an empty space where he had been standing.

That such a thing could actually happen, that it was allowed to happen, that it happened. David was never healthy again after that illness early last year. They said: David is going to the South, with Berthold. With Berthold. Ben said: he and Berthold spend all their time together. Yes, Ben. Since his youth, he has been with Berthold constantly. From me he went to Berthold -, I never got him back. And then you heard: They are back in the country, but he hasn't been cured. And suddenly this: Both his lungs are affected. But your concern disintegrated, dissolved: such things happen to others. Somewhere else -, that is where these things happen. This is the way life resists death, by denying it in the face of knowledge. But David is dead. Now nothing can change, he cannot choose another path. The years are gone, his life is gone. As children we asked Father: 'Why are so many things repeated in the Torah?' 'What God repeats is irrevocable. This means that it has been decided irrevocably.' This is how the word came to me. Everything to do with David is now irrevocable. He came towards me in the snow -, he said: this is my future, this is going to happen. And his life seemed to soar like a rocket above mine. The years sailed in like ships entering the harbour, but they were never loaded and they never left it again ... their rigging was dismantled and their yard arms were pulled askew for their silent sleep, and his life became an abandoned harbour full of dismantled, unused ships.

Once, as a child, I knew death. I shall never forget it. The knowledge was waiting for me in bed after the day of the storm and

I wanted it. I wanted to know death for a moment -, I was young and pushed it away again when I knew it - get away from me. 'One day the black sand will …' There was a white stone in the earth, enclosed by the earth -, and in the stone was a kernel -, but it isn't me. It's David, my brother, my little brother. They opened the earth, they enclosed him in it, they closed the earth.

We were born at the same time, this month we would both have been thirty-one. Now only I will be.

He never took an exam. At first they said: 'He can't find the time, he'll postpone it.'

Later on they said: 'His health won't allow it.'

Then it became something mysterious that one person shied away from asking another, avoided touching on. And now he is dead.

'At four o'clock, mother, Ernestien is coming to fetch us, with Tonia.'

'And we'll finish the doll's hat today.'

'And I'm going to read to her till supper time.'

Ernestien is blind. She hit her eye on the corner of a table when she was bending down for a stick of chalk that had rolled away. They waited too long before operating … then she lost the other eye … for years now she has lived like a grey, patient, little blind woman. That was how life finished with her, -, in one second. Her one and only life.

Ebner is married to Anna Keuls. He got to know her at evening school. 'One day I was engaged. The next I was married.' She treats him like a silly boy. She is incapable of experiencing wonder at anything. Ebner reads something in the paper … a crime, someone blinded. He says: 'This is really very curious … how people act … how people are … here a man who murders a little girl for her golden earrings … here a pastor who speaks of an earthquake as God's punishment for a caricature in a Sunday paper … don't all these things make you wonder …'

Anna interrupts him: 'What do you mean, wonder …? These things happen every day … you hear them spoken of all the time …' 'Yes, Anna, you are right, they are all very ordinary events, I now realize, but before you said so, it suddenly all seemed so wondrous to me …'

She has a view on everything. Ebner says: 'Since I have been married, I feel I am a vacillating fool.'

Oh, Ebner, I know that so well! We are spread wide and thin in our doubt, we evaporate in our meditations … They are narrow and solid in their self-assurance. They are unbending, they are immovable, they make us inferior to them, they blow us over. 'A vacillating fool …' We both laughed. Silly boy, where did you get that phrase from?

'Mother … Ernestien said: Tonia would have been allowed to bake us an apple cake, if she had known yesterday.'

'But yesterday I didn't know myself.'

'No, the letter only came yesterday afternoon, didn't it?'

'Yes, the letter came yesterday afternoon.'

Heleen's letter. An unknown strong hand, and on the back of the envelope an unknown woman's name -, but the place where David lived in the circle of the postmark, black and strong. And I stood there with that letter and with my hat still on, and I already knew: this is the girl, this is the woman, who, along with all the rest, has been sacrificed for that boy. She wrote: David has spoken to me so often about you, his twin sister, and about the old days and about the old things. I really wanted to see the old things, I wanted to walk past the old places, with you, I also want to go to his parents, to your parents with you …

Soon, over there, we will meet, each of us coming from our own direction … we each came from our own direction, to him.

The driving snow swirls past. It scarcely touches the earth; this is how wolves run, urgently, hungry dogs, scarcely touching the earth, as though running towards a goal, but there is no goal, there is only amazement and uncertainty, the solid earth will not grant it rest, the dry bushes shake it off, with their frozen rustlings.

'And the snow so hurts my face, and it blows so in my eyes …'

'Oh, mother, she is so little still …'

He looks up at her.

Yes, she is little. You are little yourself. You are both little, both helpless, both unknowing … but my strength is your aid, and my knowledge is your security. Come, mother knows what to do. We open the large, wide coat, we all three creep inside it … we pull it closed over all three … and now we are a broad, hairy beast with three pairs of legs. This is how we create the Wonder for ourselves …

Twenty-five years ago. There was a lesson in the lesson-book that began like this: 'Is that an umbrella walking along? No, it cannot be, it has no legs.' There was a picture with it. It forces its way in leaps and jumps though those twenty-five years, it comes back to me, I can see it: 'And the boys are called Hans and Frans.' There was also: 'Watch out that you don't take off into the air together with the umbrella.' This took hold of me. Miss Looman was in front of the class. I can smell the class. Next door they were singing: 'To the woods, to the woods …' The sun was shining, outside green branches were waving … ; or was it only the green branches in the song? David sat in the farthest boys' row. We were smaller than Eddy. Now Eddy calls me mother. And David is dead.

They clasp their arms round me, under the coat, they are mine.

Last week Agatha said: 'Don't you ever fret about their future? And don't you constantly think, how will they grow up, what will they have to bear?'

'No, Agatha, I do not fret about their future.' No. This one and only grace has been granted me, that the future cannot disturb me. Years and days make their way to me out of it, steadily, gradually, they roll toward me as though from a closed horizon. All my life, I have been anxious about everything, -, but this is my share in the blessed numbness. Even as a child, voices of wind and water tortured me with their whisperings, they overwhelmed me. The 'Haidarabad' invaded the harbour and the brown men came ashore, under the lightless sky they walked along the lightless water, they walked along the high sea wall, in bare feet, in a loud noise of raw jeering and clattering clogs -, I walked among them and I thought: this is a foreign town for them, all our faces are strange faces, all our houses are strange houses … and my heart was a powerful lens, in which everything was concentrated, their intense homesickness, their defenceless suffering, and it seared me … ; because they looked so grey and there was only lightless water, a lightless sky … and tears poured from my eyes, but their ship is their home … for my despair needed this consolation.

Sympathy destroyed me, - with the living and the dead, with the bones in the charnel house behind the old church. Gratitude ground me down, bliss crushed me … Spring burst upon me … I was the starry firmament … I was the sunset … I was it all, I bore it all. The cows lowed their complaints to me in the summer night, out of the meadow-dew, but I did not understand. Not a single thing left me in peace. Everything flowed towards me, and flowed out of me -, I was the flowing heart of all things. I suffered injustice, I avenged injustice -, I was burned with the martyrs -, I joined in with the plotters … I have forgiven all things, and committed all things … created all and destroyed all. Ships foundered in me, and nothing happened that I had no part in. It all ran its course right through me -, for every deed, I bore a share of the responsibility … The lonely objects, the lonely trees, the lonely waters, the lonely thoughts, all of this bore in on me unceasingly, so as to be released from its loneliness in my comprehension, in my understanding, so as to be united with all the other lonely things, in the Oneness, all of it in *my* comprehension, always in *my* understanding, and I wavered in the storm and I fainted in the breaking waves, and I could not do it … I have never understood anything, mostly not even the fact that I understand nothing … I have seen nothing, heard nothing, and only once have I attained this knowledge ... since I was small, life has conspired in me, all things have conspired in me and against me ... But the future leaves me in peace.

'No Agatha ... you won't infect me with this. They are healthy, their eyes are bright, they sleep peacefully and I do what I can.'

Ben said: 'But now you have another ideal, now you have found your new ideal in mother love, in motherhood.'

It was with the Ebners, and we had been talking about socialism.

'No, love for your children is not an ideal, it is an instinct.'

Anna Ebner said: 'I call that cynical. Animals have instincts. Motherhood is the highest ideal for a woman.'

When Eddy was born, milk came into my breasts, love into my heart. They were in me for the child that was of me. Milk and love are one-and-the-same. One and the same. It is the double instinct, in which that which seeks to perpetuate itself in a thousand ways does so in two ... And this is what we humans are good at. This is what we humans are good for ...

'I don't understand, Anna, why you are so resistant to this. I can't see why this way should make things any less 'beautiful'. If you really are so keen to speak of 'beauty' ... for me this is the most beautiful thing of all ...'

'How can you think it beautiful, how dare you call it beautiful ...'

'Because I carry it in me, because it carries me. Finding beauty is discovering oneself ...'

'And what about art ...?'

'Well, I think that it must be the same with art.'

Anna said: 'This is feverish talk. You read too much. For a woman, you read much too much. I can see the strangest books here. And it won't get you anywhere. I say the same thing to Ebner every day. Life is much simpler than you both make it, in your feverishness.' Suddenly you see Anna Ebner as the greatest marvel. Someone who calls life simple. Someone who says: 'It won't get you anywhere!'

But Anna would defend herself with: 'That's something that happens every day.'

Ebner laughed. Was he thinking the same thing?

Ben said: 'Why do you always take pleasure in dissecting everything, pulling everything to pieces?'

Like the character in Van Eeden's *Little Johannes*. And you smile, while you undo the knot in your shoelace. The weak, soft poet. 'The Truth will set you free.'

It was later that evening. We undressed. We do not look at one another when we undress. I do sometimes look at myself. I look at my shoulders, my soft shoulders. Sometimes I kiss my own shoulders. Ben winds his watch, he folds his clothes neatly over a chair. I am going to be thirty-one years old. My youth is passing me by, passing through me.

'Why wouldn't you want to call it an ideal? Why do you call it an instinct?'

'Because ... "The Truth will set you free."' But you don't say it.

Lotje, recently: 'And do you find it easy to talk to your husband?'

Defiant little Lotje! She has been married to Hugo for a few years already, now at last they are expecting their child, they are radiant.

'Well indeed, Lotje, I can talk to my husband perfectly well.' But you don't say that, however. Nor do you say this:

Since I have had children, humanity's problems are my children's problems. The big problem of Opposition is Claartje and Eddy's problem -, and so it is no longer a problem: my children may not suffer, my children may not go under. If they were going to suffer, if they might go under because of a principle, then they must denounce that principle. I shall myself forge the false arguments for them, I shall spin the sophisms for them -, such crafty arguments, such unrestrained sophisms, that they will start to despise their own ideal. I shall belittle all their ideals, just like Anna I shall say: 'You won't get anywhere with these', I will drive them to where I know they are safe, in the corral of plain happiness, in the embrace of idleness, which I have forgone for myself. Because I am a Mother, because that is why I became a Mother. In the Mother, the Human Being is lost, the Human Being is bankrupted. And then again, perhaps not. Perhaps also this is a case of: 'The way up and the way down are one-and-the-same.' But this at least I keep to myself -, at any rate, I reserve the right not to call it 'idealism'. You do not say this to Ben. All you say is: 'What would you think, Ben, if the bookbinder stamped the wrong names on the spines of your books? Like you, I do not like wrong names. In my way I am orderly - as you are in your own way ...' And Ben does not reply, you don't expect him to. You take the heavy counterpane from the bed, to fold it up, but you make a mess of it, you have to do it again, you were not concentrating on what your hands were doing, you are thinking ...

This dual order of things - this is what you are thinking - keeps us separate. And this is why nothing has ever been realized of those dreams ... those old dreams ... sweet, glowing dreams, soft, burning dreams ... because for you only the one order exists, and for me only the other. You feel unhappy at an untidy desk or if your books are not in their places, but you breathe the chaos every day and you don't feel panic. The chaos of the unexamined, uncomprehended life ... of conflicting opinions, unconnected pronouncements, a vast system of things hidden, things unanalysed, things misrepresented … the chaos that suffocates me, the way I would suffocate in a wild wood, if I couldn't carve out my own narrow little path. But behind me it grows over again. Uphill and downhill, the path is one-and-the-same.

Hop o' My Thumb found the white pebbles again, but the birds took the breadcrumbs … it's in your books today, it'll be in your books tomorrow, and yesterday it was there as well, but in my mind it dies and is reborn, every day anew, every moment different …

We never took any more from each other's arms than wretched shame and defenceless aversion because I understand only the one order of things and you only the other. This is why things can never change. A man and a woman stand next to one another beside an open window. They are small and high up and lonely above the metropolis, in a purple evening mist. And she thinks: actually, this is beautiful, such a strong, fine church tower over there, rising into space, heading for heaven. And he asks: 'Irene, can you still make out from here what time the clock says, on that tower?'

'That, mother, is why my marriage is unhappy.'

It is a boy's birthday, it is Spring, he is eighteen. He wakes and the double joy unfolds in him … because of the girl, Sylvia, and because of his little figures of animals moulded in malleable clay. And he hastens to his workshop to see them again. And opens the door and hesitates in the gloom and the balance shifts. In that one second his life is decided, his one, his only life. Will he laugh or stamp his foot -, will he flee or stay? In the soft backs of every one of the clay animals, she has stuck a green Palm Sunday sprig, upright, as a celebratory decoration, for his birthday. And he stayed and he married her, but right into old age, Mark Lennan was unable to find peace …

They are playing peekaboo under the coat, they are tugging me backwards and forwards, up and down … o you dreadful, naughty children …

'And we've been doing it for a bit and you didn't even notice …'

'Now both of you come out from under the coat, as a punishment.'

'We wanted to stop anyway, we're nearly at school!' Here it is more sheltered, and dark like evening. The angular, solid church building deflects the wind, but also blocks out the light from the houses, where the lamps burn all through the short days.

Shivering under her scarf, the tall, scrawny Froebel teacher leans in the open doorway. Claartje waves exuberantly to her, and she smiles at the child, with a little bow to the mother, but her eyes aren't laughing.

Tense, staring, too-shining forget-me-not eyes. They are set like jewels in her pale head and her white neck has a bulge ... goitre ... Jaap saw it straight away, that first day ...

There, in that winter street, behind the dark, solid church, with her too-shining eyes ... in the pseudo-ecstasy of goitre ... but I must hurry to the tram ...

To the left the quay, to the right the water -, behind me the dark roof, which traps the sounds, the trains' dungeon, in front of me the rails ... across the dry, dark earth, between the indefinite snow shapes, they carve their way to over there, to my old home. And here I was troubled by Andy, here more than twelve years ago I was tempted by Andy. And all that had been born, had grown, in me, circling in the dark around a destination not yet revealed to me ... and the burning desire to release me from myself and hand myself over to another ... at that moment it could have crystallized around her, as it later crystallized around ... as it still now circles within me. No not around her as she was, with her stories like burning visions, her scorching hands, suddenly I feel that hot hand again. At that moment I found myself undecided. Before we are born we are undecided, that is what physiologists tell us. We are undecided, we live undecided ...

Later on we are undecided yet again: before puberty. The rebirth that is puberty. I remember once as a child feeling myself in an undecided moment while balancing as I walked the log: on one side was soot and on the other flour. The mayor was celebrating twelve and a half years of marriage. And old Mr Van der Zeyde stood watching and he said: 'Yet there is no such thing as chance. None of what happens here is due to chance.' Everyone teased him, they always called after him in the street, you pointed him out to one another: 'Do you see that gentleman? That is Mr Van der Zeyde, who doesn't believe in chance.' *'Du bist am Ende was du bist.'* But that precisely is chance -, what has been allotted to you. People do not grasp this.

We were late developers, David and I ... we were undecided for a long time.

It still smells like it used to in the train, but a great deal has changed too, the city grew out into the polder, the railway was moved, further from the water, a small deviation that gives everything a different aspect -, small deviations change everything -, and in all these small deviations the old picture is gradually lost. Factories are smoking along the water's edge, once, in my childhood there was nothing there but reeds and green meadow, you could only get there by barge, there wasn't even a path. How slender the young trees were, how enormous the harbour seemed, a great lake ... how much is lost as one grows older. It falls away from you -, but it isn't really like that, you leave it behind as you make your way. All the lost things speed towards the rattling train, as they fly past they tap on the windows with rapid, fleeting fingers -, old emotions, old desires, old questions -, the old longing I had for spotlessness. Wind and fog, light and smell, I was their playground, they played through me, like the school at midday with all its doors and windows wide open. I hated the winter, the hard frost -, now I can long for winter sometimes, because it is quiet and makes no claims on me, does not remind me of what I have lost. Spring and Summer and Autumn make their claims, they speak to me -, they remind me of what I no longer possess. Of my powerlessness, I am no longer close to them. I have probably made some progress in my understanding of the world, but for this I have violated the old connection, broken the old tie. And every year, the days and the hours remind me of this as they come full circle. Say I had a friend on another planet and I had to describe Spring to him ... in the strip of meadow behind the poorhouse above the sluice gate, enclosed by blue ditches, there I waded through grass and filled my apron with flowers, there for ever it is eternal Spring, bliss ... Autumn: the first light on the first day of the Feast of Tabernacles. We go with Father to the synagogue. In Does's market garden that we call the 'monkey enclosure' because of his seven sons with monkey faces, the dahlias bend under the dew, their little white quills, their little red quills, their little red-and-white quills are bulging with dew and everywhere there is a faint dripping of hidden moisture and otherwise it is quiet, because it is early, we do not meet a soul ... Today it has snowed, I saw the snow, I can still see the snow now -, but the snow living within me, the snow of the old connection, of the old ties ... that is my own bluish, private snow, I am standing alone in the alleyway by the water butt ... and it is Sunday afternoon ... and I cannot hear a sound, but suddenly, in the distance, a steamboat calls from the harbour, a last farewell, now it is about to leave. 'Les neiges d'antan.'

The little train lurches, the track rises to the bridge. My entire youth is already in the past. Is it true that we renew ourselves every seven years ...? One and the same ... one and the same ... the track goes ... up and down ... the wheels have taken over the refrain from me ... we wax ... we wane ... one and the same ... oh, if we could, if we might ... all that we once possessed, all that we now possess ... in one breath, all at once ... one single moment. But it is not possible. We are limited.

'So you deny progress, Evolution?'

'Yes, Hugo, how would I otherwise ...? Once something took me by storm, it was this: Totality and Evolution are in conflict with one another.

Eternity excludes progress. Totality is that which eternally remains itself, that which revolves into itself, eternally opening and closing ... the Kaleidoscope.'

'But surely you can see progress ... better working conditions ... child protection legislation ... more humane administration of justice ...'

'You can always see growth ... but not death. What is dead is buried. We know what we have, - but we can no longer remember what we have lost ... we cease knowing it. As long as we remember something, we have not lost it, as long as we can name it, we still have it.

'Do you remember, Hugo, how at school we taught the children about plants that put up suckers? They grow on one side and die off on the other ...'

Then Hugo's eyes lit up in his boyish face. 'Oh, Eva, now I'm with you! The suckers gradually move the plant forward ... it grows ... it dies ... but growing and dying, it makes progress ...'

'No, Hugo, you're not with me at all. Because you are forgetting one thing ... you are forgetting that the earth is round ...'

'But how do you live ... how can you live without this belief, without this certainty? I wouldn't be able to live like that.'

'No ...' says Lotje, the little one, the defiant one, with her funny upturned nose. 'We couldn't live like that.'

Precisely! I cannot live like that. In order to live I must deny my insight. Because my insight denies life ...

Hugo said: 'And yet you still believe in Evolution! I undertake to prove it ten times over in the space of fourteen days from your own words.'

Oh, Hugo ... you could have happily said: fifty times, a hundred times. And why did you only speak of: Evolution? Why not also: free will ... and guilt ... and causality ...? For all things are equally in conflict with the Insight ... everything that we cannot live without is in conflict with that Insight toward which we raise ourselves up, in which we raise ourselves up ... moment by moment.

Always and everywhere ... the eternal pendulum swing, the same conflict ... always ... everywhere ... division, fracture ... We raise ourselves up towards the Insight; we raise ourselves up in the Insight ... this is Death.

We must surrender it, let go of it, in order to live ... it lets go of us, in order that we may live, it surrenders us to chaos. And you read of earthquakes ... how in a second they destroy the work of centuries, how they alter landscapes, make islands disappear, appear ... so it is with the one, the single second of Insight, a lightning strike, a quake disrupting the face of the world. This is what I experienced when one night this thought took me by storm: Evolution opposes Totality. I thought: it is easily said … but now I must revise everything … renew everything … now no word, no judgement may remain unrevoked … they are all illusion …

The man who taught the Persian ruler chess asked for a reward: two grains of corn for the first of the sixty-four squares, four for the second, sixteen for the third … and each number multiplied by itself, right up to the sixty-fourth square. It was easily said, it was just as easily granted, except that there was not enough corn in all of Persia. They were not able to fulfil this task, nor could I. Life sticks to our feet like clay, it holds us fast like quicksand, we never sink completely, nor do we ever free ourselves. That night I thought: 'Now I must revoke each word, now I must revise each judgement.' Error and foolishness, ejected through the front door, creep in again through the back door … There are people, who think that they practise 'Pure Reason' … There was a man, who attached wings to himself to fly to the sun -, they melted away and he plunged back down. These people haven't even been close enough to the white heat for that to happen …

There is Heleen -, she has already seen me and she knows I am Eva. It's you … yes, it's me. We do not know each other yet, we approach one another. Without David we would never have met -, and will we now stay together? If so, we will have come together through a great accident of chance. Her eyes feel their way, her eyes search, her eyes construct, she does not see me, she is searching for David in me, she wants to see him in me, make him live again.

'You are his sister, Eva?'

'Yes, I am Eva … Heleen.'

'You look like him.'

'It would be amazing if we didn't look alike.'

We walk side by side. We walk past the crude fence of heavy tar-blackened planks -, high as a wall it stands against the landscape -, there is one opening and Heleen stops. Well, Heleen, this is where we stood as well and we looked at the village strung out far beyond the meadows. Look, the houses are so far apart that between them you can see other villages further away. We called those 'The Villages of the Sea Beggars'. In summer it smelt of water and grass and in winter of hay and manure. This is what made us -, we were made, David and I, from these long, flat meadows, from these winding ditches, windmills and sheds … the smell of grass and water, hay and manure. The trees groan … the first grumbles of thunder … the railway bridge rumbling in the evening from the polder, distant music in a frightening dream … years ago, many years ago, Father was ill, our lives were haunted by dangers, which Father had kept under control. Rivers swell … ice breaks … we walked here in the evening, David and I, and then as now, the trees groaned like this.

'But you have … your eyes are different, Eva …'

'Yes … we have … we had different eyes.'

His eyes are closed. They closed his eyes, they closed the earth above his closed eyes. This cold earth.

Heleen is tall, and slender, she has a narrow face, she is certainly no younger, perhaps a little older than the two of us.

My years have fallen away from me. Every time I come here, the years fall away from me -, and what I had lost is restored to me -, but what I gained, I have handed back … the way you have to hand in your umbrella at a museum!

'This is our school, Heleen. And look, we sharpened our lead writing-sticks against that slanting stone edge … we sharpened them to get the longest, the best, the sharpest point. And we played marbles here as well, in the same grooves. But there was also a ditch, so we had to be careful. And when the sun shone, there were shiny specks in the black-grey, tightly stamped earth. On the other side of the ditch was a flower grower. We sharpened our leads in the scent of flowers -, we smelt spring flowers … summer flowers … autumn flowers one after the other … first we smelt the lilacs … later the roses … and last of all the chrysanthemums … and then we moved up a class. And in the winter it was all covered with rush matting and straw …'

And now we are standing here together, Heleen and I … and David is dead.

'Sometimes we found last year's leaves in the ditch, perfectly preserved, a network of veins, more beautiful than gold, brownish gold, if the sun came out for a moment. Usually they fell apart in your hands … but once we fished one out and took it home with us … for our museum. We had a museum in the attic … in it we had a cedar cone and a palm frond, from the Feast of the Tabernacles.'

Heleen … I haven't yet absorbed the knowledge that he is dead, it is coming towards me out of the distance.

'This is the synagogue. Yes, it is small … to us it was big … so much happened there, it was so connected to everything, all through the year. David went with Father through this door, I went with Mother through that one. I went upstairs, he stayed downstairs, and we nodded to one another. And everyone prayed and sang for themselves before the service began …'

The slides on the ice shone … it was a day like today, soon there will be an evening just like then. In old Breg's little shop a prune lay squashed against the window by a mountain of grey dried peas that had buried it, it lay in a wreath of water droplets. The lamp shone across the snow, under the lamp stood the sled, with little Levie in it. He waited so patiently, he was looking up into the lamp with his bulging, brown eyes. He died the same winter -, twenty years he's been dead now. Old Zadoks was his grandfather … he was so poor … his bottom lip hung down …

He came out of the door, he hid the turves under the seat in the sled, he had buttoned his coat over the pieces of coal … I was the only one who knew … I was the only one to see him take them, see him … steal … from the cupboard in the Jewish school … The eaves dripped, deep, yellow holes formed in the snow … we called them little graves, David and I.

Oh Heleen … I can't go on … now I know …

David is dead.

There was one moment in the room at home, by the window that looked so dark when Ben told me, … I saw David collapse onto the ground … at that moment I knew it, but afterwards I didn't any more. There was so much between me and the knowledge, but now I know. David, my brother, my little brother …

'There's a place by the canal, Heleen, we often used to sit there together. Then it seemed far to us, but it isn't all that far, we'll go along the harbour …'

So we go along the harbour.

'Heleen … how long did you know my brother, actually?'

'About three years, perhaps a little longer. But we didn't see each other often. That boy kept us apart from one another, he hated me, he hates everyone, he hated David too. It was out of hate that he … that he … he destroyed him. Oh Eva, he is a depraved boy, he is a cruel, cynical boy, he knows no sympathy, hurting is his pleasure. He was like a parasite on David, he sucked him dry …'

'Heleen … there is our seat … it isn't a seat, it's a heap of beams, rotted away and hollow on the inside, it's full of caverns, and the sand blew into the caverns, and seeds blew in and from sand and seed came flowers, sometimes there were bindweed, faded pale-pink field bindweed, which look so pale anyway, paler than pale, and purple vetch, garlands which seemed to have no beginning and no end. Are you dressed warmly enough, Heleen … shall we sit down here, then? It's our old spot.'

'He could never bear the thought that David was intelligent, that David was gifted, more intelligent and more gifted than he was. He couldn't take any exams himself, he couldn't work, he couldn't submit to it, he was too feeble and also too haughty for that. And that is why he didn't want David to take exams either. And didn't like it that David was a gifted poet … did you ever know that?'

'Yes, I knew it as a child, as a girl, but he didn't want to say so openly. We invented a boy: Theo Vermeer, but he understood that I understood. I now find it difficult to believe that Theo Vermeer never existed. Maybe we both imagined him quite differently, David and I …'

Streams flowing in me, flowing in him, out of which Theo Vermeer took shape … An old figment of our imaginations … Das Ding an Sich!

'Once we sat here, on a day like this, but it was later in the day and it was also much calmer, there was no wind -, it was a New Year's Day, the first day of the new century, of this century, the day after we both turned eighteen. And we sat here and he read a poem to me … but I didn't listen properly … I was thinking of something else … if I had listened better, maybe I would have remembered more of it … now all I know are the last two lines … I can see it, there were poplars, there was a moon, and across the whole sky arcs of colour, the sky was an archery target of coloured arcs, and in the middle was the moon as bull's eye, a misty, damp, white bull's eye. And these were the last lines:

At his window he stands staring
In his white shirt all alone …

'Who …?'
'It was a boy.'
'Berthold …?'
'No, he hadn't got to know him at that stage. Although the message had come the same day. It was still a dream then.'

'Eva, it has always remained a dream, Eva, you mustn't think bad things … you mustn't think ugly things of him … you mustn't think that there was something between him and Berthold … Berthold *is* like that, with others, not with David. Rumours went round about them, and Berthold didn't deny them, out of cruelty, out of egotism, that was how he kept David cut off from the world. And David did not contradict him, out of pride, out of indifference. Not even to Berthold's father: 'You may think what you like.' And after that, Berthold left home, and they started to live together, to travel together … and this is what gave rise to all the gossip. Did you ever want to believe it … did you believe it, Eva?'

'I didn't take much notice of it …'

'You didn't take much notice of it …?'

'That's right, because I don't think it is all that important. I mean: compared with things that really are important, the big problems, the problems of existence ... philosophical problems, problems of conscience. Sexuality itself ... regardless of relationships ... it feels unimportant to me in a certain sense, I mean: it is important for an individual, that is why I say: unimportant in a certain sense. But I'm not putting it clearly. I want to say this: it stands outside intellectual and ethical problems.'

'You mean to say -, that you may not condemn anyone for this?'

Are we close to one another, or is there a chasm? I know nothing of her, she knows nothing of me.

'It is a misfortune, Eva, to be like Berthold.'

'It doesn't have to be a misfortune ...'

'But it *is* ... sterile ...'

'And why ... sterile ...? It isn't all about children. Feelings ... and passion ... inspiration ... that is all reality, it is all outcome.'

'Oh but Eva ... the other way, the normal way ... man-with-woman, this is better, is so much more beautiful. You will have to admit this.'

'I don't know, Heleen. Don't ask me these things. I don't know anything about them.'

No, she must not ask me these things. I know nothing about them. It is the rock on which my understanding founders, it is the blind wall ...

'But you are married, you have children. You have two children, don't you ...?'

'Yes, I am married. I have two children. And yet I know nothing about these things.'

'You mean the other way ... deviance?'

'No, I mean the normal way ... the natural way.'

She is silent ... she gave me a brief sidelong glance ... now she is staring out across the water, across the polders, with her luminous, grey-blue eyes, her wide-open eyes. What does *she* know ... what will she ever know? I scarcely know her. If I knew her better, I would say this to her ... I also had a man friend, I had too many of them, I had two: the first was Jaap and the second was André. Anna Ebner says of me: Eva is a flirt, a flirt of the first order. She says it laughing, because Anna Ebner is not malicious.

No, I don't understand it, because it is ambiguous. People speak of 'low pleasures'. Johannes Viator calls it: Bodily Sin. Only love renders bodily desire good. 'But also, in a deeper understanding, love for the child, the unborn.' 'The permitted and inevitable outcome.' Always the same: having to apologise ... 'Desire can sometimes be so strong ...' Desire, but also always: shame. 'The consequences of their love made themselves felt.' Chaos. Cacophony. I know nothing of them. André once told me of a woman, who pursued a man right into his own home, who took him by surprise, forced him. But he did not love her and was repelled by it … and she returned, and she forced him again, and it was so repulsive to him, she was so repulsive to him, that he chased her away. She must have repelled him so much that he was able to tell another man the story of how he gave her up. For how else would André have known it? 'But André, why did she do it then …?' 'Because she had sunk low …' Because of her desire? And what about me …? And sometimes no words are adequate …

For a man, the one thing seems to merge into the other, seems to go with the other. Not for me. There is a gulf, an abyss, a darkness, an unbridgeable space. I do not see the link, the compelling connection.

Jaap didn't reproach me with it, but he didn't understand either. I might kiss him, but it disappointed me after the very first time. I wanted to do it again, and again I was disappointed. Each time I was more deeply disappointed. I allowed him to go a long way and my heart pounded out the old judgement: debauchery, adultery - debauchery, adultery. I thought of Ben, I thought of Jaap, too … I did want to make Jaap happy, but there was no imperative, it didn't matter to me … the gulf remained, a darkness, an unbridgeable space.

André was full of reproach, that afternoon in his room. He said: It is a scandal, you are mean and ungenerous. You are just like that woman in Zola's novel … '*Tout ce que vous voulez, mais pas ça …*'

'Oh, André …'

'Yes, that is what you are like …'

Later on he said something that was even worse, that wounded me deeply, so deeply it scorched like a bullet wound. Our last conversation, - the next day he went away. He said: 'The French have an expressive word for what you are, but I won't say it.' 'Come on André, tell me, you can't keep it to yourself, it's burning your lips, just say it.' 'Well you will be shocked by it. Yet I want to say it to you, because it is what you are: *une allumeuse* … a tease …' I felt slapped, branded. 'The Scarlet Letter.' André said: 'Can you forgive me, for saying this to you?' He was stumbling over his words. Oh André, who do you think I want to arouse? I did not ask him this. I was silent … I couldn't remain insulted for long: men are different. Later, in my thoughts, I did ask him: Who do you think I wanted to arouse, actually? Myself, only myself, I was always trying to arouse myself. But the other caught fire while I remained cold. Cold. Now I am thinking that man's word. Cold -, because in this direct, this limited … Cold -, with my ardent heart …

I sometimes think that I can experience desire … I meet a man and I like him and I cannot think of anything but him, he kisses me, and I am disappointed … but I am reluctant to admit it … he kisses me again and I am more deeply disappointed … but I am even more reluctant to admit it. Each kiss disappoints me, each word disappoints me, but I still don't want to admit it. *Allumeuse … allumeuse …* the other catches fire but I cannot set myself alight. And I submit to what I do not desire -, I allow it so as not to be ungenerous. But I cannot allow everything … I cannot betray Ben for something that has no meaning, no reason, no necessity … it makes as little sense with Ben, but I hide behind marriage. I am bound by the marriage dogma, it protects me … in this way people have bound their entire lives to dogmas, protected them with dogmas.

Always I have found my own path, made my own laws, away from the common paths, outside the common laws -, only in this one area have I never known what's what -, never understood what's what. No-one should ever ask me about it, I'm at a complete loss.

Heleen sits beside me, she looks out over the water and the polders, her grey-blue eyes shining -, wide open … I can hear her breathing - she breathes where he breathed, in this way she tries to unite herself with him, in the atmosphere that nourished him, him and me. We are nourished in our early years … 'So this is where you two walked, where you often sat?'

'Yes, we usually came this way …'

'Eva … I could have saved him, I could have made him happy. He didn't want that. I begged him to give me his poems, so that I might publish them, he didn't want that either. Eva … read this letter …'

She was about to place the letter in my hands, but changed her mind. She moves towards me, she points …

'Here, read this part … "I can bear anything and I can accomplish anything, by rejecting it all. As long as I reject it, I can find peace. Let me pay the price. Heleen, let me pay the penalty, do not prevent me, do not distract me from this, because it is the only way in which I shall find peace … "'

'Eva, to be quite clear … Look, read this as well: "The Christians are so proud of their high-minded morality. Offer your left cheek to him who strikes your right cheek. They forget one thing: depravity. Berthold is my partner in this -, it is moral insanity. We are both morally insane. He because of what he does, I because of what I tolerate. I destroy the highest in myself, in order for the lowest to rampage in him. My work and my laws, my Tablets of Stone … And there is only one thing that makes this unbearable situation bearable -, that I do penance for it every day. The suffering, the deprivation, the denial, that is my only share-of-happiness. That is how I pay off my debt, how I absolve myself. I wanted to be offered even more, so that I could deny myself even more … '''

'Do you understand this, Eva …? You, his twin sister?'

'Yes, I think I do understand …'

The black crows wheel and skim the low white polders. Heleen withdrew into David's letter. I think that I understand it … I know it … it carries me with it … the one, the eternal swing of the pendulum … the eternally disturbed, eternally recovering, never restored equilibrium. At school we learned about storms and about trade winds. A depression creates the storm, there was a deficit. Deficit equals Debt -, debt makes one thirst for penance. That is how a storm is created. The pangs of conscience are the depression, the feeling of a deficiency that tries to redeem itself through penance … that is how the Storm is created. Those who sell short must pay back, those who take too much make restitution, this is how the storm exhausts itself, this is how equilibrium is restored. Storms and trade winds … deficit, surplus … this is how equilibrium is restored. He sought harmony in misfortune. For life to be bearable, he had to inflict death upon himself daily. I knew this about him, even before I read it, I think I have known this about him for years. The swing of the pendulum … the eternally disturbed, eternally recovering, never restored equilibrium. In some people, guiltless happiness is enough to disturb the equilibrium - they inflict death on themselves in self-denial. I have known this -, as a child, I could not be happy -, it very quickly became too much for me, I soon looked for a reason to be sad -, I fled the oppression of happiness for the depression of sadness, this see-saw is called: melancholy. It is all the same: storms and trade winds. A deficit that supplements itself, surplus that empties itself. The Duty urge also, the duty urge, without content, aim, or reason! Duty is Debt, the desire to pay daily for Life with Death. To inflict Death on oneself in Life … in Mortification, in self-sacrifice, in self-denial … foretaste of Death … Life-urge pitted against Death-urge … the swing of the pendulum … the eternal, the only. All things. Berthold, the proud one, considers himself short-changed by life. The storm within him is moving in a different direction …

'No, Eva, this is not right … it isn't true the way you put it. Just think of all those people who do not reflect, who are selfish … thousands and thousands who give short measure, who take too much and yet do not think they must pay or do penance …'

'The others do penance for them. Where one person pays too little, the other pays too much. And so equilibrium is restored again.'

Sometimes there is *one* who must pay for the whole world, and who will not find rest until he has paid for what millions over the centuries have failed to expiate. He spills his blood ... spilling is a form of giving ... and so equilibrium returns. Storms and trade winds. I shouldn't say that, they would reproach me saying: you are making something exalted down-to-earth. No ... this way I am making something down-to-earth into something exalted.

The water flows around our feet -, the solemn water. Not a murmur rises from the depths. We watched the first day of the New Century marching past us, David and I -, it marched through us -, we were marched through it.

All things pass through us, pass over us. I have known this in many senses -, but it was never revealed to me quite like this before, a new clarity burst open in me just then. And it is all contained in this one thing: Totality. Because it takes such a hold of us, wherever it touches us - if it touches us! - this is why we fancy it to be ours alone. Totality - eternally blossoming tree, eternally bubbling spring, tree of life, deathspring, eternally unfolding comprehension, skyrocket against the night sky, bursting into never-ending multiple colours ... Wondrous existence, in which this very thing is unspoken, is forgotten. Among people it is safer to talk about anything but this ...

'No, Eva, this is not right, it is unjust that one person should do penance for the other, it is illogical too, that one should pay for all. One -, I know who you mean. I was brought up with it -, that is why I have resisted it since childhood. I stamped my foot in protest at it. It ran completely counter to my sense of justice. It still does.'

Yes -, what Heleen says is right. It does run counter to what is called natural justice, that *one* might be able to do penance for others, for many. Because what is called justice only knows an imposed penalty and a forced payment ... because the so-called crime is not a real debt and generates in the perpetrator not the storm but rather the payment of the debt. But whoever feels the world's debt weighing on himself as though it were his own debt, for him there is no other settlement than the ultimate payment: death penalty, death ... the martyr has chosen his own fate, otherwise he is no martyr. And whoever quenches his own urge for his own penance, how could he be the poorer, how could it ever be disastrous for him? He gains the very best of all, he gains peace. One person chases riches, another chases absolution, and there is nothing in the world that surpasses the thing that mortals chase after. Seeking pleasure -, avoiding pain. But each person knows only the price of what he is after, not of what others are after -, and this produces the confusion -, the unfounded praise, the undeserved blame … Each one is convinced that he has chosen the best share. Each one has chosen, for himself, the best share. Justice is not only what serves us!

'Maybe, Heleen, maybe you will come back to this one day, along another route.'

First acceptance without a fundamental grasp … then rejection without real understanding -, finally the understanding that is both acceptance and rejection -, that is neither rejection nor acceptance.

'But let's assume it is like that, that one person can do penance on behalf of another. Is this a reason for him to prevent his poems from being published? Surely it was his duty towards others to do this. By giving his poems to humanity, he would have done a part of that penance, as he calls it, as you understand it … do you see, Eva, that it doesn't fit?'

'If it were true that a poet composes poems for others! But do you think that is true, Heleen? Just think of this word: Immortality! Just think of this: "But I shall rise again in splendour in my poetry."' No, no … whoever tries to inflict death upon themselves cannot at the same time chase after immortality. He wanted to go under … he had decided this for himself … in this sense, too, he inflicted death upon himself … He wanted neither children nor poems as his legacy …

The wind has died down … somewhere an excess has emptied, somewhere a shortfall has been replenished. The sky is tired, and out of its tiredness snow falls, out of its failure of will, out of its indifference …. White and still and wide the polders sleep under the indifferent sky.

Oh, Heleen … I thought I knew he was dead, at home in the small room, by the window, when Ben told me -, just now I thought so again, we were standing together in front of the synagogue - but I did not know. Only now is it approaching me, I can feel it focused on me like a sharp point, a glowing white point and it penetrates the fibres of my soul, it pushes … it pushes, deeper it forces its way into me. I want to scream, I hear the echo of a scream, that came out of me, that tore out of me … Jaap and Ben were knocked back by it, and then Eddy was born … But now I do not scream … and like a receding wave, like a pain dying down, it fades away, and it may never return. Because I will first go to Father and Mother, and soon I will go home …

I heard the echo of a scream -, I am standing here by the water, I brush the snow from my coat, I see the crystals bursting in a melting snowflake. We were on the point of flying at one another when Klaas the watchmaker came along, struggling through the icy, grey snow. We stopped him and David asked him: 'Is this still the fourth or is it the fifth

Hanukkah-evening? She says: the fourth -, I say the fifth, and we were about to start fighting over it.' Klaas stood laughing which made the pendulum clock resting on his shoulder look like a seesaw: 'And whoever wins is right. So you'd better give it all you've got, because it's the fifth evening.' And a snowflake landed on the rough fabric by the third button on his coat, a snowflake which was melting, and as it melted, the crystals burst and became transparent, and became luminous light. I thought … a thousand miracles … miracles everywhere, and in me the fullness swelled, the plenitude of life, all too full, too abundant, and my forehead was covered in sweat …

David, my brother - my little brother … you brought death to yourself, but in me you still live, you still revive, every moment you revive, for we both shared the same beginnings …

'Heleen, what do you think, shall we go to my parents now? They are expecting us about now …'

8
By the Sea

The long, low boat lies at an angle to the end of the jetty, its bow facing outward, in a silvery summer morning light, in a slight haze, in the satiny, pearly water of the Wadden Sea. Nestling on the distant horizon, the low, flat coastline, a grey strip the width of a finger in which little towers have been planted, forming one straight line in one flat plane. In clear weather the shoreline is different, then the distances are evident, even colours are visible.

In the past, distant villages on a misty horizon always reminded me of what we used to call 'transfers'. They, too, conceal bright colour in mysterious haziness. You stuck them on saucers, on white walls, on the back of your hand -, you pulled away the opaque membrane covering the layer of colour, you stared breathlessly at it.

The similarity with today is so striking and so amusing because I know what is behind the mist: a flag flies from one of those towers, one of the little towns is gaily decked out, there is the glinting brass of music marching past flashes of gold from ear ornaments seen through the lace of caps. An exuberant crowd presses through the narrow little streets and the sound of horses snorting is all around -, I know that so well, I know it all from my childhood, the pleasures and revels, the delights, the enchantments of a midsummer country festival, a special high day, right at the height of holiday happiness, with games, parades, trotting races, and all the children from the island who are staying here, who live here, they will travel over there, the boat is like a mother hen, calling her chicks, it could be heard as far as the North Sea beach, right on the other side of the island …

Eddy and Claartje are going with Heleen, the children call her aunt, they have become attached to her. We mostly spend our holidays together. At first she was driven only by the need to talk about David, to find him again in me, and she revealed this to us with an almost cool honesty, but gradually it changed. This is how things take shape, this is how attachments are formed. The great differences do not disappear, but as you grow older, you allow attachments to count for more, they have their roots in different soil, they spread their own warmth out over your life -, we have become a place, a home, for her, the children and I.

The tide is rising, you can hear it thundering more insistently over there, where the heavy, cold waves are ... and you see the boat begin to get restless, it cannot wait much longer, it glides across with the tide, it will glide back with the tide, this evening. This evening, after today. Oh ... today. But for the moment I am still theirs, I still belong to them, my two. Claartje leans on her arms over the side, she stands on her own, she stares over the milky, glistening sea, but her eyes are focused inward, and she hums, I can't hear it, but I can see it, it's a familiar habit of hers. I did it too. I stood by the rail and I stared across the channel, across the pale reeds, to the bright green of the meadows, to the boys in the blue water by 'polder seven'. Their naked, wet backs sparkled in the sun -, and I hummed and the deck shuddered beneath my feet and the thick iron bar vibrated in my hands, because of the boat churning water as it swept round the bend, and all became one, and all the gates were wide open, they had to be ... This was how I was formed -, this is how she, too, is being formed. Each person is formed differently by the same things - and the same by different things. All kinds of flowers grow in the same ground. We take what we already have and we see what we already know. There are things in the distance, in the most distant distance, that you can only make out with your gaze turned inward. There is Matthijs, the brother of little Mansje who is always in love -, he's the plant collector, bird-lover, he is looking over the rail at the sea, he sees different things from Claartje. Inside both of them their world is being formed -, they are building their worlds, their worlds build them. If they meet again later on, when they are as old as I am now, they will speak of this summer by the sea, just like Anatole France's Pierre Nozière, speaking about the old days with his school friend -, they did not have a single memory in common. They grew differently in the same soil.

Oh, Mansje ... have you managed to stand next to Eddy again? And how adoringly you look up at him. You look very sweet like this, you are adorable in your adoration. He is a dear boy, he is sixteen, he is mine. I wish I could see his eyes, but I can only see yours, he is standing with his back to me - oh, I gave birth to you, that large, broad back, almost the back of a man - and I am too far away to read in your eyes how his look down at you. He tells me a lot, but he tells me nothing of this.

Perhaps he would tell Claartje, because the two of them are very close … but she doesn't want to hear. She walks away if Mansje starts talking about her crushes. Claartje still lives in complete calm, in the harshness and incomprehension this calm brings with it: 'All those boring books about boring love.' I repeated that this week during our evening cup of tea on the terrace. Mrs Zeegers got embarrassed, she coughed, she blushed; her Attie is said to be 'boy-crazy'. She is big and strong, noisy, full-blooded, and her mother is a little ashamed of her -, but Bart is pure innocence and this rescues the family honour, he is fourteen and even last spring he maintained that a cow can have a calf without the help of a bull … oh, it was ridiculous: four mothers competing over the sexual immaturity of their children.

'Mother … we're sailing, we're off …'

'See you tonight … see you tonight …'

Yes, tonight! First there is: today -, but for now I am still theirs, they keep their rights as long as they keep hold of me; when they let go of me I will belong to myself. And they let go of me and they sail away in the bobbing boat, over the pearly, silvery sea …, and now the coast will soon open itself to them, in red roofs, green meadows, and the little towers will step out of the row and each will find its place, and change places and finally stand still. Then they will drive through the flat, green, sunny countryside in decked-out carts to the little town with all its decorations …

'You're just too late, Mrs Borger.'

She stumbles in her long, wide, black lustre skirt and her plump, pale face is already perspiring.

'It's going to be hot today.'

'Oh yes, it's definitely going to be hot, the heat is already breaking through the coolness …'

We stand side by side. Hadn't I just been thinking about her? I saw her standing there, coarse and large in the dusk, beside a table where a tea light was burning. All over the terrace, tea lights were burning, there was the murmur of the adults' evening chat, the children had gone to bed … Oh, it was ridiculous. Four mothers of growing children, four middle-aged ladies. Eva … Eva … don't be childish … for you know better, for all your forty years you are no 'middle-aged lady' and you will never become one, you know perfectly well that you are Eva! We boasted about the sexual innocence of our children.

Mrs Zeegers crowed victoriously over her story of the cow that could calve without the aid of a bull. But Mrs Van Delden was not to be outdone with her story of the ducks. It was indeed an entertaining tale. Her boy put the drake in the pen, after the duck had laid her eggs. 'Otherwise she won't sit on them and we won't get any ducklings.' I was on the point of asking: what is the matter with us, that we take pleasure, that we all without exception take pleasure in the immaturity and naivety of our children? That we are proud of this, that we are almost ashamed when it isn't like this?

But I did not ask. For they already suspect that I am not altogether an ordinary 'middle-aged lady'. 'But we didn't give anything away' ·, said Nora, when I had known all about her and Ben for quite a while. People always give things away without realizing. Middle-aged ladies do not reflect on things. And I do want to pass for a middle-aged lady in their eyes as far as I can … really I much prefer to fly kites and play marbles with boys, or play robbers in the dunes with boys and girls, and I know that my heart can soar like theirs in the excitement of the game of 'Shepherd, leave your sheep a-wandering …' I also prefer talking with men, but it is better for the children that here, for these weeks, with these staid papas and these critical mamas, among whom I have never learnt to feel at ease, I am a 'middle-aged lady'. Forty years old! 'Next time you reach a number with zero, you'll be fifty.' 'Yes, Eddy …, then I'll be fifty.' A chilly hand placed itself between my shoulder blades and made me shiver momentarily, but that was all. Next time I reach a number with zero, I'll be fifty. Why not …? Why would you shiver …? I shiver because everything has passed and nothing has been accomplished. Nothing accomplished, you say? … what about your cherished indifference? Well … this is what I am, indifferent, beyond all expectations, I really am … this is an accomplishment. You ought to be exceedingly satisfied at that. Exceedingly … Well, I am exceedingly satisfied. People are crowding in front of the fairground tent, but I walk past. They squeal and wriggle and gasp. I know what's going on inside. Nothing worth seeing. I mean that particular … tent … that Punch and Judy show …

And then suddenly old Mrs Borgers raised a warning finger: 'Things can suddenly change.' She said it in such an ominous and oracular fashion ·, I couldn't help thinking of Mrs van Naslaan, I thought that everyone would laugh, but no-one at all laughed, and it was just like twenty years ago. I had left the little town for the big city and I thought: let me always and in all things be like the others. Now the children make this necessary once again.

We took an unoccupied chair from a neighbouring table and she came to sit with us and talked about her life and I realized that it was tragic. She was widowed before the birth of her son and she thought she could keep him to herself all her life. At the age of thirty-five he had never been in love, but last spring he became engaged, and last autumn he was married. She is not capable of loving the wife, nor is she capable of hating her. Most of all she would like to hate her, but can't manage it ... Things can suddenly change ...

Yes, things can suddenly change. Change may already be close to them, maybe not Claartje yet, but Eddy definitely, the first stirrings, the first disruptions, the first experience that others have your happiness and peace of mind in their hands and that their power is not in proportion to their worth and worthiness, or to your own worth and worthiness ... Isn't it dreadful ... that this sentiment should spontaneously formulate itself in me ... is this really how you experienced things? Yes ... and you came through it! Change may be close to them, without them knowing. He was close to me and I did not know it ...

He had been staying here on the island for days and I suspected nothing ... and they were talking about him and describing him and from their words nebulous images formed, but it wasn't him.

Deep golden lamplight shone out of a window, and Mansje pointed into the distance ... 'Look Claartje, over there, there is where he lives, the interesting gentleman, there in that little villa on top of the last dune!' They were walking close together along the narrow boardwalk, in the twilight, in their white dresses, brown arms around one another's shoulders, thin, dark snakes across the luminous white, but Claartje tore herself away: 'Oh you and your Interesting Gentleman.' And she raced ahead, and squeezed her way through the others to the front, with the little ones, with Klaas-the-Seal-Catcher and his mouth organ. We were on our way to the big beach in the evening, a rare event, a party, we would see the sea phosphoresce in the dark. 'Mr Borger promised that this evening the sea will phosphoresce.' 'Did the sea promise you this, Mr Borger?' He blushed, he was silent -, he is no match for Greeve's irony, they say he is knowledgeable, but he comes across as exceedingly dim. The children bring him the most unappetising, dreadful things from the beach, from the dune, as curiosities ... he takes all their nonsense seriously ... his young wife stands there and smiles, but his mother breaks up the group and her voice is hoarse with hate.

And Doctor Laroche treated everyone to cake, Baker Bartels's pale, soft honey cake -, the boys were allowed to go and buy as much as they wanted. He turned the trip into a party, the old bachelor, the lanterns were his idea too, and they burst cheering into the little general stores and they briefly returned the village to chaos, just as it was beginning to recover, at the end of a long day in the high excitement of the six holiday weeks, and Klaas-the-Seal-Catcher had to go in front with his mouth organ, he was like an Orpheus, with his bright eyes and his sun-bleached hair, in a throng of restless fire globes, yellow, red, speckled, and tiger-striped lanterns, because they all wanted to walk beside him. He is the postman, he is the luggage transporter, he is always ready for anything, he doesn't seem to sleep for the entire holiday -, everyone calls him Klaas-the-Seal-Catcher, but how he came by that name, no-one knows. And he pulls us along after him in a long crocodile, following the sentimental tunes from his mouth organ - it reminds me of rowing on the dark river with Father thirty years ago, among tall illuminated boats, when the King had been King for forty years, though we thought the sparkling colours deep in the water were the best thing, and another little boat sailed past ours with a man sitting in it who was playing the same tunes on his mouth organ, and now, I would suddenly like to know who that man was … We walked one behind the other, along the narrow boardwalk that has been laid over the dunes and down into the hollows from the Wadden beach right across to the big beach by the open sea. The bare slopes up are soft, feet stamp the planks deep into the sand, every day they have to be lifted out again, but in the wide hollows with vegetation they spring back with every step. And the globes were shining brighter and brighter, an intense, self-enclosed glow … and the sound of the sea was coming closer and closer, the sea crashed towards us, the dune valleys were growing wider and wilder, our descents were getting steeper and steeper, again and again we descended into the night and the silence, only to climb yet again towards the day and the crashing … This immense darkening sky above us … this terrifying sea stretching before us … this eternal earth, where each of us appears for his one, singular moment -, this earth which draws us to it, draws us into the light, embraces us and then banishes us, back into the murky depths from which we had emerged, for we each have our one, singular moment … and two 'middle-aged ladies' were talking behind me about their children's school reports. Eternal earth, eternal impenetrable secret … and all the time we were getting closer to the crashing, it was getting closer to us and it was as though I had never before heard what I have been hearing incessantly for so many days and so many nights. Scents rose up from the valleys, they whispered around me, they wanted to encircle me, they crept up on me, they touched me as though with fingers, but the gates are closed. Smell is smell, sound is sound, wind is wind, and that is it. 'The Cosmic Spirit, who was very much an artist' … I know all about that. Opium makes you dream … dreams deceive. At school Eddy learns about 'cooling mixtures …' there are magic mixtures too … but not for me.

From the outside the tent looks nice enough, but there is nothing to see behind the striped canvas. It flaps in front of an empty space -, ghosts have no substance. Yet I couldn't help but notice there were some openings after all, and I thought: if I surrender to them it will be under cover of darkness. I was so safe walking along, I was right behind Eddy and Claartje, I thought: these two are mine. Mine -, they are mine. There are prettier girls than Claartje, there are sturdier boys than Eddy, but these two are mine. They are Ben's too, I do tend to forget that. I forget him as a father, for I never knew him as a husband. Since Nora brought little Noortje into the world, he comes to us much less, she keeps him away from us, perhaps she's right. We parted as friends -, and still there are moments when I can't grasp it. Sometimes it comes over me, like a daze -, surely it isn't really true that we divorced? We were together for so many years, even here on the island, in the old days -, the boardwalk had just been laid, the post came every other day - it was unreal and solid. Unreal and solid. Anna Ebner said: 'I am completely shocked -, I thought you were happily married -, even though you were a flirt, Eva, because you were, even though you denied it. Even though you aren't any more, now that you're allowed to be. And I never thought it would be Ben who strayed.' No, I never thought it would be either, Ben himself hadn't thought it would be -, it was Nora really. We were: Ben and Eva. Eva and Ben. Ben, Eva and the children. Ben and Eva and Eddy and Claartje - Eddy, after his father, Claartje, after my mother. We had the children and we had the house and we had Miss Rika -, she called Ben 'master', she called Eddy 'the little boy' -, to me she said 'my missus' and to Claartje 'wretched child', and of course she liked the males best, that's what old ladies do. We had the furniture and the vases and the clock, and the prints on the walls, everything in its set place, and the basket with the butcher's, baker's and grocer's books. And the milk bottles in the porch. And the calendar with the birthdays on it. The wild duck cage. But I knew that. That we never escape the wild duck cage, I knew that. And there were days, when I forgot the wild duck cage, forgot the wide-open spaces, there were days and evenings like this. I wove mats with Claartje, I did sums with Eddy and the veranda doors rattled gently -, but I didn't sense the open spaces. I thought: it was an illusion, they aren't there, just like … the other thing.

Then you think of love letters you once wrote, no response of the heart confirms the memory, it must have been an illusion. Jaap says: it's like the day after, when you think about what you did when you were drunk, and you believe it because you know it, but nothing is so lifeless as a knowledge you don't feel. They always returned. The wide-open spaces did not remain silent for long. They raised their voices and I realized how weak the power of imagination is in us. But this was not because of the wild duck cage, it has nothing to do with the wild duck cage, each one of us has a gateway to the open spaces -, it comes from the strength of our desire, the pressure of our longing, our unbearable homesickness.

Ben was right to break up our lives together in time, and marry Nora -, what he was seeking, what he felt was missing was available. It's all the same to me, because I reach for the unattainable anyway. What I seek is nowhere and everywhere. Nowhere and everywhere. I don't like travelling anyway … I like to stay where I am, to return to where I've been before. This is where I get to know the ways to the open spaces. As soon as you are in a place where you cease to see anything except what you can see by looking inwards, then the ways to the open spaces will be clear for you. I would even prefer not to leave the village ever again, and I will stay there, unless I have to accompany the children on journeys.

He let me have the children, and we went away and we got some of the furniture, we took the piano with us, we took Miss Rika with us. And for a long time afterwards, the ghosts of old shapes, of lost light, lingered around the furniture … reminders of the places where they had once stood. If I was sitting upstairs reading and Claartje was downstairs practising the piano, then child and piano sometimes suddenly leapt back to the old house and she was sitting between the windows and I could hear the murmur of the street, the man with lemons from one direction and the man with briquettes from the other and everything that I would otherwise never have remembered … and sometimes I could hear the rattling of the veranda doors and the whispering of the spaces around the green-gold poplar tops and the Andante from Schubert's Unfinished … until my breath had been held so long that it weighed on my heart, until the welling tears forced their way from under my eyelids … but now the piano has belonged in the little house for a long time and we belong in the village. Now when I think 'home', it is this little house, the village that expects us back in the autumn. The children are happy there, with their playmates, at their schools, we buried Miss Rika there. In the evenings I often walk up and down along the gravel road outside the house, in a golden glow of sunset.

Behind the outstretched fields of rye lies the main road, with the tram and the bicycles you can't hear, only see. There is a bumpy field where the wild sorrel glows in a haze of flowering grass -, and there is clover, a cool-silvery green among the russet-gold rye. Oat plumes make a dreamy, metallic sound as they brush against each other, that sometimes reminds me of the tiny bells on the Torah scroll, in the synagogue, long ago. The wind, made visible in glossy waves, strolls towards me across the fields ... and I watch the strolling wind, I watch the glowing sky and over there is the city. So many years of my life were spent there. I let these years slip through my fingers, like a stream of dry, glinting sand. As a child you could sometimes occupy yourself for hours doing that. You grabbed a handful and your hand was full to bursting and you let it run out and your hand was empty and you did it again. And your eyes stared, your mind was empty, and yet it stayed with you for days. It stayed with me for years. Now, I let the years of my life run through me like this. The children have cycled off and the gravel road is deserted, twilit white, it stretches away between the bright green hedges; a long, low farmhouse shuts out the view on one side, the red brick glows more warmly than the field of sorrel, the thatched roof shines like a silver pelt. And I watch the shifting light, and I walk right along the edge of the crop fields, the stalks are taller than I am, the wind pushes them against me, I let them run gently through my fingers, and along with the wind, the years flow through me. I gather them together in one handful, and I am full to bursting with all those years like my hand was with sand -, then I grabbed more than I could manage, and now too, a human being can only hold so much all at once, can only grasp so much all at once, can only be so much all at once. Holding is grasping. Understanding is being. The years are stacked up in me to my throat and I would like to cry, but they are flowing and this flowing removes the tension. They flow first fast and then slow, there are years that mean everything and years that mean nothing. The old years always weigh heaviest, the years in which I was formed, in the old set-up, the old covenant, and I lived in the little house between the seventh and eighth lamp post ... and I grew up and I moved to the city, to the school by the water, to the attic room at Bertha and Saar's, later I moved in with Ernestien, and I married, and just like the colours of a soap bubble ... or a box of Bengal matches when you struck a green one, a yellow and a red one in turn ... or humming tops which change their note if you strike them with the flat of your hand ... time and again I feel like a different Eva while at the same time I know that I was always the same Eva ... and my hand is empty. The wind strolls across the fields in rusty-silver gleams, it comes to me across the tops of the ears of corn, the oats rustle, the rye whispers, the children have cycled off, the gravel road is deserted, and once more I grab my handful of years, they flow like a stream of dry, glinting sand and my hand is empty.

'To prepare oneself …' How did Montaigne put it? 'That to study philosophy is nothing but to prepare oneself to die.' Actually, it's not completely true, it may not even be true at all, but it is a nice thing to say to yourself, to say inside yourself on the deserted, twilit white gravel road, at sunset: 'Death, where is thy sting …' You have not gained your freedom unless Death holds no more terror, until in the fullness of life death loses its terror … I reach out sometimes of late, in precious moments, to taste Life-and-Death in one -, Unio Mystica.

And we walked in the dark to the big beach, the scents rose up from the dune hollows, the children stamped on to the boards, off the boards, and the closer we came, the more the rhythm disappeared from our footsteps, because we could no longer hear the mouth organ. The heavy crashing tore the tunes to shreds, the wind carried them away, into the dark valleys, sometimes right past your ear and you caught one of them briefly. We were walking faster and faster, because Mr Borger had said: 'If we don't speed up, the moon will have got there first.' And they all shouted this to one another, half laughing, half fearful, it ran along the cavalcade, from Klaas-the-Seal-Catcher, past the children in their luminous, light clothes, to Doctor Laroche, who was bringing up the rear with his swimming things under his arm and a red lantern in his hand. Eventually a girl grasped the words, moulded a rhythm in them, put a tune to them: 'Speed up soon and beat the moon', and everyone joined in, we trotted along laughing, so that the sand crunched and the boards danced beneath our feet, until there it was at last, the sea, between the tops of the last dunes. Orange-red light shone out of the little villa. 'That's where he lives, the old gentleman.'

'You and your old gentleman, he isn't old at all.'

'His hair is grey.'

'But he isn't old.'

'He's got … heavenly eyes …'

That is Attie's voice and Claartje nudged Eddy and burst out laughing. 'Did you ever hear anything so idiotic?'

'His wife can't walk …'

'Yes she can … I've seen it with my own eyes.'

'But she can only walk for a very short distance.'

'Because she had a stroke.'

'Because she has a bad heart …'

'Her heart stopped beating when she heard that her son had been killed in battle.'

A sharp, harsh laugh.

'If her heart had stopped beating then she would be dead now.'

'Her son …? Their son, surely …?'

'No, not their son, only her son, because she was a widow before.'

'I suppose that makes her an orphan now that her son is dead …'

'Oh you heartless boy …!'

'I say, Matthijs, do you know what the wife of a widower is called?'

'She's from England.'

'Oh no she isn't, she speaks French.'

You are full of imaginings, you don't know where they came from, a shadowy world composed of an array of the weirdest shapes. At school we learned how the Eger, Inn and Danube meet near Passau -, the Eger is yellow, the Inn is green, the Danube is blue. Endless streams flow towards you like this, crossing the years, your whole life through … their voices called up shades from that shadowy world … but it wasn't him, I couldn't see him.

One of the mothers said: 'Yes, he really does have extraordinary eyes.'

'Oh, please tell me, are they blue or are they brown?'

'Well really, Attie -, I don't exactly know.'

He was close by me and I didn't see him.

And the moon had got there first - it hung pale reddish in the heathland on the horizon, it rose as though trapped in bloody membranes, and we reached the sea, and they were momentarily dumbstruck after the fullness of their jollity, in front of this dark, thundering grey-silvery surf, almost swallowed up by the night, visible in luminous strips, that for days on end has been their playground. And we went down to the very edge of the beach and we stood in the dark wet sand and we peered towards our feet looking for the sparkling edges, the phosphorescent seams of the ebbing waves, but one after the other rolled out of the surf, tumbled sleepily landwards, but not a single one brought with it from afar something of the wondrous light …

'Oh, Mr Borger … and you had promised us so definitely …!'

'Yes, I had indeed! But who can know everything in advance? Not a single person. Nature is always capricious.'

'Well, don't think you'll get away with it that easily!'

With their long, bare arms, they wove a circle round him, they jeered and booed, they stuck their tongues out; his young wife laughed, but the plump, pale face of his mother was contorted in anger. Her eyes spat hatred, at the young wife, at the uncooperative sea, at all those shameless children. I could be like that … maybe ….

They were soon consoled, they shared the cake, they threw themselves on top of Klaas to 'bury him alive' and a lantern caught fire.

We rejoined the path through the dunes -, I glanced round briefly at the red-gold lamp in the window … something I had read as a child surfaced briefly, I wanted to grasp it, but it evaded me, and the thundering receded. The air around us grew milder again and scented, after the briny chill at the shore, and the moon had freed itself from the reddish tendrils, the bloody membranes in order to ascend, naked and pure, to the apex. It had already risen above the edge of the wide hollow and transformed it into a dream valley of shadows and silver light, and right in the middle we saw Minnie van der Elst and Betty, her unmarried sister, and Paula and Jack and Greeve, who they call 'the cynic' here, like Miss Korff did to Penning, years ago at school … the school by the water, with Leendert and Truitje, who have been grown-ups for some time and the 'old boss' who is long dead now. I was 'Miss', I wore a large, striped pinafore, and it was twenty years ago … He does resemble the other cynic a little, both in character and looks, this Greeve, but more distinguished. He is actually rather attractive. It felt good to think this, because it leaves me cold. I have been liberated from all that.

We saw them sitting there, and they heard us walking past and looked up and saw us and called to us. Greeve called me. He has a blond beard, and light blue irises with dark blue edges. Betty looked up, she looked at me, she looked at him, she looked from him to me. I thought: this leaves me cold. I have finished with all that. The gates are closed for good, closed before they opened, closed before anyone ever entered. No men. 'The Cosmic Spirit, who was very much an artist …' but I have seen through the little game.

'Will you come and sit with us?'

'I'm with the children.'

'Oh, Mother, we can go back with Mansje and Matthijs and their mother.'

'Yes, indeed, they can come back with me.'

'What about you though?'

'I have to go back to the hotel anyway, Miesje always wakes up at this time for her drink.'

The ground was warm, warm and spongy, I was sitting half in shadow and half in moonlight, it was as though the whispering wind and pounding sea had been completely eliminated -, it was so still there in the hollow. The sudden stillness made me dizzy. Suddenly there seemed to be a great deal going on around me and outside of me. I reached, I reached … but I couldn't feel it, I couldn't grasp it. Greeve sat watching me. Once I would have, once I would have … been unable to ignore it. It did not affect me. I thought: this does not affect me.

They were talking about the 'vegetarian married couple'. The phrase was coined by Doctor Laroche. 'Doctor Laroche, this is not nice,' said the vicar's wife the day before yesterday, at tea. 'But, madam … they are literally vegetarians as well!' 'Yes, they are literally, but that is not what you mean.' He smiled -, not even the vicar's wife could resist that smile.

Minnie van der Elst had run into them that afternoon, at the beach. They were walking with little fingers linked, but when they saw her, they let go of one another, blushed, and rushed headlong back where they came from. A married couple! What would the world come to if everyone behaved like that? And why would you need to get married if you insist on that way and no other? I had also repeatedly seen them out walking -, as it happens just the previous evening. And I had indeed asked myself: how did all these people here get to know about it? Who is the originator of these rumours? They are lodging with 'old mother Bos' in the ancient gabled house -, they each have their own room there. Every night they lock their doors, against each other, against that … They don't want it, they have not been able to reconcile themselves to it, they have opted for a celibate marriage, a vegetarian marriage, says Doctor Laroche. All the talk happens around them, they have no part in it. They are both tall and thin, sallow and blond, they could be brother and sister. They could not find the way, they could not build the bridge. None of us finds this way, none of us builds the bridge, no-one has ever consciously accepted what he once consciously rejected -, we flee into the refuge of marriage, we find salvation in the dogma of marriage. A man rationalises it like this: it's why you get married. He doesn't stop to ask himself if it is lust or love that drives him towards his wife. The woman rationalises it like this: it's how you get children. And she stops being ashamed of her animal side. Marriage is their protection. In the Church they no longer have to think about God, in the Party about justice, in the State about morality and in Marriage about celibacy. These two are different -, no marriage can make the impure pure for them and the animal divine - they reject impurity.

And the vicar's wife said: 'But what about children?' No, vicar's wife, this won't do! No human being on earth was conceived out of duty. Nor do we eat meat to so that we won't be overwhelmed by animals. No-one may demand the latter of vegetarians, no-one the former of … vegetarian marriage partners.

And we sat on the dark, spongy ground and we heard the children stamping along the planks, some distance away by now. We sat in the deep hollow in moonshadow and silvery light and the moon grew smaller, seemingly more compact, more brilliant, as it rose in the sky. And Minnie van der Elst said: 'They are distancing themselves from nature.' But she blushed, even before she had uttered the words and she glanced shyly at Greeve. He is an intimate friend of theirs. She and her husband despise one another by daylight and embrace in the dark. Greeve has already brought him back to her, and her back to him more than once. 'But why, Mr Greeve, why don't these people divorce?' 'Yes indeed, madam, why don't these people divorce …?' His words speak volumes. This is something remote from me … that bodies meet while minds do not … Hell! And they live in it, so it is not their idea of hell. But it doesn't bring them satisfaction -, just like other people, a bearable marriage provides the justification and they will in the end be driven apart.

'I think so too,' added Paula, with a hot blush and burning eyes. 'You are right. They are distancing themselves from nature.'

'Nature …'

'Yes, Jack … Nature! Why do you repeat that after me so disparagingly? You repeated that so mockingly.'

He did not answer, shrugged his shoulders in endless, reluctant impotence. He stared up at the silver sky, I could see his fine profile, his thin lips, his straight nose. Dear boy … dear, dear man … I knew exactly how you were feeling, what you were thinking. The scents surrounded us, we could hear the children and the mouth organ in the far distance. I could see him breathing, I could see him thinking: Nature. This pure sky, these sweet, pure scents, this immaculate moon, all this is moving, transporting … and then that. All of it is: Nature. Oh dear man, you will never get there. No more than I will. You will never find the way, never build the bridge out of chaos … you will not reconcile shame and shamelessness, what the stable boy's words were alluding to and the Tallest Towers … no more than I … I sent my thoughts in another direction, so as not to be thinking of the same thing as him at the same time as him in the same way … And we were silent. We sat at the bottom of the hollow, between the rough, dark sides, like a small troop of ants that had come tumbling down from all directions, all jumbled up -, we were complete strangers, but this formed a bond between us for a moment. 'These things, which cause so much sorrow and distress.'

And Paula sought his eyes, her full, red lips apart, but he doesn't like her, so he didn't sense it, and he didn't give his eyes to her. She gave hers to him, her cheeks were burning. She is twenty-three, she is full-blooded and noble, perhaps she will build the bridge, perhaps she will find the way. Not if he is unwilling. If he is unwilling, she is lost. Because she is not sure of herself ·, thanks to those other two, the celibates, she feels ashamed. And so she is a thousand times closer to me than to them …

'Oh …' said Betty all of a sudden, in the silence. 'Oh …' said Betty, 'I understand it so well, I understand it so w …' She stopped, as though someone had hit her on the mouth, as though a sharp knife had cut the word in two, sliding along her lips.

'Why did you stop?' Minnie asked.

'Because we are … in a group of married and unmarried people …'

'Well …' said Jack and he gave Betty a quick look.

'We aren't small children.'

Paula spoke angrily, instantly blushing bright red again, but she regretted it immediately ·, Betty is well into her thirties.

'We are modern people …'

'Why do you understand it so well, Betty?' Greeve asked this in his usual sardonic manner, but with an unexpected gentleness, which made her sister take notice. She was sitting in the full moonlight, she seemed so helpless, slowly the pained expression at her sister's clumsy words disappeared, she was almost beautiful, she appeared no older than eighteen. I thought: perhaps this is the moment … If he only sees her now as beautiful, then she can be ugly again tomorrow, then the spark will have flown, the seed will have been sown … if he can just see her now as beautiful. She looks delicate and soft in this moonlight ·, tomorrow the sun will make her bloodless and angular, and she has ugly red sunburn, but perhaps it will be decided this evening. The height of the moon will determine her life, her one, her only life, life will now decide her fate ·, mother or infertile virgin … Can she feel this, she is sitting so motionless in the light that renders her beautiful, so that he looks at her as if he is seeing her for the first time …

'Well, Betty …?'

'Well … I mean … you want to do so many other things together. Together you want … oh, everything. Together you strive for … everything. And why does it always come down to that, actually …?'

It sounds almost tortured … it has been locked inside her for a long time.

'Then they shouldn't touch each other at all …'

Again the passion, the blush. This is a kind of struggle. For whom … for what?

'Oh … Paula … you walk like that with little fingers linked with your sister, with your father, with your brother …'

'You don't suddenly let go …'

'No, Minnie … there was no need for them to have … done that … anyway.'

Unemphatic. Nobody responds. Greeve laughs. 'And why did they get married then?'

'Indeed, Betty, why did they get married?'

'For all the rest. Because you need each other, because you complement each other, because, as man and wife, you are different from one another in so many ways.'

'And all without any connection to that other thing that they … the veget … that those two reject? Is that what you think?'

More sharply sardonic, less gentle … and he suddenly looks at me again, and the moment has passed. Now the moon is almost directly above the hollow, we are in its full light, we are sitting in a circle, our shadows fall behind us, mingle around us. All these people are worried, some more, some less, some because of uncertainty, some through fear -, he because of his aversion, she because of her desperate desire, and Greeve because of me. Only I have finished with all of this. Then, unexpectedly, Paula turned to me.

'And may I ask what you think?'

'*Et vous, madame, qu'en pensez vous?*' Where did this bizarre phrase spring from? Claudine … So shall I respond as Claudine …? '*Moi, je m'en fiche …*' No, for it isn't like that. True, like the moon just now, I have freed myself from the reddish tendrils, but there is still the glow of old dreams -, like the afterglow of sunsets. An echo rose in me, as though from the depths: 'No-one should ask me these things, I know nothing of them.' But I was silent.

'Do you believe that it is even possible between a man and a woman … Platonic love?'

'Platonic …' mocked Greeve, the classicist. 'Thou shalt not take His name …'

'Is it possible …?'

And I remained silent, for what could I say? Greeve looked at me, steadily and fiercely.

'Those who know say nothing -, those who speak know nothing.'

For goodness sake, you know less than nothing about me … But I was silent.

'Sphinx' cried Minnie van der Elst.

'Oh, dear people … we do make things difficult for ourselves … The Greeks certainly had things much easier, compared to us. They knew how to live, they really knew how to live. "Human honour and nobility …" sorry Betty.' Pure sarcasm … oh, she's about to cry.

When Greeve says: 'Greek' or 'the Greeks' everyone puts on an erudite look -, even Jack turned towards him. Paula asked: 'What do you mean by that?'

'By what …? Honour and nobility …?'

'No, no … the Greeks … How did they live …?'

'Well indeed … how …' And he smiled and looked at me with his light blue irises ringed with dark blue. And then he suddenly flung himself backwards, and lay on his back on the ground, his fair-skinned face upturned towards the moon, his voice rising vertically as though he was addressing the cool, clear sky. 'At any rate without this Judaeo-Calvinist moralising.'

'Judaeo-Calvinist …?'

He sat upright again.

'West European, if you'd rather …'

And then a footfall in the distance on the boardwalk and someone whistled: the opening of Tchaikovsky's 'Pathétique' symphony. And everything changed instantly. The Inn is green, the Eger is yellow, the Danube is blue, each river flows toward the others with its own colour, flowing over everything, mingling with it, united with it, with the moon, with the shadows in the hollow: the opening of Tchaikovsky's 'Pathétique.' Unknowingly we had waited for this, it will now belong with this evening for ever more.

'Who's coming …?'

'Doctor Laroche. I can tell from his steps.'

It was the doctor, in his blue linen suit, with his head like a shiny round cheese. His swimming suit under his arm, his red lantern in his hand.

'He stayed behind to swim.'

'Are you lot planning an overnight stay in that hollow by any chance?'

'No, no, we're going home.'

'Yes, we must go home …'

At that moment I didn't know that he was so close to me. And I leaned far out of the second-floor window, all my life I have loved leaning out of an upstairs window, half in the wild duck cage, half in the open air, and the moon hung above the Wadden Sea, a boat glided right across the ruffled silver causeway, you could hear the gentle, wet slapping sounds against the wooden sides of the boat … and in the distance the force of the breakers, reverberating through the sleeping island.

I thought of nothing … of something … of everything intermingled … I felt my eyes open wide and staring. And I knew that something was approaching, something difficult, not something light, and it paused in front of me - it was Greeve's words …

'Without this Judaeo-Calvinist sexual moralising. They knew how to live. They really knew how to live.'

And the Things of the Body which cause them so much sorrow and distress …

Not them. Us, all of us. We play with words like 'atavism' and 'convention' -, but this is deeper. You root out atavism, you rise above conventions, but this has spread, has choked our entire life with its roots, with its tendrils. All lives -, children's lives, people's lives. 'Without this Judaeo-Calvinist sexual moralising.' I thought: why does this make me downcast, so strangely and intensely downcast? I dived to the bottom of this dejection and surfaced with this: in my view of the world, I had thought people to be alike -, functions organized in like ways, organisms functioning in like ways. This deep distinction that Greeve's words carved out between people -, unsettles my view of the world, this takes my breath away, I feel a sense of panic … and yet I was certainly not hearing it for the first time this evening. But it is indeed for the first time that it makes me so deeply downcast, takes my breath away … Once as a child I had to go through thick smoke, hanging across the whole street, it took my breath away, but I came through and I could breathe again … I came through and I could breathe again, I even breathed as though I had never breathed before, I wanted to shout across the night sea, across the wedge of light, I wanted to shout it to the hidden shore: Oh night sea, wedge of light, hidden shore … all this difference is in essence sameness, in the way that the different types of light at Pole and Equator are in essence the same, in essence one. Everything anchors itself firmly in Life, everything tears itself loose for Death. They anchored themselves firmly in life with their desiring senses, and with their deep and penetrating thought they tore themselves loose for Death. The self-denial, the self-betrayal of thought. Raising up … dashing down. We anchor ourselves firmly in Life with unshakeable dogma, theological dogma, scientific dogma, and in self-torturing abstinence we tear ourselves loose for Death. The self-denial of celibacy, the mortification of the flesh. Always everything different, always everything the same. Organisms functioning in like ways, functions organized in like ways. Never before had I felt the Pendulum Swing so magnificently and so simply. Oneness, Eternity, Totality eternally enclosed in itself, collapsing, closing in, opening out. Urges that are functions, delusions that are functions … lust and revulsion, fear and joy, certainty and doubt. It is fulfilled in the foolish Borger's foolish pursuit of useless knowledge, It is fulfilled. What must be performed emerges here, emerges there, as a Delusion or an Urge ...

There they sat in those ancient times by their ancient seas and here we sit in this century by our sea and everything is and remains the same for eternity, people and their passions, seas and their motion.

And the full moon hung above the Wadden Sea, boats floated across the silvery causeway rocking softly and I could not move from the window ... and still I did not know that he was so close to me. Nor the following morning.

I went to the sea, it was a bright morning, a cool morning, the children stayed to play tennis, Heleen had letters to write. The sea rose high and great and dark out of the horizon, against the pale strand. Norderney ... 'Sei mir gegrüsst, du Ewiges Meer.' Why is this phrase so beautiful, so beautiful that I can't help thinking it every day and that it brings tears to my eyes nearly every day? I try to grasp this by repeating it, but it will not be grasped in this way and it escapes me. Small and alone I stand before the sea, the sky ... I surrender to them, they take me out of myself. Sea and sky take me out of myself. Across the blue waves, my eyes anchor themselves deep in the horizon, I am as wide as I can see, I stretch as far as I can think ... my nebulous thoughts lose themselves in my unbounded being -, imagine compact, tiny clouds stretching into thin mists ...

And then suddenly I returned to myself and became once more the tiny compact cloud of a human being with its tiny defined thoughts -, for I saw that I was not alone. Another human being stood there surrendering to the sea and sky and I thought: that could be Mansje's 'Interesting Gentleman'. And he came towards me and he came closer and we saw one another and we recognized one another ...

It had rained that morning, but towards midday it cleared up. Slow, patchy mists rolled across the pools, wound themselves around the trees, hovered over the damp bed of mutedly colourful zinnias ... and placed themselves like a hand on my shoulder, like a hand on my throat in the autumn stillness of the park, so that I could scarcely walk and scarcely breathe ... Music sweeps us to the top of mount Nebo and we see across the Promised Land stretching from Jericho to Zoar, and we are what we see, but we cannot inhabit it -, this is what our eyes once confided to one another ... A lamp shone next to the chestnut tree, but the crown illuminated itself, for every hand-like cluster of leaves was golden, and all the delicate slender hands were linked, a golden dome above the golden dusk glow -, a leaf gleamed at my feet, I inhaled chrysanthemum, I tasted damp -, I inhaled and tasted something that has no name and no shape, I stood in wonder at how it could all be like this, I waited in the calm of the quiet street beside the lit lamp, I had rung the bell of the narrow house with the yellow door, Ernestine's house, and in me the wonderment grew, I stood there encircled in a rustling whisper, I thought: I shall never forget this moment ... and it was twenty years ago and now at last here I am back with you. I do not know where you have been and you do not know where I have been, but now we are here together again. And on that bygone autumn day I dreamed a yellow ochre evening sky above the East Lake ... the gentle little grey waves reflected the yellow light, the thick foam they produced clinging to the pale reeds, two birds flying towards one another, they are going to entrust to one another the secrets of the wide open spaces.

But we two walked past each other, I thought I would hear the thread snap, but it didn't, for we spoke to one another and we walked beside one another along the beach, and we did not know one another's name. He said it first: so who are we, then? And because I hesitated between Ben's name and my maiden name, I simply said: Eva ... I saw him blush and that made me flustered, but it was already too late, he said: 'Then my name is ... Marius ...' By 'then' he meant ... if you are called just Eva.

He is ten years older than me and they had got their facts right: he is married to a French woman and she never recovered her health after she lost her only son in the war. She was a widow with a child when they married, and they never had children together. They live in France for part of each year, by chance they came here to the island, for a short period that is now nearly over.

And I told him about Ben, and we couldn't stay afloat. We also mentioned books that we had read and weren't amazed that they were the same ones -, in itself it means so very little really, and we could not keep ourselves in the air, we each became a compact little cloud, and we drifted down, which lowered my mood. I looked across the sea, which loomed high and huge and dark blue out of the horizon. '*Sei mir gegrüsst, du ewiges Meer* ...' All beauty is intent. - These words formed in me in an instant. I looked up at him, I wanted to ask him, it seemed natural to me that I should ask him: 'Isn't it true ... isn't it true ... that all beauty is intent?' But suddenly he stopped.

'Oh ...' he said, 'That's it ... that's exactly how you looked, when ... when ... that afternoon at the Concertgebouw ...'

'How ... how did I look ...?'

'Like you do now, with a question in your eyes, in your ... eyes. What was it you wanted to ask me then, what do you want to ask me now?'

Like hot air balloons rising through the air ·, they could maintain their height no longer, they came closer to the earth, but when they cast off all the remaining ballast they are soar triumphantly into the spaces. Like when your finger finds your first child's first sharp little tooth, and you are elated ... it is obvious that these teeth must come through and these things probably happen every day, but you had never experienced it yourself before. A few days later he said: 'Couldn't we just once spend a whole morning, a whole afternoon together ...?'

Today ... it is today.

The children have gone to the country festival, they are now half way to the mainland. Perhaps not even that far yet, I walked so fast from there to here. In those short moments I have thought so much, I need to sit down here, against this sloping dune, in the sun, it's still so early. The children are looking in the direction of the mainland, with wide, longing eyes, patches of green slide into the sea towards them, little spires have stepped out of the row ·, each finds its place, like in a game of musical chairs. Decorated carts wait on the bare, high dike. They are sailing over the pale blue sea away from me - beside the great dark blue sea on the other side of the island stands the one who waits for me.

To Heleen I simply said this: 'Twenty years ago, Heleen, I walked past a man who I should have got to know, and he walked past me. But people must be properly introduced to one another ...'

The earth pulls us up from the eternal deeps, pulls us into the light ... and it is over ... we return once more to the eternal deeps, into the vaults which hold the eternal secret. And each moment of emotion, of intensity, all deeper understanding and all wonderment are born in that one, that only instant. But people must be properly introduced to one another. And school reports are also very important.

'What did you ask, Heleen? I was just thinking of something else.'

'Have you met him again, this man ...? Is he here?'

'Yes, he is here ... and I wanted to ... I was going to ... with him ...'
Heleen looked up, she looked at me, I was silent. I believe that in these things we ... one person is quick to think another ridiculous, and the other is quick to think the first one hateful. Where did I read once that contact with other people's intimate lives repels us, that is why we are so hard on each other? Animals creep away when faced with each other's hate ... wherever did I read such a thing?

Never did I suspect that I would ever want to entrust so much of myself to another person. To hand myself over to another person. I am filled to the brim, like rising water -, all of me, even what I had thought had died away, and what seemed forgotten or already spoken of, or eroded, or put aside ... And yet I don't know what I want to say to him. I want to say everything to him, but I prefer to say nothing, if I can't find the right thing to say quickly.

We were little and at home there was a great mystery. Every evening after supper, Father shut himself away in the little side room and stayed there until very late writing on large sheets of paper. Father had deliberately had the smith make a new key for the door which didn't shut properly. But we peeped through the curtains from outside in the street. Finally, early one morning Father took the boat to the city -, the large sheets of paper went with him in a small case. And we besieged Mother, we ambushed Mother, we could always persuade Mother to do things, we swore that we wouldn't reveal Father's secret, not even under torture. 'Oh, Mother, do tell us, go on, tell us, what did Father write on the large sheets of paper, what is going to happen to them today?' 'Father has written a book, Father has written a real novel, it is called *Rabbi and Antisemite*, it is set in Spain, there are palm trees and mountains in it and gardens with fountains and the people there wear robes -.' We wanted to ask ... ask ... ask ... and we did ask, we asked too much. Mother closed her ears to our questions, but we didn't ask the right thing, I certainly didn't ask the right thing, because I can still well remember that I thought: this fullness in me, this breathlessness, which can't be anything other than a bundle of unasked questions, it won't get better, whatever I ask.

A hundred lives have revived in me, I have filled up with this rising tide, I have everything to say to him ... but if I can't say it all in one and the same instant, then I would rather tell him nothing ... we should have found the one right question then, too, about Father's book, but we didn't.

There he is and his eyes are searching, but he can't see me yet. His face has become tense with alertness, the taut face of a stern man. That is how they see him, the two 'middle-aged ladies' who walk past him arm-in-arm in their stiff linen dresses, and they look at him, and they turn round again, but he doesn't notice. He has sent his eyes out hunting, hunting for me, and they have caught me ... and a sun rises across his entire face, and they both look round at the same time, to see who the smile on his lips and in his eyes is for. Yes, me ...! Me, Eva, that smile like an emergent sun is for me ...!

Eva, Eva, don't race down the slope like that, you are almost a middle-aged lady yourself. You have a son of sixteen and a daughter who is fourteen. You are an old person to your grown-up children, what a foolish old person you would be to your grown-up children, to your dear, to your cruel grown-up children if they could see you like this.

I hold your hands tightly and our hands are warm and oh, I have so much to say to you. My whole life, my life ten times over, my ... life with its ups and downs. I want to confide it all in you, it wants to be liberated from me, and that is why my hands shake, my legs tremble, my lips quiver so ... but it must be possible for me to hand myself over to you in an instant ... everything all at once ... in one minute ... Actually, shouldn't there be ... a formula ... for such a complete handover ...?

'Yes, I think there should be, for such a complete handover ... as you put it ... a complete handover ... I can't help laughing at you ...'

'Do I make you laugh ...?'

'Yes, I can't help laughing at you. Come.'

He leads me by the hand up the slope. Yes ... further ... further ... I want to go further ... but we must still be able to see the sea and the sun. Beach life stops by the row of abandoned bathing carriages, we are alone in silence and emptiness, alone with sea and sun. The emptiness, the loneliness of the old dream, now at last we are going to confide our secrets in each other. Bending towards his secret, handing over my secret ...

'You already know a lot ... you know about my marriage ... my children ... his next marriage, and his child ... I've already told you that. I already know quite a lot about you ... And yet ...'

What if I were to tell him about Father's book ... how I asked, and asked and still didn't ask the right thing ...

'Listen a minute. I was quite small and my father had written a book. And I besieged my mother, but I didn't ask the right question. Do you understand that ...? Can you help me..? To find the question ... and the answer ...?'

'Yes, I understand ... And I think that I can help you to find the question and the answer. I can even do it without words. Like this ...'

'Oh ... is this the way to confide everything in one another ...?'

'Yes, this is the way to confide everything in one another ....'

Yes ... you ... you know all right ... I have told you everything. My hands no longer shake, my lips no longer quiver ... I am released from myself ... in one second my lips have confided everything to your lips, yours have confided everything to mine. Twenty years have been spoken.

I want to lie beside you in the sun, I have never before lain beside a man, I have never before kissed a man …

Oh Ben, poor Ben … for years we slept side by side in the same bed and I really did not know what it is to lie beside a man till now at last I am lying here above the sea, in the sun, on the sand, beside him … It still hurts me now, that I will betray you, that I am casting you out … But people in balloons cast everything away, they have to.

'You understand that I don't literally …'

'Yes, I understand … Nor have I ever lain beside a woman, nor have I kissed a woman … nor do I mean this literally … oh it's even less true for me than it is for you … But all those years, twenty years, we have saved this for each other. Let us now share it …'

Your voice wraps round me, your voice is as deep and as sweet as the old dream … your voice points the way back to the dream denied, I am lying on my back in the sand, and my eyes are closed, you are sitting upright, but you bend towards me, I feel you approaching.

I drink from your lips … 'Tamalone kissed Mevena who didn't know how to kiss, until her lips began to move …' I have never understood this, yet it has always stayed with me. My head lies on the warm, soft sand … your mouth, kissing me, your sweet, burning mouth, presses my head more deeply into the sand … with each kiss my liberation becomes complete. Oh you … you know this … that words are not necessary, that it can't be done with words … Oh you … you know this … your kisses are neither too soft nor too forceful … you kiss me with such solemnity and such … such determination … and so you build a path to me, to that part of me that I did not know myself and that no-one has discovered. This is how bees find their way without hesitation to the heart of the flower … Why only you …? why you …?

Further and further we want to go, and you lead me by the hand … and here there is no hint, no sign of people remaining: waves, birds, clouds and us, on a deserted beach … Oh the eternal, the endless, lonely embrace of earth and ocean … and here is where we want to stay.

And I lie beside you in the warm, soft sand … and you build your path, the path to me, through kiss upon kiss, in a determined solemnity … but this path cannot lead anywhere. With these kisses you drive me into bliss, beyond bliss and you drive me to despair. You drive yourself to despair too, because this is not yet fulfilment …

There was a gulf, a darkness, an unbridgeable space, I myself could not find the path and no-one could show it to me. I dreamed the One, the Oneness, but neither he nor it was present … this despair when we enter each other with kisses reveals it to me. The sweetest of all despair at the inadequacy of the sweetest of kisses ... 'The Cosmic Spirit, who was very much an artist' ... We must find a way through this despair ... we must know this despair ... and together, carried along by this despair, across the gulf, into one another's arms. And the light shines through, and my face glows at what I suddenly realize ... the formula for complete surrender is the very thing ... that I have been looking for all my life and have shrunk from all my life, and glorified and despised in one and the same breath of my being.

Eva ... Eva ... you are almost a middle-aged lady. You are solid and untouchable. You closed the gates before anyone ever entered. For years you walked on past the circus tent, you laugh at the mousetrap. Ghosts have no substance. You have grown-up children.

I lean against him. I have put my cheek against his cheek. Our faces are warm and damp. 'I have grown-up children ... two of them. I have two grown-up children.'

'Yes, I know them, your two grown-up children ... Eva ... I have to tell you something: I am leaving here tomorrow.' Oh but this makes me happy! I don't want to admit it to you, but this suddenly makes me exceedingly happy. I also know why: because this is what you came here for and then you must go away again. To reveal this to me, that is what you came for, and I desire no more than this. I don't want to go the way of everyone else. *The Way of all Flesh*, about the ill woman, the dead woman. Others would force us along that path before we realized it ourselves or wanted it. Not us together in the wild duck cage. Exaltedness ... but even exaltedness is a function. I too can sense that it would collapse and that is why I am so very happy that it will become irreversible as soon as tomorrow. And that we do not even know each others' names ... People who have not been properly introduced.

'Not each other's name and not where we live.'

'But isn't this foolishness, Eva ...?'

'Complete and utter foolishness, except for this one thing, except for that one thing.'

He cannot understand this, he looks at me and is amazed at this sudden peace.

Now I would like to tell him this ... I would like to tell him this in words, leaning quietly against him, the wind in my hair, high above the great, blue sea, in full sun and as though in a dream, I think the words in which I would explain it to him, so dreamily ... dreamily ... so dreamily, the way we, the children and I, would lie there in earlier years, on winter Sunday mornings in the half light, the three of us in my narrow bed, between the blushing rose-red curtain and the brown-stained wooden partition. In each arm I held a child, on each shoulder lay a head, and I had to make up stories to go with the ever-changing, shape-shifting dream-images in the wood-knots, the satiny patches, naked and pale in the brown stained wood. Stretched wide open, our eyes peeped out of heads thrown back on the pillow … and there were female figures in ghostly folds of veils, deep ocean stretches, cantering dream horses, wonderful forest plants, hazy sunsets … and dreamlike, so dreamlike, without much coherence … tenuous threads of scattered fictions, as we lay there squeezed between the brown wall and the rose-red twilight of the curtain … I was eighteen, the last year with my brother, David, in the little town. And a much older man, a man whose eyes were soft, blue flames, put his arm along the back of my chair, around my shoulders and it lasted for only a moment. He said, 'Oh you know very well, you know very well, I like you best, you are the only one …' a thousand birds fluttering round me … a thousand white flowers … a thousand vows … *Kol Nidrei*. All the vows. Lift me up above the tallest towers … and the room was full of silver-grey light … the housekeeper came in carefully with cups of coffee on a tray, with brown biscuits on a plate, but he didn't understand. My heart was so oppressed it hurt with its own pain, tugging at its pain like an independent being. I heard it moan: I do not want this … I do not want us to carry on eating in each other's presence. I want to break free of this low life … Let us, oh my boy, let us … be noble. The word fell to me from the staring stars, but that was later, that was in the small dark garden, with the wind blowing in the ivy …

And this was one thing.

The other thing was written on the inside of the stable doors and inside was the man with the hard, red cheeks who spewed it out, when he saw girls, and it was uttered at school in whispers that made your eyes blink and your forehead clammy … and in my own deeply hidden, deeply hated pleasure. There is a way leading upwards out of the slavery of the contemptible -, there is a way leading downwards out of the impatient tugging towards what is noble … and somewhere must be the crossing-point where 'high' merges, emerges, submerges, into 'low', 'low' into 'high', life-in-death, all-in-all. I have never been able to find that crossing-point, because I have never managed to follow either path to the very end, though I did venture again and again on to both … there remained a gulf, a darkness, an unbridgeable space.

I was married, I have two children from my life with my husband … but I could never grasp it fully, it never acquired meaning. Not even that … well-concealed, deeply-hated pleasure. Minnie and her husband, they despise one another by daylight, they embrace in the dark. We never despised one another by daylight and never found each other in the dark.

I had a man friend, I had many, I had two of them -, Jaap was one and André was the other. The gulf remained, the darkness, the unbridgeable space, and in his pain, André once called me a tease. Oh ... André ... who did you think I was trying to arouse? He said 'Cold, that is what you are, cold ...' Cold? With my ardent heart? But I could not take the one path and I didn't how to get there by the other one.

And now, at last, and as unexpectedly as the sun breaking through, now I have understood. I came to you, I thought: I want to tell him everything ... A thousand birds fluttering round me, a thousand white flowers, a thousand vows ... that's how it was ... And that one question about Father's Book, the one, right question, which would have pacified us ... we didn't find it. And I want to entrust to him all my different lives ... my tenfold life ... my turbulent ... my ever turbulent ... my oh so turbulent life ... Because there is such an extreme tension in me, and my equilibrium has been completely destroyed. And so the Storm arrives. The eternally disturbed, eternally restored equilibrium ... Storms and Trade Winds. My brother, my little brother, David -, he had to bring death upon himself, in atonement ... that way equilibrium is restored. We flee from happiness into unhappiness, we do that to ourselves, I did it as a child, it's called: melancholy. A single individual must pay for what millions do not have in their power, for their inability, their impotence. One individual, and Heleen called that unjust. Not so. Because this universal obligation is his one and only desire. Desire is function, function becomes desire ... I knew this yesterday evening; the moon shone over the sea, little boats glided on it, the shoreline was invisible. You said: This is the way to confide in one another. And you kissed, kissed, kissed me. But the extreme tension remained and increased. I remember standing by the window as a child, as a girl, I stared at the brown planks, I was not aware of seeing them and I never forgot them, they lay on top of the silver-grey water as though on quicksilver, I was still trembling a little from the chair tipping over and my hands were cold, he looked at me in wonder, our lives unfurled next to one another in the silence -, the way a soap bubble blunders about till it bursts, is the way my heart blunders towards fulfilment, it blundered about then as now. But when you kissed me it seemed for a moment as though I had given expression to those twenty years and my hundred lives, but the tension remained, the tension increased and grew into despair. And this sweetest of all despair at the inadequacy of the sweetest of all kisses, this is what carries me across the gulf, through the darkness, beyond the unbridgeable space, into your arms to that point where the two paths merge, in a mist, in a silence, in a valley. Only this way is everything said and everything given and said and given all at once.

This and this too … and this too … and all the rest. You say: I was little and my father wrote a book … you say … how soft and sweet your lips are … I can understand how Tamalone was able to teach her, Mevena, who couldn't do it before … and isn't it true that beauty is intent …? *'Cette odeur de tabac blond et de muguet avec un peu de cuir de Russie qui imprègne les vêtements de Renaud et ses moustaches longues … pour m'enivrer plus … pour m'enivrer …'* This and this too and this too … Life was played out right through me, and I had to take all the guilt upon myself. And I want to reach higher than the tallest towers … The dual order of things kept me and my husband apart … you understand … or you wouldn't have been able to kiss me like that. This and this too and this too … whatever else inhabits me: unquenched fevers, untamed urges, unredeemed promises … the intangible longing for what has no name and no form. This and this too and this too … you are my darling … you are my darling and I wanted you to demand of me more than is human … my blood … all my blood … more than all my blood … for there is in me such an extreme tension and my equilibrium has been completely disturbed … and this is what will help it return once more … I know that it can only return this way. I know that this is the only way to confide wholly in one another and that this is the formula for a total surrender. All is one, one-and-the-same.

Totality … eternally blossoming understanding, rocket against night sky, bursting into endless myriad colours. Tree of life, deathspring. Eternally disturbed, eternally restored equilibrium. Storms and Trade Winds. The unbending urge towards duty -, the hot thirst for penance, the longing for mortification … the one-and-the-same, expressed through emotion in endless forms. And that which presents itself as Despair … the Storm-of-Storms …

The cosmic Spirit, who was very much an artist … one person must take the upward path from lowliness, the other person must take the downward path from on high, but all must arrive at the spot where life is complete in the storm of storms.

And because this one thing, uncomprehended till now, untasted until today, is suddenly absorbed like a flame into Totality, because my emotion chimes in with my understanding, and my understanding confirms my emotion, so that now for the first time it truly enters my life where emotion and understanding may not remain separate or Totality will shrivel to a word, I am now sailing into the safe haven before your eyes, so that my calm amazes you …

And tomorrow you are leaving here, with your ill wife, and tomorrow this will be irrevocable -, it really must be, otherwise I would revoke it.

My knees are weak. I see him in the distance, but I don't call him back. Eva … Eva … this is worse than exaltation … this is lying and madness … Tomorrow I will regret it, tomorrow when it can't be changed. This evening the children return. With the tide the boat sailed to the other side, with the tide the boat will sail back again. I have hours until evening. I look for a dip in the heart of the dunes, a deep wide hollow, where I can lie down full-length on my back, my hands behind my head on the purple-green floor, under the dark blue roof -, but I must be able to hear the sea there, I must still be able to feel time and space there.

This is peace, this is harmony. You should really break out in a sob, wring your hands and sob. You let him go and you can't even call out to him and you don't even know his full name. You hesitated between Ben's name and your maiden name, and then he had no alternative but to say that he is called Marius. Such tiny hesitations, such deep-seated whims determine the direction of your life, his life, her life and that of my children. I shall wring my hands and sob, I shall sob bitterly, and regret it once it is irrevocable. But now there is this, the reason why you lie here so calmly, - you have made your peace with life, and are turning back to life completely at peace. Not in unassailability, but in surrender. You thought that life had put you in the wrong, but life has proved you right … this knowledge of being proved right by life is the harmony that surpasses all. Unio Mystica. It came over you that evening, by the open window, and now it comes over you again. Once you dreamed the Oneness, the One, with heavenly earnestness in his eyes, with the heavenly smile around his mouth, standing in the ring of children, holding the ribbons, the silver ribbons, in one hand. He is: the one who knows them all, who they all know, but outside of him they do not know each other. He is: the Meaning, from which everything receives its meaning, the Magnet around which all things arrange themselves, loose iron filings and hard steel … You dreamed the One and you thought your dream an illusion. This is what you said as a child: a dream is an illusion. But this dream is no illusion. The very sweetest despair at the inadequacy of the very sweetest kisses, drives you across the gulf. 'The formula for complete surrender.' He said: 'I can't help laughing at you …'

I can't help laughing at you. Never has a man said such a sweet thing to me in such a sweet voice. It pushes me into bliss, it makes me shiver, as I lie here following the black birds across the silvery-luminous blue. 'I can't help laughing at you ...'

And you, my old enemy Shame, now you will never again disturb me. You who dared to haunt me wherever I went ...

The violins trembled at what had been consummated, the narrow windows caught the silvery light, tall white furrows in the grey of the wall, I held my breath along with hundreds of others in the silence, we experienced the moment, endless, unbearable, until the invisible choirs were reborn in a sigh and the chorale's crescendo filled the spaces beneath the twilit vaulting:

Wenn ich einmal soll scheiden
So scheide nicht von mir ...

And my demon Shame touched me between the shoulder blades, so that I shivered. You ... you dare to sit here, dare to identify yourself with this fulfilment ...? Stop and think ... what did you hope would give you your fulfilment? You ... dare to sit here? And all those others, hundreds of them? Those others, hundreds of them, have nothing to do with you. I am your Shame.

No longer my shame, no longer any shame, because these things are all the same to me. This ... and this too ... and this too ... and all the rest. I want to call him to me in the dark in my loneliness, I want to lie in his arms in the dark, I call his voice, - 'I can't help laughing at you ...' I call his lips ... alone, in the waking dream, in his arms, I drive myself to despair, alone, in his arms, through the despair, across the gulf.

And you, Johannes Viator, stupid prophet, will o' the wisp above the marshes, twice you appeared to me. Once in the little attic room and I trembled before you. Years later you entered through rattling verandah doors and I accounted for my life to you. Now come here, for the third time, here where I lie, so that I can sit up and expose you as a liar face-to-face. You do not know, and I do. It is not love that makes bodily desire acceptable. Bodily desire makes love acceptable. I could tell it abroad. But if they should ask me what it means, I would refer them to St. Paul: He who has ears to hear, let him hear.

This evening the children return, another ten days or so and we will be going home, then summer will be almost gone again. In the village under the damp trees the quiet of early autumn awaits us. The corn was taken from the field some time ago, stored inside, and the potato leaves have yellowed, every morning the dew lies caught on the purple cabbages in cool, clear, flat droplets. Across the heath, the flickering flames are lit, red-brown, yellow, red … they in their turn waft away, they in their turn are extinguished … and then it is winter. Where the summer breeze brushed the tops of the corn ears in a silky glow of sunset, and the sorrel glowed reddish under the silver blur of flowering grass, the grey fields lie frozen under the grey sky. And it is late evening, the moon shines above our roof and the children are asleep ⸴, I walk outside for a moment, out of the warm into the cold. I walk up and down the white gravel road … in the silence I hear my own footstep … I have left the front door open, the lamplight floods into the garden, right up to the hedge. I do this so often in winter. And every whisper of wind blows the quiet towards me from the heart of the village, in a smell of straw and manure … silence, the very deepest winter silence. And it's not altogether right what Montaigne says, and actually … it's not right at all … but it is pleasant to say it within yourself, to say it to yourself in the silence of the late winter's evening, with the moon among the poplars, above the roof, above the sleeping children, and the light that streams out of the open house into the garden … and a door slams, and a bolt is drawn across … and the ultimate goal of all wisdom is the calm contemplation of death.